Preserving Intellectual Freedom

Preserving Intellectual Freedom

Fighting Censorship in Our Schools

Edited by
Jean E. Brown
Saginaw Valley State University

National Council of Teachers of English
1111 W. Kenyon Road, Urbana, Illinois 61801-1096

Manuscript Editors: Robert A. Heister, Hamish D. Glenn
Humanities & Sciences Associates

Production Editor: Michelle Sanden Johlas

Interior Design: Tom Kovacs for TGK Design

Cover Design: Jim Proefrock

NCTE Stock Number: 36710–3050

Library of Congress Cataloging-in-Publication Data

Preserving intellectual freedom : fighting censorship in our schools /
    edited by Jean E. Brown.
        p.   cm.
    Includes bibliographical references and index.
    ISBN 0-8141-3671-0
        1. Academic freedom—United States. 2. Public schools—United
    States—Curricula—Censorship. 3. Language arts—United States.
    4. Literature—Study and teaching—United States. 5. Educational
    law and legislation—United States.   I. Brown, Jean E.
    II. National Council of Teachers of English.
    LC72.2.P74   1994
    379.´55—dc20   94-19860
                                                                        CIP

Contents

To Robert and Eileen Ross,
for confirming my belief that great teachers
have a lasting influence on their students,
with my gratitude, admiration, and fondness

Acknowledgments

As with any edited volume, this book is the collected work of many people. I thank the contributors, especially those who have been involved since I became editor in 1989.

This volume was originally suggested by Jim Davis in 1988 when he became the first chair of the CEE Commission on Intellectual Freedom. He has been generous with his insights and assistance throughout the process, as was demonstrated by his willingness to contribute the afterword. We have also benefited from the interest and encouragement of the CEE Executive Committee, first under Bob Small's leadership and more recently under Joe Milner's and Carol Pope's direction. Also, the comments of the NCTE Editorial Board members and the peer reviewers were insightful and helped bring the manuscript to completion.

I appreciate the time and suggestions offered by three of my colleagues at Saginaw Valley State University. Elaine C. Stephens, Mary Harmon, and Eric Gilbertson read and offered perceptive suggestions about parts of the manuscript.

I extend a special thanks to Michael Spooner, formerly senior editor at NCTE, who was helpful in conceptualizing the manuscript's structure; to Michelle Sanden Johlas who, first as acting senior editor and more recently as production editor, has always been supportive; and to Bob Heister, director of Humanities & Sciences Associates, who as manuscript editor did a thankless job with great grace. I especially appreciate their insights, humor, and professionalism.

Jean E. Brown
Saginaw Valley State University

Introduction

Jean E. Brown
Saginaw Valley State University

As our title, *Preserving Intellectual Freedom: Fighting Censorship in Our Schools,* implies, this book is designed to reflect issues, approaches, and sources of support for educators who encounter attempts to control and abridge the open flow of ideas. The book is consistent with the general objective of the National Council of Teachers of English to promote "Intellectual freedom at all educational levels," as articulated in the Strategic Planning document.

The Conference on English Education of the National Council of Teachers of English established a Commission on Intellectual Freedom, giving it the following charge:

> to examine and make recommendations concerning the effects of censorship efforts on the English curriculum in literature and also on the teaching of composition and language; to examine and make recommendations about censorship in relation to the preservice and inservice preparations of teachers of the English language arts, and to explore the adequacy of preparation given such teachers to deal with censorship issues and situations.

This volume is the product of work by this commission, and a number of the contributors are among its current membership. The commission's first chair, James E. Davis, suggested that one of the ways in which we might meet the commission's charge was by publishing a collected volume addressing issues of intellectual freedom. As NCTE members know, Jim Davis moved on to other responsibilities in the Council, but his continuing contributions to intellectual freedom are reflected in this book by the afterword that he has contributed. Ironically, many of the issues and concerns that were explored in *Dealing with Censorship,* which was edited by Jim Davis in 1979, are still as relevant today as they were fifteen years ago. In that context, we have entitled this book, *Preserving Intellectual Freedom: Fighting Censorship in Our Schools,* to indicate the ongoing nature of the efforts of those of us who support the free exchange of ideas.

This collection is designed to articulate and address some of the issues that we face. The manuscript is divided into five major sections. In the first section, there are four chapters that explore general areas of concern for intellectual freedom. In part I the chapters include Philip Anderson's exploration of the conflict between the limits of technological models with the improvement of critical thinking through aesthetic experience. Jean Brown explores the impact that attempts to achieve political correctness have on intellectual freedom. David Moshman explores the role of faculty in protecting student rights. Kathie Krieger Cerra explores the concept of selection versus censorship as it is manifested in self-censorship. The four chapters in part I illustrate that issues of intellectual freedom surface in a number of different ways. From this general overview of problems confronting educators, we move to specific exploration of the impact of censorship problems in the varied aspects of the school curriculum.

In the first four chapters of part II, Hugh Agee, Margaret Sacco, Jim Knippling, and Mary Ellen Van Camp examine problems of censorship in the teaching of literature. These chapters are followed by three other chapters that address problems with intellectual freedom in other aspects of the curriculum: Allison Wilson discusses the impact on intellectual freedom by the restriction of free expression of ideas in composition courses; Roy O'Donnell explores issues concerning language study; and Ellen Brinkley addresses the challenges to intellectual freedom confronting the whole language movement by the religious right.

The book then addresses courses of action that can be taken as teachers confront censorship. Part III begins with a general overview by Jean Brown and Elaine Stephens as they advocate establishing an intellectual freedom group in each school to help teachers and librarians handle censorship problems. In the next two chapters, John Kean addresses the problems that can confront secondary teachers and recommends approaches to address them, and then Adrienne May and Paul Slayton make suggestions about providing support and education for in-service teachers. In the final chapter of part III, Bob Small and Jerry Weiss provide information about groups and organizations, along with their addresses, for teachers and schools when they face censorship problems.

Part IV of the book includes three chapters that explore censorship experiences. In the first chapter, Dee Storey presents a number of scenarios describing censorship situations. In the other two articles, public school teachers explore the impact of censorship. Lynda Kapron and Rita Paye describe their own experience when their high school literary magazine was censored. C. Jane Hydrick discusses a censorship simulation that she created for her third-grade students.

In the final section of the book, the authors of the three chapters examine the legal implications of issues concerning intellectual freedom. The first chapter of the section is an overview of court cases concerning issues of freedom in schools written by Lief Carter and Daniel Carroll. The breadth of their examination provides the foundation for the next two chapters. Mel Krutz looks specifically at the impact of the *Hazelwood* decision as it serves as precedent for numerous other court cases seeking to limit student rights. In the final chapter, Ken Holmes looks at the impact of *Hazelwood* on high schools.

If we are to meet the challenge of censorship, we must act rather than react. This book seeks to provide support to preserve an environment that values a free exchange of ideas and diversity of opinions.

I Intellectual Freedom and English Education

The four chapters in this section each explore different issues that are of current concern for English educators and teachers. While most discussions about intellectual freedom focus upon the issues of overt censorship, each of these chapters explores a broader perspective.

Philip Anderson provides a broad framework for exploring concepts of intellectual freedom within the contexts of enhancing aesthetic experiences in an environment rife with the impact of technology and attempts to define and control learning experiences. He advocates the recommitment of English educators and English teachers to provide aesthetic experiences to improve the critical thinking of students as a means of responding to censorship.

Jean Brown addresses the current discussion of political correctness. Central to the discussion is the question of whether or not policing language will, in fact, alleviate traditional abuses or if it is an infringement on intellectual freedom.

David Moshman, in his chapter, presents the position that academic freedom should be clearly and coherently defined if it is to be an effective response to attempts to censor. He further believes that the primary responsibility of teachers is to protect their students' First Amendment rights.

Kathie Krieger Cerra addresses an often-unrecognized issue of intellectual freedom, the issue of self-censorship. In her chapter she shares the results of a study she conducted in 1988–89. Initially, she sought information about selection policies, but the findings lead her to recognize the self-censoring aspect of behavior.

1 In Defense of the Aesthetic: Technical Rationality and Cultural Censorship

Philip M. Anderson
Queens College, CUNY

> They think that things are all right,
> Since the deer and the dachshund are one.
>
> —Wallace Stevens

Intellectual Freedom and the Nature of Censorship

Censorship in the United States is a battle over cultural definition and intellectual freedom, over who controls the culture. Censors want nothing less than to limit the content and the form of the culture as a means of controlling thought and behavior. For English educators, the censorship issue requires more than reactively attending to individual censors. In the end, censorship challenges the need for literary texts and creative expression in the culture at large. Censorship impugns what we do as a profession; it questions where our responsibilities lie.

Censorship is anti-intellectual in nature. Religious censors do not believe in reading more than their religion's holy books. Moreover, censors from other perspectives wish to control and limit the way in which children, and adults for that matter, read the books they are allowed to read. The students' and the teachers' intellectual freedom is in danger when "approved" commentaries and interpretations are enforced in the schools.

Limiting and controlling forms of language experience are as much a censorship threat as limitations on the content of teaching. English educators must struggle to provide literary experience, aesthetic language experience, and promote writing as creative expression. And, most important, English educators must resist the increasing attempts to reconceptualize human thinking and behavior in technological forms, structures that are controlling and limiting by their very nature. This technical frame of reference is the chief danger to literary study and aesthetic forms of expression necessary to cultural understanding.

3

English Education and Cultural Form

The functions of English education necessitate the preservation of the aesthetic in the face of technological reductionism and anti-humanistic social philosophy. As to the responsibilities of English educators in the postmodern world, I would argue the following tenets:

- The primary function and justification of English teaching is the promotion of aesthetic experience and aesthetic forms of linguistic development.
- Aesthetic language experience is necessary for cognitive growth, and aesthetic experience in general is necessary for cultural understanding.
- Censorship monitoring in the English classroom should be concerned with linguistic and cognitive *form* as much as with content.
- Certain forms of linguistic and cognitive behavior are antithetical to aesthetic experience. Since aesthetic forms are necessary to language development and an integral part of human culture, promotion of non-aesthetic forms for aesthetic activities in schools is a form of cultural limitation, and therefore, censorship.

English educators perform their roles by preserving and promoting aesthetic forms in the culture, both aesthetic ways of knowing and aesthetic forms of representation. Mere attention to cultural content does not meet this responsibility. John Dewey's (1916) "process" definition of culture, "the capacity for constantly expanding the range and accuracy of one's perceptions of meanings," is necessary for educational purposes, it being a more useful definition than any static "content" idea of culture (145). Dewey's vision of culture is both progressive and creative, and not tied to an authority's delineation of cultural content.

Given Dewey's definition of culture, I offer this definition of a censor: *a censor is one who seeks to limit the cultural experience of another through the use of limiting forms of thought and language, or who limits access to creative expression.* Limiting forms of experience promoted by various educational and social authorities are dangerous to intellectual freedom.

Conservative school reformers, most notably E. D. Hirsch, Jr. (1988b), have revived the outdated criticism that Dewey's "content-neutral" educational philosophy is somehow responsible for the alleged sorry state of American education (19). Below, I will discuss how conservative education critics subscribe to the notion that education is "process-neutral," thereby promoting a technological delivery system. This false notion of neutrality in the forms of education presents a greater threat to culture than any content-neutral argument.

Two recent developments in educational thinking undermine the aesthetic domain of English teaching, both emanating from technological reconceptualizations of human activity. One trend promotes cognitive science as a basis for educational psychology, i.e., artificial intelligence models and computer models of human thinking as descriptions of human cognition. The other trend reinforces the use of technical models for school curriculum, especially now that cognitive science precepts are used to legitimize those models. Hirsch's "cultural literacy" model exemplifies the second trend. Both trends are manifestations of technical rationality.

The philosophy behind these trends is not new. Even Matthew Arnold (1867), the progenitor of modern English teaching, warned: "Faith in machinery is 'our besetting danger'" (1960, 49). Our "faith in machinery" as educational practice is a form of social control and linguistic deprivation, and therefore, a form of censorship that teachers frequently, though unwittingly, support. English educators are responsible for monitoring and resisting the invasion of technical rationality into the English classroom.

Technical rationality is a form of practice and thinking defined by technological reframings of human activity, informed by theories of technology. Technical rationality, also referred to as *technique,* to quote Jacques Ellul, "is the rational and unblinking search for increased efficiency and greater productivity" (in Burnham 1984, 6). Technical rationality applies technological form to human activities, both behavior (social and behavioral engineering) and cognition (artificial intelligence and cognitive science).

Maxwell Goldberg (1972) first warned English teachers about this threat over twenty years ago. David Dobrin's (1989) recent examination of *technique* in the writing field raises serious questions about the limitations of technical forms in composition instruction. Patrick Shannon (1989) has explored the same issue with regard to reading instruction in elementary schools. I've written about the misuse of technical rationality in the teaching of literature on several occasions (P. M. Anderson 1979; 1980; 1990). And, the limiting effects of technical rationality on professional development in general has been explored by Donald Schön (1983). Technical rationality is not a future threat, but a real and pressing threat to humanistic conceptions of education and culture.

Technical rationality applied to human behavior is a limiting conception of human behavior, and, as theories of technology suggest, designed more for control than growth. English educators' primary focus is in the aesthetic realm of culture, not the technical. In fact, English educators may be the only hope for the promotion of aesthetic language experience in American culture; the other arts are frequently considered "frills" in school budget decisions. Curbing technical rationality does not mean abandoning the use of computers in English classes, though; for instance, we cannot confuse word processing, a text *management* system, with human composing. English teachers should be wary of prophets espousing technological views of humans, especially when they use computer models as an "explanation" of human cognition.

Technical Rationality in the Curriculum

Technical rationality has now produced the field of cognitive science, a field in which computer science models of human behavior and thinking are used to describe and explain humans. Cognitive science presents us with a new version of the psychology and sociology that produced teacher-proof materials under B. F. Skinner's behaviorism in the 1950s. Cognitive science promotes experts dictating the curriculum, as in the concept of the "expert-system," one of the hallmarks of artificial intelligence research. Cognitive science researchers frequently blur the distinction between human thinking and computing, confusing ideas with information.

Technological visions of process, information-processing visions of thinking, and technical modes of communication and systems of thought are based on theories and rules of technology:

- All systems can be reduced to sequential, and often hierarchical, steps.
- Concepts are reducible to discrete information components.
- Technical systems of communication and thinking are designed to control information and ideas, not to generate them.
- Technical systems produce monological systems of communication, i.e., one-way or nondialogical communication.

One of the more illustrative recent examples of the application of technical rationality to an educational problem is the argument put forth by E. D. Hirsch, Jr., resulting in *Cultural Literacy: What Every American Needs to Know* (1988b). Hirsch's curriculum model is defined by technical rationality and governed by the theories of technology cited above. Hirsch doesn't need a *Metropolis*-inspired machine environment to bring his technical system to fruition. All he needs is the technology of the printing press combined with the technology of cognitive science and technically determined systematic instruction. On the other hand, Hirsch's information-based model would be easy to build into a computer program. His emphasis on early memorization of cultural data (by third grade all the "baseline" cultural data are assimilated) is a computer programmer's idea of how learning and thinking (or "information processing") work.

As with many conservative commentators, Hirsch is a skillful writer who couches his prescriptions in humanistic terminology. If Hirsch had said we need to enter schematic data into the memory banks of our children in order to program them in a socially controlled way to support the labor needs of the military-industrial complex, the membership of NCTE would be after Hirsch with rakes and pitchforks. Instead, he says we need prior knowledge as a necessary condition for cultural literacy in a democracy, and some English educators say he has a "point."

It would be fair to say that most professionals in the field of English education have reservations about the cultural literacy model, if only intuitively. NCTE passed a resolution decrying basal readers (another product of technical rationality) as a substitute for children's literature, and another resolution questioning the implications of the notion of cultural literacy ("NCTE," 1988). And, the point that English educators tend to concede to Hirsch is, in Hirsch's words, "literate content is absolutely essential to the higher skills of reading, learning, and thinking" (1988a, 19).

Of course, this statement ignores method and form, and these aspects of Hirsch's educational model define the problem. Hirsch's contention that the specific content of the cultural information list doesn't matter (as when he invites teachers to "make up your own list") further reinforces his true emphasis on method: memorization of cultural knowledge (or in the cognitive science jargon: programmed input of cultural data) is the key educational concept in "cultural literacy."

But, Hirsch's model belies his stated democratic intent because the technical form he employs limits possibilities for learning to read to culturally approved forms as well as culturally approved content. He doesn't discuss teaching method because it reveals the controlling, and limiting, nature of the model he employs. He claims that form of instruction is unimportant (as long as the content is "learned," by which he means "memorized"), strongly suggesting that he believes the process is neutral, or technical, in nature.

Additionally, he is only presenting one half of the curriculum, the technical half, then claiming that the other half of the curriculum, the aesthetic half, is dependent upon it. Learning in a technical mode does not prepare one to learn in an aesthetic mode, just as reading basals does not prepare one to read literature in an aesthetic way. Hirsch is describing a data-processing model, not a human-thinking model.

Reading research in general is becoming increasingly immeshed in cognitive science models (Smith 1988). The work of Richard C. Anderson, from whom Hirsch draws much of his reading research, certainly reflects these trends (Hirsch 1988b, 51). Anderson was one of the authors of *Becoming a Nation of Readers* (1985), a highly publicized educational document published at the height of the Reagan-era reform reports. Interestingly, cognitive science is also the basis for some important writing research from that era, that of Flower and Hayes (see Dobrin 1989, for a critique). It is important to keep in mind that reading as a "skill," reading as separate from literature study, is a fundamental technological rethinking of literature study in the first place.

Hirsch extensively employs cognitive science jargon, borrowed from current reading research: e.g., "integrated *chunks*," "habitual schemata," and "cognitive overload" (1988b, 55, 68; 1988a, 19). He apparently envisions the mind simply as a computer, as in this descriptive reference to cognition: "the floppy disks in our minds would quickly fill to capacity, and we would have to erase them periodically" (1988b, 36).

Hirsch also quotes extensively from artificial intelligence (AI) pioneer Herbert Simon's work, and claims unequivocally: "AI models actually work" (1988b, 60, 62). For what? For whom? With what consequences? There is considerable debate, and less certainty, about the efficacy of AI models in the scientific community (Gardner 1985; Johnson 1986). But Hirsch is certain that artificial intelligence paves the path to educational reform.

Hirsch draws on instructional models from reading research, rather than on literary response models (a question raised about *Becoming a Nation of Readers;* see Sims, in Davidson 1988, 63). As I have argued previously, most of reading research, and especially its practice, in the twentieth century represents a technological reconceptualization of literature study (P. M. Anderson 1979; 1980). Hirsch could be said to misuse recent research in reading, but he claims that Richard C. Anderson approves of his application of the research (1988b, viii).

An NCTE monograph identified certain anomalies within the report, especially: "One of the major problems with *BNR* is the inconsistency between the theory of reading espoused and the suggestions made for beginning reading instruction" (Bridge, in Davidson 1988, 51–52). I would submit that the discrepancy between the seemingly holistic description of human reading behavior and the suggested remedies, which appear atomistic, is that the technical rationality philosophy of the AI models is invoked for some of the material, resulting in a "quality control metaphor [suggesting] standardization of the instruction and of the processes and products of reading instruction" (Bloome, et al., in Davidson 1988, 8).

Technical rationality, of which Hirsch's cultural literacy model has all the characteristics, makes it appear logical that reading is decoding, followed by literal comprehension, which then leads to higher-level inference and interpretation; and, writing is learned by first mastering the sentence, then the paragraph, then the essay. Interestingly, Hirsch writes that he does not believe any of these notions in the text of *Cultural Literacy*, but the model he proposes follows these principles. This tendency to determine and limit forms regardless of democratic or aesthetic intention is also a characteristic of technical rationality. Also, there is the possibility that Hirsch's system belies his rationale purposely for political reasons.

Technical Rationality and Political Conservatism

Hirsch's work also typifies why technical rationality appeals to conservative educators, especially those who promote its "efficiency" and "control" criteria. Ironically, these efficiency notions were originally promoted by the Progressives these folks claim to be attacking (Callahan 1962). Nonetheless, "knowledge is not just power; it is also speed," says Hirsch in one article (1988b, 18), and the index for *Cultural Literacy* lists an "efficiency of communication" entry, among other efficiency key words.

Most of Hirsch's professional life has been spent trying to eradicate complexity and dualistic thinking in education. Like most technologists, he is looking for a unified theory, such as his theory of "grapholect," that aims at a single, controllable end (1977). Hirsch is so caught up in technological frames of thought that he even evokes technology as a determinate of educational policy, claiming, "Because of the demands created by technology we need effective monoliteracy more than ever" (1988b, 92).

The nondialogical form that technical rationality employs guarantees a limiting and controlling educational model. Paulo Freire (1970) has written eloquently about the undemocratic political consequences of nondialogical, i.e., technical, structures of communication in education. The philosopher Jurgen Habermas (1970a; 1970b) has provided a cogent analysis of technical rationality in communication situations, clearly demonstrating the primary aim of technological views of humans and society to be the removal of dialogue from the social process. And, in what turns out to be an apt criticism of "cultural literacy," Habermas points out that technical visions of society and communication remove the ethics category from discussion of social issues (1970b, 112–13).

A nondialogical form of education is censorship even when it carries the best of stated intentions. Technical rationality presents a worldview that is reductive rather than constructive, and promotes a hierarchical one-way system of communication. Rather than being "content-neutral," technical rationality presents technological systems as "neutral." But, technology is never neutral, given its controlling form; technical systems embody the controlling intentions of those who employ the system (Habermas 1970b).

Conservatives are not just looking for unified content, but unified process (a "one-best-way" which is also "one-way-only"). Ironically, theories of cybernetics and technology suggest that the simple dream of total technical control of communication is not possible. As the father of cybernetics, Norbert Weiner (1967), observes, "Just as entropy tends to increase spontaneously in a closed system, so information tends to decrease" (158–59). Technical systems are high-maintenance, and more time and energy is spent on regulating the system than on meeting the goals of the system. Hirsch's arguments for "efficiency" are not really served by the closed system he proposes.

Technical models are inadequate when applied to human learning in general. Again, the threat is not new. Over thirty years ago, Carl Rogers provided a trenchant analysis of the behavioral engineering models promoted for learning by B. F. Skinner, the behavioral messiah who tried to replace teachers with foolproof teaching machines, quoting Skinner to the effect that:

> As the use of science increases, we are forced to accept the theoretical structure with which science represents its facts. The difficulty is that this structure is clearly at odds with the traditional democratic conceptions of man. (Rogers 1961, 390)

Skinner goes on to say that the democratic social philosophy is "out of date and indeed an obstacle" if it prevents us from "applying to human affairs the science of man" (Rogers 1961, 390).

Cognitive Science and Human Thinking

The cognitive science view of human cognition is a part of the "science of man" represented by behaviorism and cybernetics (Weiner 1967), both technological reconceptualizations of human behavior, and shares their inherent biases:

- Cognitive science posits the basic units of human thinking as data, not as ideas (Roszak 1986).

- Computer modeling of human cognition produces reductivist models of human learning (by definition).

- Technical models of learning define reading and writing instruction exclusively as a goal-driven technological system (i.e., "reading or writing as problem solving").

- Technical communication systems, which tend to be "closed" systems, require high levels of maintenance, so more emphasis is put on maintaining the system than on transmitting information (Mueller 1973). In other words, the technology becomes the object of attention, e.g., filling out work sheets instead of reading, studying test-taking procedures, taking cultural literacy tests instead of reading literature.

The artificial intelligence research already being applied to the classroom, providing specific views of the structure of thinking, is highly suspect even within its own limited domain of "intelligent behavior in machines." Many commentators express concern about the lack of an undergirding theory of mind and the reliance on computer programming as a substitute for human thought processes (Gardner 1985; Johnson 1986).

Provocative theorists such as Douglas Hofstadter (1979) are considered outside the AI mainstream because they do not have appropriate computer programs to show to other AI researchers. According to Johnson (1986), "If you don't have an acceptable program to show, philosophers may take your ideas seriously, but AI researchers will not" (290). Johnson also quotes John Seely Brown, director of the intelligent-systems laboratory at Xerox's Palo Alto Research Center, on cognitive theory building using computer modeling: "All too often you find scientists simply building a program that actually generates some interesting behavior—interesting problem-solving behavior, interesting knowledge acquisition, interesting learning—and saying, 'Aha, this is the model of the inner mind!'" (141).

Most problematic for English teachers is the AI approach to narrative thinking. A review of the AI books on narrative, according to Bizup and Kintgen (1993), reveals that AI researchers are developing narrative theory without consulting any literary-critical work on the subject. My reading of those same books reveals a lack of any reference to reader-response studies. I would submit that current narrative theory in English studies, and reader-response research, do not fit technological frames of reference, and therefore are not useful to AI research.

Aesthetic Models and Language Development

The way in which a technological model of the curriculum affects the language development of our students can be seen by comparing the nature of language learning with technological systems theory. Research on language development from Vygotsky (1962) to Britton (1970; 1976) to Howard Gardner (1982) demonstrates that:

- Dialogue is necessary for language development.

- Language tasks are approached holistically, not hierarchically or sequentially.

- Reading and writing are constructive and creative activities.

- Reading with an aesthetic stance (as defined by Rosenblatt 1978) and writing in the role of spectator, i.e., writing "poetic discourse" (as defined by Britton, et al. 1975), are necessary parts of learning to read and write.

- Aesthetic use of language is not determined by articulated prior knowledge or analytical abilities. For example, metaphor production can precede metaphor analysis developmentally (Gardner 1982, 166).

How does technical rationality fit this research? Technological systems are monological by definition, since AI computers do not "actively" participate in meaning making. Cognitive-processing models (and much of developmental reading) are reductive, sequential and hierarchical, despite all the talk about "schemata" and "parallel processing." Technical systems are designed to replicate data and control response. Technical models require, or at the least promote, efferent reading and transactional writing. Finally, Hirsch's argument says that articulated prior knowledge is necessary for literary understanding, though there is ample evidence for the role of tacit understanding in literary response.

Technical rationality applied to reading, writing, and thinking represents the antithesis of current language development theory. To apply these technical frames to human language learning means limiting and controlling education. *Exclusive use of technological models in English teaching amounts to cultural censorship.*

To combat this form of censorship, this limiting form of educational technique that impinges on intellectual freedom, we need to look no further than to two well-known theorists: Louise Rosenblatt's theories of reading and James Britton's theories of writing. Both theorists insist that aesthetic forms are an integral part of literacy, and both assert that the aesthetic is not dependent on the technical (see Anderson and Rubano 1991). Technical and aesthetic discourse are interrelated in developmental terms, but not in a hierarchical relationship.

Rosenblatt's theories show us why applying SQ3R (an example of technical rationality in reading and study skills, as well as efferent reading stance) to literature study or asking the infamous "What facts does this poem teach you?" question are detrimental to democratic education (1976 [1938]; 1978; 1980). Britton's vision of poetic discourse, of writing in the role of spectator, shows the aesthetic as a necessary part of verbal expression and psycholinguistic development (1970; 1975; 1976). Supporting these English educators, the curriculum thinking of Elliot Eisner (1985; 1993) provides a curricular justification for the necessity of aesthetic forms of representation in schools.

English educators need to promote "creative" writing and aesthetic reading in the curriculum based on models of human learning, not reductivist computer models. We need to allow for unarticulated response, unresolved ambiguity, collaborative learning and dialogue. We need to worry less about comprehension and business communication, and more about aesthetic reading and poetic writing.

Cultural censors prefer controlled education. Censors prefer a testable curriculum because it is a controlled curriculum. Censors prefer standardized tests about literature content because it promotes efferent reading, and, as I have suggested, using efferent models exclusively to read literature is censorship. Censors do not like *whole language* because it flies in the face of the technical rationality of basal readers. Educational programs developed under technical rationality cannot assimilate ideas such as "invented spelling." Whole language has become a target of censors, and some educators are losing jobs over support of whole language (Berger 1993).

Technical models are of a fundamentally different nature than aesthetic models. Aesthetic models are dialogical and generative; technical models are monological and replicative. Technical forms of thinking do not lead to aesthetic forms of thinking any more than memorization of parts of speech leads to learning to write.

Instead, aesthetic reasoning is necessary to break the self-replicating nature of technical rationality. Readers cannot read aesthetically if the only reading model at their disposal is a technical (efferent) one. Aesthetic knowledge cannot always be translated into a non-aesthetic, or technical, form. Conversely, nothing is legitimate under technical rationality unless it can be turned into a technical form.

Conclusion

AI and cognitive science models are technological models and technological models are designed for *control*. Controlled vocabulary is not a
panacea for teaching reading, and controlled cultural data are not an
answer to the "problem" of reading literature. When English teachers
cooperate in putting our students in "reading" classes and make them fill
out work sheets, we are censoring, both because the work sheets keep
them from reading, and the technical form of language experience we
provide is limiting by its nature. When we study formal grammar *instead*
of writing, we are censors. When we require students to memorize
cultural data as a prerequisite to allowing them to read, we are censoring.

We are limiting an essential part of our students' linguistic and social
development when we assume the technical (the efferent stance in
reading and the transactional function in writing) as the foundation of
aesthetic reading and response. The job of the English educator requires
the engendering of aesthetic forms of thinking while providing aesthetic
experiences for our students. American culture's faith in machinery is
leading us down a slippery slope where the aesthetic is only for those
who can articulate culturally approved data, or into a world where
aesthetic experience is only an educational frill.

There is a role for technical forms of thinking, but it is not the English
teacher's primary function to emphasize it. In fact, almost every other
subject in the school promotes technical frames of reference, as do the
external administrative and testing interests. But, aesthetic experience is
the key to critical thinking as well as creative thinking, and aesthetic
experience (akin to the relationship of science to technology) breaks the
controlling and limiting influences of technological systems.

Despite all the patriotic talk in the recent conservative educational
agenda about freedom and access to middle-class culture, John Dewey
spelled out the best criticism of the "superficiality" (Hirsch's sought-
after educational goal, 1988b, 16) explicit in the cultural literacy movement:

> If [the student] has not powers of deliberation and invention, he
> must pick up his ideas casually and superficially from the sugges-
> tions of his environment and appropriate the notions which the
> interests of some class insinuate into his mind. (Dewey 1908, 438)

Censorship and social control cannot stand against a defined program
of aesthetic experience. If English educators emphasize the aesthetic,
then we are already taking a stand against censorship. If we promote the
research that defines aesthetic reading and poetic writing, and if we do
not participate in the neglect and trivializing of the aesthetic in our

classrooms, then we are fighting censorship in the best way possible. And then, if we are successful, our students will be able to tell the deer from the dachshund.

Works Cited

Anderson, Philip M. 1979. "The Ethics and Aesthetics of Literature Study in the Secondary School: A Sociolinguistic Approach." Doct. Diss. University of Wisconsin–Madison.

———. 1980. "Technical Rationality and the Future of Secondary School Literature Study." *English Journal* 69: 43–45.

———. 1990. "Removing the Language and the Art: Three Trends Transforming English in the 1990s." *English Record* 41(1): 1–13.

———, and Gregory Rubano. 1991. *Enhancing Aesthetic Reading and Response.* Urbana: National Council of Teachers of English.

Anderson, Richard C., et. al. 1985. *Becoming a Nation of Readers: The Report of the Commission on Reading.* Washington, D.C.: National Institute of Education.

Arnold, Matthew. 1960 [1867]. *Culture and Anarchy.* Edited by J. Dover Wilson. Cambridge, MA: Cambridge University Press.

Berger, Joseph. 1993. "Fighting Over Reading: Principal and Methods Under Fire." *New York Times* (17 November): A1, B6.

Bizup, Joseph M., and Eugene R. Kintgen. 1993. "The Cognitive Paradigm in Literary Studies." *College English* 55: 841–57.

Britton, James. 1970. *Language and Learning.* Baltimore: Pelican-Penguin.

———. 1976. "Language and the Nature of Learning: An Individual Perspective." *The Teaching of English.* 76th NSSE Yearbook, Part I. Edited by James Squire. Chicago: University of Chicago Press.

———, et. al. 1975. *The Development of Writing Abilities (11–18).* Schools Council Research Studies. New York: Macmillan.

Burnham, David. 1984. *The Rise of the Computer State.* New York: Vintage-Random House.

Callahan, Raymond. 1962. *Education and the Cult of Efficiency.* Chicago: University of Chicago Press.

Davidson, Jane L., ed. 1988. *Counterpoint and Beyond: A Response to Becoming a Nation of Readers.* Urbana: National Council of Teachers of English.

Dewey, John. 1916. *Democracy and Education.* New York: Macmillan.

———, and James Tufts. 1908. *Ethics.* New York: Henry Holt.

Dobrin, David. 1989. *Writing and Technique.* Urbana: National Council of Teachers of English.

Eisner, Elliot W. 1985. *The Educational Imagination.* 2nd ed. New York: Macmillan.

———. 1993. "Forms of Understanding and the Future of Educational Research." *Educational Researcher* 22: 5–11.

Ellul, Jacques. 1964. *The Technological Society.* Translated by John Wilkinson. New York: Vintage-Random House.

Freire, Paulo. 1970. *Pedagogy of the Oppressed.* Translated by Myra Bergman Ramos. New York: Continuum.

Gardner, Howard. 1982. *Art, Mind, and Brain: A Cognitive Approach to Creativity.* New York: Basic Books.

———. 1985. *The Mind's New Science: A History of the Cognitive Revolution.* New York: Basic Books.

Goldberg, Maxwell H. 1972. *Cybernation, Systems, and the Teaching of English: The Dilemma of Control.* Urbana: National Council of Teachers of English.

Habermas, Jurgen. 1970a. *Knowledge and Human Interests.* Translated by Jeremy Shapiro. Boston: Beacon.

———. 1970b. "Technology and Science as 'Ideology'." In *Toward a Rational Society: Student Protest, Science, and Politics,* translated by Jeremy J. Shapiro, 81–122. Boston: Beacon.

Hirsch, E. D., Jr. 1977. *The Philosophy of Composition.* Chicago: University of Chicago Press.

———. 1988a. "The Best Answer to a Caricature Is a Practical Program." *Educational Leadership* 46: 18–19.

———. 1988b. *Cultural Literacy: What Every American Needs to Know.* Updated and expanded edition. New York: Vintage-Random House.

Hofstadter, Douglas. 1979. *Gödel, Escher, Bach: An Eternal Golden Braid.* New York: Vintage.

Johnson, George. 1986. *Machinery of the Mind: Inside the New Science of Artificial Intelligence.* New York: Times Books.

Mueller, Claus. 1973. *The Politics of Communication: A Study in the Political Sociology of Language, Socialization, and Legitimation.* New York: Oxford University Press.

"NCTE to You." 1988. *English Journal* 77(6): 87.

Rogers, Carl. 1961. *On Becoming a Person.* Boston: Houghton-Mifflin.

Rosenblatt, Louise. 1976 [1938]. *Literature as Exploration.* 4th ed. New York: Modern Language Association of America.

———. 1978. *The Reader, the Text, the Poem: The Transactional Theory of the Literary Work.* Carbondale: Southern Illinois University Press.

———. 1980. "What Facts Does This Poem Teach You?" *Language Arts* 57(4): 386–94.

Roszak, Theodore. 1986. *The Cult of Information: The Folklore of Computers and the True Art of Thinking.* New York: Pantheon.

Schön, Donald. 1983. *The Reflective Practitioner: How Professionals Think in Action.* New York: Basic Books.

Shannon, Patrick. 1989. *Broken Promises: Reading Instruction in Twentieth-Century America. Critical Studies in Education.* Edited by Paulo Freire and Henry A. Giroux. Granby, MA: Bergin & Garvey.

Smith, Frank. 1988. *Understanding Reading: A Psycholinguistic Analysis of Reading and Learning to Read.* 4th ed. Hillsdale, NJ: Lawrence Erlbaum.

Vygotsky, Lev. 1962. *Thought and Language.* Translated by Eugenia Hanfmann and Gertrude Vakar. Cambridge, MA: MIT Press.

Weiner, Norbert. 1967. *The Human Use of Human Beings: Cybernetics and Society.* New York: Avon Books.

2 Policing Thought and Speech: What Happens to Intellectual Freedom?

Jean E. Brown
Saginaw Valley State University

For advocates of the free exchange of ideas, discussions of "political correctness" are fraught with irony. The term has been institutionalized to the degree that it appears in the new edition of *Webster's College Dictionary*, where it is defined as "marked by or adhering to a typically progressive orthodoxy on issues involving especially race, gender, sexual affinity, or ecology." The term has come to be used, both positively and negatively, as a label to identify and categorize both its proponents and opponents. For example, any instance of racial or gender insensitivity may be considered as "not PC." Those instances of "insensitivity" frequently are manifested by irresponsible labeling of individuals based on their race, gender, or sexual orientation, a practice that most people would find offensive. The inherent irony is that those who advocate "political correctness" object to the denigration of being labeled; yet, they resort to the same practices. The irony is further compounded by the opponents who label political correctness as the "new fundamentalism" (Taylor 1991, 34). Taylor further says:

> But curiously enough, in the past few years, a new sort of fundamentalism has arisen precisely among those people who were the most appalled by Christian fundamentalism. And it is just as demagogic and fanatical. (34)

The issue of political correctness is frequently discussed in both the news and entertainment media. The news media seem to be among the most vocal opponents of the movement by reporting as characteristic some of the most outrageous examples of political correctness. Accounts of the movement in the popular news media frequently focus on the sloganeering that unfortunately has come to characterize the public perception of political correctness. This sloganeering also makes the movement an easy target for quick jokes on situation comedies. This glib reaction focuses on the enforcement rather than exploring and recognizing the value of the underlying principle of the movement which is to monitor language and behavior toward previously disenfranchised groups so that they are included in society. It is a topic that engenders vocal responses both from those who practice it and those who condemn it. The irony is that the stage upon which the debate about political correctness is being enacted is primarily our universities, where the tradition of openness and a free exchange of ideas has long been a hallmark. Regardless of one's position on the subject, the issue is highly controversial and widely debated. In this chapter, we will explore an overview of what it means to be politically correct, a case for political correctness, a case against it, and its impact on intellectual freedom.

What Is Political Correctness?

In simplistic terms, the political correctness movement is said to be a reaction against the dominance of white males in our culture. It seeks to promote the use of unbiased language and attitudes on campuses by administrators, faculty, and students. Political correctness seeks to eliminate prejudice. Proponents of political correctness claim that they seek to alleviate past abuses and discrimination by inculcating tolerance, as they define it. The hotbed of discussion about political correctness began in higher education, where there is an attempt to establish and adopt codes of appropriate speech and behavior to embrace minority groups that previously have been systematically disaffected from the mainstream of Western culture. The objects of this type of discrimination are largely those groups in our society that have had to struggle to achieve the rights and freedoms established under the Constitution based upon issues of gender, race, or sexual preference.

Events of the last few years (the Rodney King case, bias crimes, the appointment of Clarence Thomas to the Supreme Court, the Senate Judiciary Committee's treatment of Anita Hill, the allegations against Congressman Brock Adams and Senator Bob Packwood, the Detroit police beating death of Malice Greene, vandalism in Hebrew cemeteries, and the beatings of homosexuals, for a few examples) have demonstrated that intolerance and inequity are significant problems in this country. While these examples vary in severity, they are all indicative of a pattern of discrimination that has been allowed to flourish during recent years. While these are current examples, they do represent the most recent chapters of a heritage of racism, sexism, ethnocentrism, or any other *-ism* that traditionally has sought to promote the interests of one group at the expense of others. One lesson that these troubled and troubling times has taught us is that no individual, nor any institution, including our schools, is removed from political concerns. Additionally, these events create an environment that fosters a concern for political correctness.

The issue of political correctness (PC) creates controversy. While it is widely accepted to be a movement of liberals to respond to our Western heritage which systematically excludes and discriminates against virtually all groups except white males, there are some critics who speculate that it is, in fact, an attempt by conservatives to discredit the movement. The organized opposition to the PC movement is primarily from the National Association of Scholars, a predominately conservative organization. The irony is that the conservatives are accusing liberals of repressive tactics while the liberals proclaim that they are responding to inequities of the past.

A Case for Political Correctness

The movement was designed, in part, to eliminate thoughtless and irresponsible use of language. The politically correct movement is a reaction to inequities that have occurred throughout our history. Within this context, however, the principle of freedom of speech takes on conditions of responsibility. Speech that is deliberately hurtful and damaging to individuals or groups that are not a part of the mainstream must be eliminated in order to begin to address the abuses of the past. Political correctness exemplifies the tenet that "the ends justify the means" because any short-term sacrifice that is made now in limiting freedom of speech will be more than compensated for over a period of time as a more tolerant and open acceptance of all people creates a better society.

The nature of the movement is to recognize and accept those who previously have been excluded; therefore, the movement is an inclusive one. Mabry (1990) responds to the clamor against political correctness by describing his experiences as a resident assistant at Stanford where he worked with freshmen. The focus of the program was to provide students with a recognition of the multicultural nature of our society. He explains:

> Attending a PC U (Stanford) is like taking a wilderness survival trek. It hurts like hell along the way, but afterwards you're glad you did it. Many white (straight) males have said they did discover perspectives they never knew existed. More than one fresh*man* thanked me at the end of the year for "making them think." And some women learned that stereotypes are forced on men, too. We all came a long way in our ability to hear each other, even if we sometimes didn't like what we heard. (55)

In other words, the process of gaining an awareness of the differences in our society, while difficult, will help students establish a level of understanding of others.

A Case against Political Correctness

Political correctness is an attempt to legitimatize intolerance, according to those who oppose the movement. They believe that it is ironic that the proponents of political correctness seek to eliminate what they consider to be our tradition of oppression while they condemn those who do not conform to their view. As history demonstrates, attempts to control human behavior such as Prohibition have failed horribly. There is no reason to believe that a movement designed to control thought and speech will have any more success.

In 1987, the American Association of State Colleges and Universities adopted a position statement on "Academic Freedom and Responsibility, and Academic Tenure." In that document, the role of the university concerning freedom is articulated:

> Within the academic community, the vigorous exercise of these freedoms—to participate in the democratic process of government as citizens, to learn and to teach what scholarship suggests is the truth, to question even what is believed to have been settled, to publish without fear of reprisal what scholarship has discovered—gives vitality to teaching and learning and is the essence of academic freedom. Without these freedoms, academics cannot fulfill their duty to their students and to society. (n.p.)

Our universities have long been the center of diverse ideas and opinions; however, those who practice political correctness reject that tradition as they seek to eliminate instances of offensive speech. Furthermore, some PC proponents argue that the free exchange of ideas on college campuses has been limited to those that respond and support the agendas of the white male power structure. Yet, the opponents of political correctness point out that the multicultural concerns and needs of society are slowly being addressed. Therefore, they believe that it is counterproductive to yield to what they consider to be an inherent danger of political correctness, a "blame" mentality. The traditional power structure of white males is viewed as the enemy. The opponents complain that whenever a position begins with a premise based upon attributing blame rather than assuming responsibility, constructive action is shackled and an environment of repression is created. The movement seeks to enforce their views to intimidate and control. Repression is not alleviated by simply changing the recipients of it.

Additionally, higher education should provide a forum for including diverse ideas that are representative of every aspect of our society. In his State of the University Address in January 1993, Dr. Eric Gilbertson spoke at Saginaw Valley State University about the nature of today's universities. While he did not address the specific issue of political correctness, his comments on academic freedom certainly provide an appropriate framework for measuring the exclusionary posture of militant advocates of political correctness. In reference to Saginaw Valley's mission, he spoke of

> . . . our role as an institution of higher education in this society [is]— "to represent and advance the ideals and values of higher education in a democratic society. . . ." The first and foremost of these is academic freedom—"pursuing and defending freedom of inquiry, thought and expression." Universities have historically stood firmly against McCarthyism, against book banners and book burners. Today, the challenges to freedom of inquiry, thought and expression are often more subtle—whether from the political Right or the political Left, whether from religious zealots or hate mongers of whatever variety—but they are no less real. This is all easier to state as an abstract proposition than it is to live in real life. It means that we will have to encourage departments and student organizations to debate controversial ideas and bring controversial people to campus.

This advocacy of a free exchange of ideas is consistent with the avowed purposes of education. Political correctness seeks to limit an exchange of ideas and provide a litmus test for intellectual freedom, thus denying the significance of diverse ideas, beliefs, and expressions not only as cornerstones of the educational system, but also as foundations for our democracy.

Political Correctness and Language

On one level, political correctness addresses language and is designed to prohibit the use of personal slurs in making reference to an individual's gender, ethnic background, or sexual orientation. While an unfortunate number of incidents of racial slurs have taken place on campuses throughout the country, perhaps none has received more attention than that of the University of Connecticut student who posted a sign on her dorm room door enumerating those to be shot on sight, including, among others, "preppies," "bimbos," and "homos." Certainly, the student's posting might most charitably be considered an example of ignorant, poor judgment, but it created a furor that resulted in the student being found guilty of violating the student behavior code that the university had enacted. The code sought to prohibit students from ". . . making personal slurs or epithets based on race, ethnic origin, disability, religion, or sexual orientation." The student was required to move out of the dorm and then forbidden to go into university cafeterias and dormitories. She was reinstated to the campus only after her attorneys threatened lawsuits. The university revised their code of conduct when they were faced with the possibility of a federal lawsuit. Other universities such as the University of Wisconsin and the University of Michigan have adopted speech codes only to have these codes struck down in federal court as unconstitutional.

The overt attempt to control or at least moderate biased and intolerant speech is in direct opposition to the provisions for freedom of speech in the Bill of Rights. However, in spite of the position of its critics, advocates of political correctness in language contend that it is designed to include rather than exclude. The proponents of PC contend that the inclusive nature of the movement reflects efforts to provide a forum for those society members of traditionally underrepresented groups.

Long ago Justice Oliver Wendall Holmes reaffirmed the basic recognition of the value of the varied range of opinions when he advocated protecting "freedom for the thought we despise." He demonstrated an understanding that our fundamental freedoms cross all ideological persuasions in our society. The free exchange of ideas is central to our democracy. Political correctness, like all forms of censorship, is a violation of that fundamental principle. As Justice Holmes understood, the issue is not that we must always agree with diverse ideas; however, it is essential that we protect the rights of those with whom we disagree to express even ideas that we find abhorrent. In ascribing to political correctness, we seek to eliminate the "thought we despise," rather than using diverse opinions as a measure against which we explore and reflect upon our own values. (See chapter 10, this volume, in which Roy O'Donnell also discusses the issue of political correctness and language.)

Political Correctness and the Canon

While the aspect of political correctness that the media most often focus upon is the use of language, the curricular implications of it are even more significant for education. In a broader context, the essence of political correctness is grounded in the belief that the curriculum needs to be revised to reflect the multicultural nature of our culture. The concern about the issue of political correctness is reflected and explored in the debate over what should constitute the canon and what should be taught. The canon is defined by both content and perspective. While the debate rages on the college campus, a review of many of the high school literature texts demonstrates a willingness to include token selections of previously underrepresented groups, such as African Americans, Native Americans, Asian Americans, and women authors. A superficial survey indicates that representatives of these groups are acknowledged in many recent anthologies; however, in her current research, Harmon (1993) has found that these groups remain underrepresented on a per author, per selection, or per page basis. On college campuses, new courses are being developed to address what the "narrow" perspective presented in traditional Western civilization courses. Stanford University led the way by developing a course entitled "Cultures, Ideas, and Values" which focuses upon the works of women and minority writers (D'Souza 1991). While the merits of the new course are obvious, the problem is that the course is not an addition to the curriculum, but a replacement for the traditional Western culture course. Their lead has been followed by a number of other highly respected universities. Advocates of eradicating the inequities of the past do not see replacing one ideology with another as a solution to the long-term problems.

Political Correctness and Intellectual Freedom

Regardless of the challenges of political correctness to language and literature, we will only be able to provide a global perspective in the schools when we have established an environment in which diversity of thought is valued and protected, and in which we are able to meet the threats that challenge intellectual freedom at present. The strategic planning document of the National Council of Teachers of English identifies promoting "Intellectual freedom at all educational levels," to be a general objective for the ongoing direction of the Council. This document further speaks to fundamental issues of diversity and pluralistic understandings. The first objective of the document reads that the Council "[s]upports programs, policies, and practices that (1) promote respect both for English and other languages and literatures that contribute to a rich cultural heritage; (2) affirm the legitimacy of native dialects, languages, and cultures; and (3) enable students to rediscover the language of their heritage and to learn other languages." This is an advocacy of inclusion rather than the exclusionary tenets of political correctness. For those who truly value intellectual freedom, the inequities of the past cannot be solved by creating new inequities:

> Political Correctness requires that students, faculty, and administration project "right" opinions about women, sexism, race and the numerous other categories of victimology. . . . The chief victim of this effort is, of course, intellectual freedom. (10a)

One facet of curriculum planning includes always a matter of selection; however, when the ideas and works of all underrepresented groups are systematically ignored, we cross the line between selection and censorship. Additionally, when the inclusion of works by members of underrepresented groups is simply tokenism, the problem remains. Until the curriculum reflects the multifaceted diversity of our total culture, we are infringing on the intellectual freedom of those who are not represented or who have traditionally been underrepresented.

Unfortunately, too often political correctness is not designed either to open the curriculum or to open minds. Curricular decisions should be made on merit, a merit that is inclusive. The direction of the English curriculum should be reflective of the best authors and thinkers. We cannot afford a material or pedagogy policy that either includes or excludes simply on a criterion of ethnicity or on gender rather than on educational merit; or on attempts to control thinking rather than encourage critical thinking.

If the whole political correctness effort were to be effective, it would need to begin with a posture of inclusion rather than exclusion, not replacing a policy of old biases with a policy of new biases. We need to move away from labeling and name-calling to acceptance and coalition building. True inclusion would not reject the contributions of the formerly "white male" majority, as some of the most vocal supporters of the movement advocate.

As we explore the implications for intellectual freedom, political correctness presents an interesting dilemma. We would like to believe that those who infringe on First Amendment rights are wild-eyed ultraconservatives who wish only to espouse their own narrow ideology. We would like to believe that attempts to limit language and the content of the curriculum are the self-serving actions of reactionaries who fear controversy and ideas that may challenge their own beliefs. We do not expect attempts to limit freedom of expression to come from the left of the political spectrum. So political correctness does not fit the pattern; it is a response to true abuses, abuses of bigotry and oppression. It is difficult to believe that all thinking people would not be appalled by slurs based upon race, gender, or sexual orientation. It is also difficult to believe that they would also not seek to have the curriculum present the most representative examples of the total human experience. The dilemma is that while philosophically we may agree with the ultimate goals of the proponents of political correctness, their repressive tactics are an anathema to our belief in the tenets of our Constitution. Ironically, the movement, through its wide media exposure, may be counterproductive. As the term is bandied about, the concerns of political correctness are rendered insignificant. As the media trivialize the term political correctness, an inherent problem is that the legitimate concerns that gave birth to the movement are also trivialized and even lost. The label PC has become an excuse for ignoring these issues that, in fact, inspired it. It demonstrates that labels obscure issues and provide an easy focal point that negates the original concern.

Works Cited

American Association of State Colleges and Universities Committee on Academic Affairs. 1987. "Academic Freedom and Responsibility, and Academic Tenure." Washington, D. C.: American Association of State Colleges and Universities.

D'Souza, Dinesh. 1991. "Illiberal Education." *The Atlantic* (March): 52–58, 62–67, 70–79.

———. 1992. "PC and How It Grew." "Focus Section," *The Boston Globe* (29 March): 78–79.

Gilbertson, Eric. 1993. State of the University Address. Saginaw Valley State University. Saginaw, Michigan. January.

Harmon, M. 1993. Doct. Diss. [in progress]. Michigan State University.

Mabry, M. 1990. "A View from the Front." *Newsweek* (24 December): 55.

Pindell, Howardena. 1990. "Politically Correct." *The Wall Street Journal* (26 November): 10.

Taylor, John. 1991. "Are You Politically Correct?" *New York Magazine* (21 January): 32–40.

3 Academic Freedom: Student Rights and Faculty Responsibilities

David Moshman
University of Nebraska–Lincoln

No one admits to being against academic freedom. Claims that academic freedom is being violated, like claims that motherhood or apple pie are threatened, thus have strong rhetorical value. When the censor is at the schoolhouse door, one can often hear incantations of academic freedom from within.

But what is academic freedom?

Is it the freedom of educational institutions from external constraints? Is it the freedom of faculty from external or institutional constraints? Is it the freedom of students from external, institutional, or faculty constraints?

Is it freedom to teach? Freedom to learn? Freedom to engage in original research? Freedom to communicate one's conclusions? Freedom to apply one's knowledge?

And how can academic freedom be justified? Is it a constitutional right? A moral entitlement? Is it created by laws? By contracts? Is it a component of quality education? A spur to social progress?

One possible answer is obvious and plausible: Academic freedom involves all of the above. But unless we can say more than this, such a broad and multifaceted notion of academic freedom is at best vague (Yudof 1987) and at worst incoherent (Byrne 1989). Although seeming to protect everyone and everything, it may, for that very reason, protect nothing.

Obviously, this leaves teachers in a vulnerable position. Today's censors are often ingenious and persistent, and may have strong political support. It takes more than self-righteous slogans to ward them off. A thoughtful and effective response to potential censors requires a clear and well-justified conception of academic freedom.

It is often noted that there is nothing so practical as a good theory. Dealing effectively with censorship in academic contexts, of course, requires written procedures, appropriate criteria, personal fortitude, good public relations, and so forth. But above all, I believe, it requires a clear sense of what academic freedom encompasses, why it is important, and how it is justified. Dealing with censorship, in short, requires a theory of academic freedom.

My purpose in this chapter is to provide a brief and nontechnical outline of such a theory. You may disagree with some of what follows. That's fine. My aim is not to provide a definitive account but rather to address some complex issues in a manner that will challenge you to explore your own views and formulate a theory of your own.

I begin with a commonly held view of academic freedom as consisting, at its core, of the right of faculty to teach as they see fit (cf. Byrne 1989; Sacken 1989; Yudof 1987). I will argue that the Constitution protects no such right and that this conception provides a shaky foundation for academic freedom. I then propose that academic freedom is better construed as a matter of student rights. After exploring the nature and justification of such rights, I return to the realm of faculty and argue that teachers should indeed have substantial academic freedom but that such freedom rests not on any special rights they have as faculty but on their responsibility to protect the rights of students and to provide quality education.

Academic Freedom as Faculty Rights: A Critique

Imagine that a teacher at a public school or college publishes a letter in the local newspaper which the governing board of his or her school finds immoral, politically objectionable, or just plain offensive. As a result the teacher is fired. Clearly, the teacher has a very strong constitutional claim that his or her First Amendment rights have been violated. But a janitor in a government building who is fired under the same circumstances would, it seems to me, have an equally strong First Amendment claim. There is no reason to suggest that a teacher in a case of this sort has special rights beyond those of any government employee. Cases of this sort do not appear to raise any special issue of academic freedom (Byrne 1989; Clarick 1990). Consider now the following circumstances:

1. A janitor in a government building is told that he is to mop certain rooms each day. He believes, however, that it would be better for the state of the building to water the plants, or to mop different rooms, or to sweep the rooms in question rather than mopping them. After repeatedly refusing to mop the designated rooms, and with appropriate due process, he is fired.

2. A teacher is hired to teach history in a public school and is told to teach the state-approved American history curriculum. She believes, however, that it would be better for her students to teach them classic American literature, or to teach European history, or to focus on aspects or interpretations of American history at variance with the approved curriculum. After repeatedly refusing to teach the state curriculum, and with appropriate due process, she is fired.

Although there is room for argument about whether the janitor should have been fired, it seems clear that he had no constitutional right to determine his own job description. There was no constitutional violation in firing him for not doing the job he was hired to do.

But the case of the teacher seems to me exactly parallel. Here also there is room for argument about under what circumstances firing her would be the proper decision, but there does not appear to be any *constitutional* reason to suggest that she has more right than the janitor to define her own job. She was fired for not doing the job she was hired to do. The academic nature of the context does not provide any basis for suggesting that her constitutional rights have been violated (Yudof 1987).

One can, of course, vary the situations. Suppose the teacher does teach the required curriculum but supplements it with her own interpretations, elaborations, additional readings, etc. It might be suggested that she is doing her job and that what she chooses to express beyond the curriculum is protected by the First Amendment. But it seems to me that the janitor, as long as he gets his mopping done, also has a First Amendment right to express his views about mopping, sweeping, the value of well-watered plants, or whatever else he chooses to address. So again it is not clear that anything in the academic context provides a teacher with special rights beyond those of any government employee. In fact, given that the teacher has a captive audience of students, and especially if the students are young, a case might be made that *greater* restriction on the teacher than on the janitor is constitutionally defensible. Everyone has a First Amendment right to freedom of expression, but no one has a general First Amendment right to express his or her views to a captive audience provided by the government (Sacken 1989; Yudof 1987).

But what if the teacher's contract, school policy, or state law guarantees substantial autonomy in deciding what to teach and/or how to teach it (Sacken 1989)? In that case, of course, the teacher has whatever rights are specified. My argument is *not* that teachers cannot or should not have such rights. My argument is that such rights go beyond what the Constitution requires.

To put the point more generally, I suggest that, although the Fi... Amendment strictly forbids government censorship of personal expression, it does not forbid government to formulate views of its own, to hire individuals to express those views, and to require such individuals to do the jobs they have been hired to do. It is thus constitutional for governmental entities to establish public schools, to determine the curricula of those schools, to hire teachers to implement those curricula, and to require such teachers to teach what they are directed to teach (Sacken 1989; Yudof 1987). Narrow specification of exactly what each teacher must teach may be a threat to student rights and detrimental to quality education (see below), but it does not, in my view, violate teachers' First Amendment rights.

Academic Freedom as Student Rights

Having thus questioned the rights of teachers, I might be expected to be even more dubious about the notion of student rights. But in fact, quite the contrary, I think the First Amendment should be interpreted as providing stringent protection for public school students' intellectual rights.

Students as Private Agents

Why do I see the First Amendment as providing stronger protection for students than for faculty? The key constitutional distinction between students and faculty is the status of the former as private agents. Faculty in public educational institutions are agents of the government who have been hired to serve the government's educational purposes and who therefore, when acting in their professional capacities, have a responsibility to do what they have been hired to do. Students, by contrast, are not agents of the government. They have not voluntarily agreed to further the government's educational aims. They are private individuals whose fundamental intellectual rights may not be abridged by the government (Moshman 1989; 1993).

Applicability of the First Amendment to Education

It might be argued that First Amendment rights are all well and good but that they have little relevance to learning; thus, they should not apply to students in educational settings. To evaluate this proposal, we must consider the purposes of the First Amendment. At least three such purposes (respect for personal dignity, promotion of truth, and protection of democracy) are generally acknowledged (Byrne 1989; Moshman 1989).

First, it is a basic assumption of the U.S. Constitution that individual persons have a fundamental right to dignity and respect. Underlying the First Amendment is a commitment to freedoms of belief and expression as central to human dignity. There is no reason whatsoever to believe that undermining students' dignity or denying them respect is necessary, or even helpful, to education. On the contrary, psychologists and educators generally agree that students learn best when they are free to form, hold, and express their own ideas (Clarick 1990; Moshman 1989; 1990). Thus, on the view that the First Amendment is intended to protect the dignity of individuals via respect for their freedoms of belief and expression, it is clear that the First Amendment should apply directly and strongly to students in educational settings.

A second purpose of the First Amendment is to facilitate the emergence of truth and the social progress that results from truth. Underlying the protection of belief and expression is the assumption that truth is most likely to prevail in a free market of ideas and that government restrictions on belief and expression should therefore be forbidden. But the quest for truth is clearly at least as central to education as to any other human activity (Byrne 1989). Government may, of course, add its powerful voice to the quest for truth by designing educational messages and arranging for them to be taught in government-run schools. The truth-promoting function of the First Amendment provides no reason, however, to question the right of students to explore a variety of ideas and perspectives, and to form and express ideas of their own.

Finally, democracy entails the right to dissent from governmental views and actions; the First Amendment was intended to guard against the natural tendency of governments to restrict such dissent. More broadly, full and vigorous democracy requires citizens with the intellectual autonomy to formulate and communicate their own ideas. Public education provides government with the opportunity to undermine genuine democracy by molding the views of each generation of citizens via government-run schools (Clarick 1990; Moshman 1989; 1990). With respect to the democracy rationale, then, First Amendment protection of intellectual rights, far from being irrelevant to the educational context, is particularly critical in the case of students in government schools.

In sum, there is no reason to construe public schools as a special domain outside the realm of the First Amendment. As the Supreme Court put it in *Tinker v. Des Moines* (1969), students do not

> shed their constitutional rights to freedom of speech or expression at the schoolhouse gate [506]. . . . In our system, students may not be regarded as closed-circuit recipients of only that which the State chooses to communicate. They may not be confined to the expression of those sentiments that are officially approved [511].

Applicability of the First Amendment to Children

It might be argued that, even if the First Amendment applies to mature students, it has little or no applicability to children. Given the three rationales for the First Amendment just discussed, it might be suggested that children have little need for dignity and respect and little ability to participate in the search for truth or the processes of democratic self-government.

Even with respect to elementary school children there is reason to question such a proposal (Moshman 1989). Children as young as age two—in fact, perhaps *especially* children of age two—have ideas of their own and a strong inclination to say what they think. Censorship of expression can be a psychologically damaging assault on personal dignity, and this is no less true for young children than for adults. Moreover, restricting access to ideas and sources of information, even when rationalized as protecting children from dangerous influences, may in fact hinder development of their ability to coordinate multiple perspectives and think for themselves. Censorship of books and curricula may thus inhibit intellectual development and limit later ability to contribute to the free market of ideas. Finally, even to the extent that young children are less capable than adults of evaluating input and rationally formulating their own views, this only heightens the importance of First Amendment protection against unconstitutional efforts to limit their ultimate intellectual and political freedom as adults by indoctrinating them as children.

With respect to adolescents in secondary schools, there is even less reason to limit First Amendment rights. Psychological research shows substantial overlap between adolescents and adults in basic reasoning abilities. Contrary to popular myths, there is no evidence of the sort of qualitative difference in intellectual competence that might justify a difference in First Amendment rights (for reviews, see Moshman 1989; 1990; 1993).

Although the Supreme Court has been inconsistent in its treatment of adolescents (Moshman 1993), an important recent ruling accords with this analysis. In *Board of Education v. Mergens* (1990), a public high school had refused to allow a voluntary student religious club to use its facilities on the same basis as other extracurricular groups. The Supreme Court had earlier ruled that the First Amendment requires public colleges to permit all student groups, including religious groups, equal access to their facilities (*Widmar v. Vincent* 1981). The high school argued that this precedent should not apply at the high school level because high school students are less mature than college students and would incorrectly assume that any group permitted by the school was thereby endorsed by the school. On this argument, then, high schools may censor student speech if they deem it inconsistent with the views or mission of the school (cf. *Hazelwood v. Kuhlmeier* 1988). The Court rejected this analysis, however, maintaining instead that

> secondary school students are mature enough and are likely to understand that a school does not endorse or support student speech that it merely permits on a nondiscriminatory basis.... The proposition that schools do not endorse everything they fail to censor is not complicated. (250)

Students' First Amendment Rights

Having suggested that students, even young students, have First Amendment rights, the precise nature and extent of such rights remain to be considered. Although detailed analysis of this is beyond the scope of a brief chapter (see Moshman 1989), I would suggest three basic sorts of First Amendment rights for students in public schools: (a) freedoms of belief and expression, (b) free access to ideas, and (c) limitations on inculcation.

First, students have a right to form, hold, and express their own beliefs. Schools may, of course, restrict expression when necessary to maintain order or to protect the rights of other students (*Tinker v. Des Moines* 1969). They may not, however, restrict expression simply because teachers, administrators, or other government officials object to what a student says or writes (but see *Hazelwood v. Kuhlmeier* 1988).

Second, students have a right of access to ideas and sources of information. Schools need not, of course, facilitate such access by purchasing or assigning every book that any student wishes to read, but they may not, in my view, take specific steps to restrict access to disfavored books or ideas.

Third, although schools are free to inculcate a multitude of ideas and values in a variety of ways, the First Amendment, it seems to me, places some important restrictions on this. For one thing, there must be legitimate educational reasons for the choice of what to inculcate. Moreover, the school must remain neutral with respect to (a) religion and (b) current political controversy. And finally, even where inculcation is acceptable, it must be nonindoctrinative—that is, nothing may be taught in such a way as to undercut the possibility of independent analysis and criticism by students.

There is room for argument about precisely what First Amendment rights entail and how they apply to issues of education. I think it is clear, however, that academic freedom for students is not just a good idea; it is their constitutional right.

Academic Freedom and Faculty Responsibilities

With student rights in mind, then, let us return to the issue of academic freedom for faculty. I have already argued against the view that teachers have special First Amendment rights beyond those of other government employees. I nevertheless believe that teachers at all educational levels should have broad and firm academic freedom to devise and select curricula and course materials, teach what and how they see fit, etc. There are, in my view, two reasons for this.

The first relates to students' First Amendment rights. I argued earlier that it violates the First Amendment for students' access to books and ideas to be restricted or for them to be subjected to political or religious inculcation or systematic indoctrination. It is, of course, possible for students' First Amendment rights to be violated by any of a variety of government agents, including teachers. It seems fair to suggest, however, that as one moves along the continuum from legislators to governing board members to administrators to teachers and librarians, one is moving in the direction of decreasing political motivation and increasing professional expertise with respect to the subject matter being taught. By granting faculty substantial autonomy and insulating them from legislative and administrative pressures, one increases the likelihood that curricular and instructional decisions will be made on educational rather than political grounds (Moshman 1989).

Faculty freedom should not be absolute, of course. In cases where a teacher is systematically inculcating particular religious or political beliefs, for example, it is fully appropriate for a school to step in and correct the situation. But such actions by a school should be the exception rather than the rule and should be carefully scrutinized and justified. Indoctrination by individual teachers is, no doubt, a serious constitutional concern. The danger to students and democracy is far greater, however, in cases of systemwide or statewide indoctrination by administrators, governing boards, or legislatures.

A second reason for supporting substantial academic freedom for faculty is that such freedom is likely to improve education. Psychologists and educators generally agree that meaningful knowledge and autonomous reasoning are actively constructed rather than passively internalized. Students learn and develop best in environments in which they have free access to multiple sources of information and are encouraged to form, express, and discuss their own ideas (Clarick 1990; Moshman 1989; 1990; Roe 1991). Teachers constrained by rigid requirements, externally imposed curricula, and threats of censorship are unlikely to create the kind of environment that fosters meaningful learning, much less the development of rationality, creativity, critical thinking, etc.

Academic freedom for teachers, then, is valuable not only because it tends to protect students' First Amendment rights, but also because it promotes quality education.

It should be noted that the above analyses apply at all levels of education. Although there is a much stronger tradition of academic freedom in higher education than at the elementary and secondary levels (Byrne 1989; Clarick 1990; Sacken 1989; Yudof 1987), there seems to me no constitutional, psychological, or educational basis for a sharp distinction in this regard. As I argued earlier, even young children have First Amendment rights, and there is little reason to distinguish adolescents from adults with respect to such rights. Accordingly, if the central point of academic freedom is to protect students' intellectual rights, academic freedom is important even at the elementary school level, and there is little reason to sharply distinguish secondary and higher education in this regard.

Although my argument has been made on constitutional, psychological, and educational grounds, the present approach to academic freedom has political advantages as well. Teachers who assert their right to teach as they see fit are likely to be seen as protecting their own interests and thus no different from any employee who argues for higher pay or better working conditions. When academic freedom is threatened, faculty may have limited credibility if they resist primarily on the basis of their own rights. Their credibility is likely to be greater if they resist censorship on the basis of their constitutional and professional responsibility to protect (a) their students' First Amendment rights and (b) the interest of students and the community in quality education.

Conclusion

I have suggested that a clear and well-justified conception of academic freedom is critical to warding off and responding to censorship efforts. Common conceptions of academic freedom as faculty rights, I have argued, are difficult to defend. Academic freedom is better construed as resting on the intellectual needs and First Amendment rights of students. Far from weakening the concept of academic freedom or shrinking its scope, this conception clarifies the nature of academic freedom and places it on a stronger foundation.

Works Cited

Board of Education of Westside Community Schools v. Mergens. 1990. 496 U.S. 226.

Byrne, J. P. 1989. "Academic Freedom: A 'Special Concern of the First Amendment.'" *Yale Law Journal* 99: 251–340.

Clarick, G. A. 1990. "Public School Teachers and the First Amendment: Protecting the Right to Teach." *New York University Law Review* 65: 693–735.

Hazelwood School District v. Kuhlmeier. 1988. 484 U.S. 260.

Moshman, D. 1989. *Children, Education, and the First Amendment: A Psycholegal Analysis.* Lincoln: University of Nebraska Press.

———. 1990. "Rationality as a Goal of Education." *Educational Psychology Review* 2: 335–64.

———. 1993. "Adolescent Reasoning and Adolescent Rights." *Human Development* 36: 27–40.

Roe, R. L. 1991. "Valuing Student Speech: The Work of the Schools as Conceptual Development." *California Law Review* 79: 1269–345.

Sacken, D. M. 1989. "Rethinking Academic Freedom in the Public Schools: The Matter of Pedagogical Methods." *Teachers College Record* 91: 235–55.

Tinker v. Des Moines Independent Community School District. 1969. 393 U.S. 503.

Widmar v. Vincent. 1981. 454 U.S. 263.

Yudof, M. G. 1987. "Three Faces of Academic Freedom." *Loyola Law Review* 32: 831–58.

4 Self-Censorship and the Elementary School Teacher

Kathie Krieger Cerra
Macalester College

A preservice teacher views, in an intellectual freedom component of her language arts class, a list of books that elementary school teachers in her state have reported challenged. Among them is Mildred Taylor's *Roll of Thunder, Hear My Cry*. "I'm reading another book by that author to the fourth-grade students in the classroom where I am student teaching. Will this book be challenged?" she asks me, the instructor. She has been reading *The Friendship* aloud to students of a multirace class, generating thoughtful discussion among the children, explaining the times in which Taylor's book is set, and helping the children to confront the portrayal of racism which they immediately recognize. I have watched her do this, admired her sensitivity and skill in generating and guiding the children's discussion. She is fortunate in that her supervising teacher has recently been teaching a unit, in this fourth-grade class, concerning social justice issues.

In our college class, we have discussed the First Amendment basis of intellectual freedom in the schools, talked about the Tinker case (*Tinker v. Des Moines Independent School District*) and Justice Abe Fortas's statement, "It can hardly be argued that either students or teachers shed their constitutional rights to freedom of speech or expression at the schoolhouse gate" (Qtd. in Hentoff 1980, 5). I have mentioned the varying results of other court decisions (Jenkinson 1979, 149). The student teacher's question arises—Am I at risk here? The following week, I ask her if she has continued to read the book aloud. She has. "I've finished *The Friendship*. We've had good discussions, and I've started reading *Number the Stars*," she tells me. She has resisted self-censorship, resisted the

Some of the information in this chapter appeared previously in Cerra, Kathie Krieger. 1991. "Teachers' Attitudes about Intellectual Freedom and Books in the Elementary School." *Minnesota Media* 16.2: 20–21, 33–38, and is used by permission. The author wishes to thank Norine Odland, professor emeritus at the University of Minnesota, for her generous interest and guidance concerning this study.

tendency to take what might seem to be the easier, safer road of avoiding a potentially controversial book, instead relying upon her skill in fostering the students' developing ability to think, to reflect, to respond to a well-written book. "I feel that the right thing to do with children is to be straightforward and to discuss things honestly," she tells me.

This preservice teacher distinguishes herself from others faced with similar situations and questions. Studies of school and public librarians which investigate attitudes and practices concerning book selection and censorship reveal a repeating pattern—censorship in tandem with espousing the freedom to read. Marjorie Fiske's (1959) study of book selection and intellectual freedom interviewed California librarians and administrators in public high school libraries and in public libraries. Although nearly one-half of the librarians expressed convictions favoring freedom to read, nearly two-thirds of those responsible for book selection reported instances where the controversiality of a book or an author had resulted in a decision not to buy the book. Of those who expressed strong convictions about freedom to read, 40 percent took the controversial nature of material into account under some circumstances (Fiske 1959, 65). Fiske also found differences between librarians who worked in public schools and those who worked in public libraries. Fiske reported that public school librarians saw themselves as isolated from the profession of librarianship and subordinate to concepts and practices of school administrators. Public school librarians were less likely than were public librarians to support freedom to read when considering controversial material.

Another study of librarians shows similar results concerning self-censorship and freedom to read. Charles Busha (1972) investigated attitudes toward censorship and intellectual freedom by sending a questionnaire to a random sample of librarians in Illinois, Indiana, Michigan, Ohio, and Wisconsin. Busha states that the most significant result of his study is the finding of a disparity between attitudes of librarians toward intellectual freedom and attitudes toward censorship as an activity. Although most librarians supported principles of intellectual freedom, 64 percent were neutral toward censorship practices, and 14 percent were sympathetic to such practices. Only 22 percent were strongly opposed to censorship practices. Busha found the neutrality toward censorship to be inconsistent with the favorable attitudes of the same librarians toward principles of intellectual freedom and freedom to read.

The studies by Fiske and Busha have something to say about self-censorship. They both embody the dichotomy among the respondents who espouse intellectual freedom and yet select actions which would support censorship. The Fiske study shows controversiality of materials to be a limiting factor to actions supporting intellectual freedom; being subordinate to a school administrator, as was the case for school librarians, also appeared to be a factor in the disparity between principle and practice. A study by Frances McDonald (1993) suggests that educational preparation of school librarians plays a role in agreeing with principles of intellectual freedom but not in applying those principles. In an investigation of junior high school and high school librarians with master's degrees, McDonald found that librarians who had been educated in institutions with programs accredited by the American Library Association were more likely to embrace principles of intellectual freedom than were librarians whose professional preparation took place in other types of institutions. However, in application of these principles, there were no significant differences between the groups.

Censorship by school staff has been reported in two major studies. Lee Burress (1979) reported on the 1977 National Council of Teachers of English Censorship Survey, in which questionnaires were mailed to a sample of secondary school teachers who were NCTE members. Burress concluded "that censorship pressure is a prominent and growing part of school life" (36). In looking at the origin of censorship attempts, Burress concluded that most censorship pressures came from parents (73 percent) and *school staff* (23 percent; italics mine.) A report of a national survey, *Limiting What Students Shall Read* (1981), concluded that challenges to textbook and library materials occur in every region and type of community in the nation, and that sources of challenges *derive from within* (italics mine) as well as from without the educational establishment. A study of Minnesota principals' views of intellectual freedom and book selection in the elementary school (Chandler 1985) reported that challenges to the suitability of library books in Minnesota elementary schools were about as likely to come from the school staff as from members of the community. These studies touch on the challenges to reading materials by school staff—the educational community censoring itself.

In *Free Speech for Me—But Not for Thee,* Nat Hentoff (1992) gives examples of censorship by school staff. In a chapter which discusses challenges to *Huckleberry Finn* in the public schools, Hentoff tells about a school administrator in Virginia who worked to have *Huckleberry Finn* removed from the curriculum, and about a curriculum director in Indianapolis who favored having the book removed from reading lists because it offends minorities. He tells of a library center in upstate New York which advised school librarians to place warning labels on biased material. He mentions librarians who decide not to order books by Judy

Blume because of the controversy which accompanies them. Hentoff's accounts of interviews with librarians, teachers, and administrators bring to life what is known from quantitative research about self-censorship among school staff.

Let us return now to our clear-thinking preservice teacher. The list of books reported challenged in elementary schools, the list (c.f. appendix, table 8) which caused her to wonder if the book by Mildred Taylor that she was reading could be the next one to be challenged, was derived from a study of elementary school teachers, which I conducted in 1989 (Cerra 1990; 1991). At the outset, I did not think of the study as one of self-censorship, but rather as a study of teachers' attitudes and practices with regard to selecting books for children and reading books to children, and the role that intellectual freedom played in those attitudes and practices. It was the findings, the teachers' responses, which made the study into one of self-censorship.

I turn now to an account of the study itself. The population was the elementary school teachers in Minnesota, grades 1–6, who were certified and teaching in a public school elementary classroom during the 1988–89 school year. I mailed questionnaires to a randomly selected sample of 452 teachers, which comprised about 3 percent of the population of 15,000 elementary school teachers. After three mailings, 375 surveys were completed and returned, resulting in a response rate of about 83 percent of the original sample.

In designing the questionnaire, I asked questions having to do with book selection and intellectual freedom, and teachers' views about elementary school students' First Amendment rights. There was a series of questions which particularly addressed the actions that teachers might take when selecting books for their classrooms, and it is the responses to these questions which led this sample of teachers to distinguish itself in favor of self-censorship.

Here are the survey items, followed by a discussion of the results for each:

> Item #1: If an award-winning book you have chosen to read aloud to your class has language which you feel might be offensive, what action would you take? (Check one)
> a. __ Select another book
> b. __ Read the book exactly as it is written
> c. __ Alter the text so it is more suitable

In response to this question, 16 percent of teachers indicated that they would select another book, 14 percent indicated that they would read the book exactly as written, and 70 percent indicated that they would alter the text so that it is more suitable. Thus, when faced with language that might be offensive, a majority (70 percent) of the elementary school teachers surveyed would alter the text while reading an award-winning book aloud. This is self-censorship, at the level of bringing the book to the children while reading aloud. Those who would select another book make a choice which is not limiting to intellectual freedom, since the integrity of the book remains, and children can presumably read it for themselves if it is available in the classroom. A small percentage, 14 percent, stood squarely in favor of the principle of intellectual freedom and resisted self-censorship, indicating that they would read the book exactly as written.

> Item #2: When you are warned that a favorably reviewed book which you have read is risky because of its subject matter, what action do you take when considering purchase of the book for your classroom? (Check one)
> a. __ Purchase the book anyway, and do not limit student access
> b. __ Purchase the book, but limit student access
> c. __ Do not purchase the book

In response to this question concerning book purchase for the elementary classroom, 16 percent of teachers indicated that they would purchase the book and not limit student access, a response which clearly supports intellectual freedom. Twenty-five percent would purchase the book but limit student access, and 60 percent indicated that they would not purchase the book. The last two responses are a form of self-censorship in reaction to a warning that a well-written book may be controversial. Our preservice teacher, although she was not faced with the question of book purchase, knew that a book by Mildred Taylor might be challenged, but elected to continue to read it to her class.

> Item #3: Would you permit the following types of children's books in your classroom? (Circle one response for each item)
>
> | | Yes | No | Undecided |
> | -------------------------------- | --- | --- | --------- |
> | a. Stories from the Bible? | Y | N | U |
> | b. Stories from the Koran? | Y | N | U |
> | c. Stories from the Torah? | Y | N | U |
> | d. Native American mythology? | Y | N | U |
> | e. Greek myths and fables? | Y | N | U |

In this question about the particular types of children's books that teachers would permit in their classrooms, about half of the elementary school teachers would permit stories from the Bible (55 percent said "yes") and the Koran (49 percent said "yes") and the Torah (49 percent said "yes") in their classrooms. A substantial proportion of teachers, between one-fourth and one-half, were undecided about permitting stories from the Bible, the Koran, and the Torah in their classrooms. A very high percentage of respondents would permit Native American mythology (94 percent said "yes") and Greek myths and fables (96 percent said "yes") in their classrooms.

Self-censorship or uncertainty seems to be the response for about half of the teachers when the presence of clearly religious material is brought into question. The last two types of books, Native American mythology and Greek myths and fables, may not seem to be items of a religious nature in the view of the respondents, although the cultures which created these "myths" did view them as part of a religious belief system. Responses to this question bring to mind Nat Hentoff's (1992, 11–13) account of one ten-year-old student's legal battle to read the Bible during free time in his public school classroom. Permitting a book like the Bible to be available in a classroom, and allowing a student to read it during free time, differs from teaching religion to students.

> Item #4: Would you reject a book for inclusion in the school library on the basis of the following subject matter: (Circle one response for each item)
>
> | | | |
> |---|---|---|
> | a. Religion? | Y | N |
> | b. Sex? | Y | N |
> | c. Politics? | Y | N |
> | d. Racism? | Y | N |
> | e. Sexism? | Y | N |
> | f. Other? | Y | N |
>
> (Please specify: _____)

In this question, which asked for teachers' views about school library book selection with regard to certain subject matter, 21 percent of respondents would reject a book on the basis of religion as the subject matter. On the basis of sex as the subject matter, about 53 percent of teachers would reject a book for inclusion in the school library. On the basis of politics, about 12 percent of respondents would reject a book, while on the basis of racism as the subject matter, 62 percent of respondents would reject a book for inclusion in the school library. On the basis of sexism as the subject matter, 58 percent of respondents would reject a book for inclusion in the school library. Respondents who would reject books on the basis of subject matter may not understand that including certain subject matter within a book does not assume agreement with the subject matter itself. Among the books that, theoretically, could be rejected by a majority (62 percent) of respondents are Mildred Taylor's Newbery Award winner, *Roll of Thunder, Hear My Cry* and *The Friendship* (the book read aloud by our preservice teacher) because of the portrayal of racism in both books. Those who would reject a book on the basis of politics as its subject matter (12 percent) could presumably reject biographies of historical figures, such as the Newbery Award-winning book by Russell Freedman, *Lincoln: A Photobiography.*

> Item #5: It is a common practice for textbooks to have excerpts from children's books. Do you agree with the practice of rewriting selections in order to satisfy reading difficulty demands?
>
> a. __ Yes
> b. __ No

This question addresses the altering of literature by textbook publishers through rewriting in order to achieve a lower readability level. In response to this question, 74 percent of teachers, or about three-fourths, agreed with the practice of rewriting selections from children's books, and 26 percent did not agree. The practice of rewriting selections from children's books for inclusion in textbooks has been discouraged by authors and reviewers within the field of children's literature (Cohen 1987; Silvey 1989).

If studies of librarians have pointed to the contradiction between belief (espousal of the freedom to read) and action (selection of actions which would censor materials and books), how did Minnesota elementary school teachers respond when asked about their beliefs concerning First Amendment rights for children? I asked the following question:

> Item #6: Do you agree or disagree that elementary school students should have First Amendment rights? (Check only one)
>
> a. __ Strongly agree
> b. __ Agree
> c. __ Disagree
> d. __ Strongly disagree
> e. __ No opinion

About three-quarters, or 76 percent of responding teachers strongly agreed (19 percent) or agreed (57 percent) that elementary school students should have First Amendment rights. Nine percent disagreed and 2 percent strongly disagreed that elementary school students should have First Amendment rights, while 13 percent of teachers indicated that they have no opinion regarding this matter.

It appears that the elementary school teachers' responses follow the pattern of other studies which show a contradiction between belief and practice. The self-censorship in action in items 1 through 4, and the agreement with publishers' altering of excerpts from children's books, contrasts with the teachers' majority view (76 percent) agreeing that elementary school students should have First Amendment rights.

In this study, teachers were also asked about the sources of challenges to the suitability of trade books during the 1988–89 school year. Of the 38 challenges reported, fourteen of those, or 37 percent, originated with teachers; five challenges, or 13 percent, originated with principals; and five challenges (13 percent) originated with the librarian. Other sources of challenges were parent, nonparent community resident, and religious group. Thus, 63 percent of the challenges that were reported originated with school personnel. This finding is consistent with other studies (Burress 1979; 1989; *Limiting What Students Shall Read*, 1981; Chandler 1985) which report that some censorship pressures and challenges do originate with school staff.

Why do elementary school teachers agree with First Amendment rights for children but select actions with children and books that, in effect, would censor? Do teachers know about intellectual freedom issues? One survey item asked if the teacher has attended at least one class period devoted to intellectual freedom. Approximately 37 percent of respondents have attended a class period devoted to intellectual freedom, while 63 percent reported that they have not attended a class period devoted to intellectual freedom. It may be that teachers' responses derive from the fact that many are uninformed and uneducated in the area of intellectual freedom in the schools.

Are teachers knowledgeable about children's literature and about professional standards of book selection? Forty-four percent of respondents indicated that they have taken one children's literature course in their teacher-preparation program, and 53 percent have taken more than one children's literature course. Other items in the questionnaire asked about teachers' current reading in the field of children's books. Of teachers who responded, 98 percent read children's books, while 78 percent read reviews of new children's books. Further questions about the frequency of reading reviews in various publications showed that, of those teachers who read reviews in *Reading Teacher*, 13 percent often do so, and 50 percent occasionally do so. Of those who read *School Library Journal*, 4 percent often read the publication and 31 percent occasionally read it. Of respondents who read special children's book editions of major newspapers, 29 percent often read reviews in this resource, and 46 percent occasionally read reviews in this resource. Of particular interest is the finding that only 2 percent of the responding teachers read *Horn Book Magazine* often, and 18 percent read *Horn Book Magazine* occasionally; 80 percent of the responding teachers never read *Horn Book Magazine*, a publication devoted exclusively to children's books.

Presumably, teachers would read book reviews in order to aid them in selection of books. Selection involves the choice of books according to professional literary and artistic standards which determine quality. The reading of well-written book reviews will turn one's attention to the quality of books for children, and hence will assist a teacher in selection. Although 78 percent of teachers reported that they read reviews of new children's books, when asked about the frequency of reading reviews in specific publications, a much lower percentage reported reading reviews *often*. It may be that the respondents' choices in terms of intellectual freedom are related to a fuzzy understanding of professional criteria for selection of children's books. A lack of firm grounding in selection of books based on quality may allow teachers to be influenced by subject matter and the controversial nature of some books.

Understanding selection, the choice of books based upon standards of literary and artistic quality, contrasts dramatically with censorship. Censorship has to do with the suppression of communication (Burress 1989, 9), and can be defined as the suppression, alteration, restriction of access, or removal of books because of the ideas contained within them (Jenkinson 1979, 66–74). On the one hand, selection has to do with choice of books because of quality; on the other hand, censorship has to do with avoiding, suppressing, or altering books because of the ideas contained within them, without regard for quality. Each of the self-censorship situations chosen by the majority of teachers in this study involved, in some way, the suppression of communication because of the ideas contained in the books.

Although this survey was an empirical study, there are some findings that reveal things not included in the questions which might be worthy of further investigation. Five of the teachers who declined to complete the questionnaire said that the survey did not apply to them because they were Chapter 1 reading teachers. It would be interesting to investigate why reading teachers might think that a study connected with books and children would not apply to them. Two of the respondents completed the survey but covered or cut off the identifying code number, even though I had guaranteed confidentiality of responses and had explained that the code number would be used only to send follow-up letters to those who did not reply. Their wish not to be identified might indicate fear of intimidation by administrators or others who might react to their opinions. An investigation of teachers' views of school climate with regard to intellectual freedom could offer insight into this issue.

Let us return, once again, to the preservice teacher, whom I have left in mid-sentence, reading aloud to her class of fourth-grade students. She has distinguished herself in terms of selecting high-quality literature and in her commitment to intellectual freedom. But her question, "Will this book be challenged?" still rings with a call for self-preservation, and of course she must be educated, as must all teachers, about professional procedures for dealing with challenges, should they arise. She must learn to ask the person who challenges a book to submit a written request for reevaluation and then to refer the challenge to a reevaluation committee, which she may have worked to establish before censorship attempts arise. She must examine book selection and reevaluation policies in her school, and may seek an active role in the selection of high-quality books for the school library. She must learn to write an instructional rationale for the books which she uses in her classroom and will need to establish a file of reviews by professional reviewers. She must learn the difference between assigned reading and available reading, and she will come to understand the value of allowing children to make choices in the books that they read and in their responses to those books. She must learn about the importance of allowing concerned parents to make choices regarding reading material for their own children, but not for all the other children in the class or in the school. She must learn about professional organizations, such as NCTE and ALA, where she can find like-minded people who will assist her should a challenge arise. In short, she must learn the politics of how to foster and defend the students' right to read.

"Books like *The Friendship* and *Number the Stars* get children to think," the preservice teacher told me. "I want to create an open environment where it is safe for children to talk about these books and the issues that they raise." I believe that this young teacher will rely upon the strength of her convictions and continue to support the freedom to read, even when she is working with a contract and the possibility of disagreement with an administrator who wants to be on the "safe" side.

In the elementary school setting, the First Amendment right of access to information can be enacted through making available a diversity of quality books in the classroom and in the library. The stakes are no less than that of an educated electorate for a democratic society, if the child is father/mother of the man/woman. The developing child tastes the fruit of free inquiry through exploring a variety of well-written resources in children's literature. Access to a diversity of resources encourages the child-reader to respond to what he or she reads and to begin to develop facility in critical reading and critical thinking. And in a democratic society, citizens who have learned to think critically can make informed decisions as voters.

Works Cited

Burress, Lee. 1979. "A Brief Report of the 1977 NCTE Censorship Survey." In *Dealing with Censorship,* edited by J. E. Davis, 14–47. Urbana: National Council of Teachers of English.

————. 1989. *Battle of the Books: Literary Censorship in the Public Schools, 1950–1985.* Metuchen, NJ: Scarecrow Press.

Busha, Charles H. 1972. *Freedom versus Suppression and Censorship.* Littleton, CO: Libraries Unlimited.

Cerra, Kathie Krieger. 1990. *Intellectual Freedom and the Use of Books in the Elementary School: Perceptions of Teachers.* Unpublished Doct. Diss. University of Minnesota.

————. 1991. "Teachers' Attitudes about Intellectual Freedom and Books in the Elementary School." Research report presented at the Annual Convention of the International Reading Association. Las Vegas, Nevada. May. ED 362 893.

Chandler, Katherine Mone. 1985. *Intellectual Freedom and the Use of Trade Books in the Elementary School: Perceptions of Principals.* Unpublished Doct. Diss. University of Minnesota.

Cohen, Barbara. 1987. "Censoring the Sources." *American Educator* 11 (Summer): 43–46.

Fiske, Marjorie. 1959. *Book Selection and Censorship: A Study of School and Public Libraries in California.* Berkeley: University of California Press.

Hentoff, Nat. 1980. *The First Freedom: The Tumultuous History of Free Speech in America.* New York: Delacorte.

————. 1992. *Free Speech for Me—But Not for Thee: How the American Left and Right Relentlessly Censor Each Other.* New York: HarperCollins.

Jenkinson, Edward. B. 1979. *Censors in the Classroom: The Mind Benders.* Carbondale: Southern Illinois University Press.

Limiting What Students Shall Read. 1981. Summary Report on the Survey "Book and Materials Selection for School Libraries and Classrooms: Procedures, Challenges and Responses." Chicago: Association of American Publishers, American Library Association, Association for Supervision and Curriculum Development.

McDonald, Frances Beck. 1993. *Censorship and Intellectual Freedom: A Survey of School Librarians' Attitudes and Moral Reasoning.* Metuchen, NJ: Scarecrow Press.

Silvey, Anita. 1989. "The Basalization of Trade Books." *The Horn Book Magazine* (September/October): 549–50.

Children's Books

Freedman, Russell. 1987. *Lincoln: A Photobiography.* New York: Clarion.

Lowry, Lois. 1989. *Number the Stars.* Boston: Houghton-Mifflin.

Taylor, Mildred. 1986. *Roll of Thunder, Hear My Cry.* Illustrated by Jerry Pinkney. New York: Dial.

————. 1987. *The Friendship.* Illustrated by Max Ginsburg. New York: Dial.

Young Adult Fiction

Clemens, Samuel. 1981 [1884]. *The Adventures of Huckleberry Finn.* New York: Bantam.

Appendix: Tables (Cerra, 1990; 1991)

Table 1: Response to the Question: If an award-winning book you have chosen to read aloud to your class has language which you feel might be offensive, what action would you take?

Action	f	%
Select another book	60	16.3
Read the book exactly as it is written	51	13.9
Alter the text so it is more suitable	256	69.8
Total	**367**	**100.0**

Table 2: Response to the Question: When you are warned that a favorably reviewed book which you have read is risky because of its subject matter, what action do you take when considering purchase of the book for your classroom?

Response	f	%
Purchase the book anyway, and do not limit student access	55	15.8
Purchase the book, but limit student access	86	24.7
Do not purchase the book	207	59.5
Total	**348**	**100.0**

Table 3: Decisions about Types of Children's Books Teacher Would Permit in Classroom

Type of Book	Yes f	Yes %	No f	No %	Undecided f	Undecided %
Stories from the Bible	203	54.9	99	26.8	68	18.4
Stories from the Koran	181	49.2	89	24.2	98	26.6
Stories from the Torah	179	48.6	90	24.5	99	26.9
Native American mythology	349	93.8	9	2.4	14	3.8
Greek myths and fables	358	96.2	5	1.3	9	2.4

Table 4: Subject Matter Basis upon Which to Reject a Book for School Library

Subject Matter	Yes f	Yes %	No f	No %
Religion	74	20.8	281	79.2
Sex	186	53.4	162	46.6
Politics	41	11.8	307	88.2
Racism	223	61.6	139	38.4
Sexism	209	58.2	150	41.8
Other	13		28	

Table 5: Response to the Question: It is a common practice for textbooks to have excerpts from children's books. Do you agree with the practice of rewriting selections to satisfy reading difficulty demands?

Response	f	%
Yes	274	74.3
No	95	25.7
Total	**369**	**100.0**

Table 6: Agreement of Teachers with First Amendment Rights for Students in Elementary School

Response	f	%
Strongly agree	69	19.0
Agree	207	57.0
Disagree	34	9.4
Strongly disagree	6	1.7
No opinion	47	12.9

Table 7: Sources of Challenges to the Suitability of Trade Books during 1988–89

Source of Challenge	f	%
Teacher	14	36.8
Librarian	5	13.15
Principal	5	13.15
Parent	10	26.3
Nonparent community resident	2	5.3
Religious group	2	5.3
Total	38	100.0

Table 8: Books Reported Challenged in 1988–89

Title	Author
Why the Sun and the Moon Live in the Sky	Elphinstone Dayrell
Bridge to Terabithia	Katherine Paterson
Grandpa's Ghost Stories	James Flora
Liza Lou and the Yeller Belly Swamp	Mercer Mayer
Be Nice to Josephine	Betty F. Horvath
Pippi in the South Seas	Astrid Lindgren
How You Were Born	Joanna Cole
The Right to Bear Arms	Geraldine and Howard Woods
The Upstairs Room	Johanna Reiss
The Long Secret	Louise Fitzhugh
Are You There God? It's Me, Margaret.	Judy Blume
The One in the Middle Is the Green Kangaroo	Judy Blume
Deenie	Judy Blume
Where the Sidewalk Ends	Shel Silverstein
Devil's Donkey	Bill Brittain
Roll of Thunder, Hear My Cry	Mildred Taylor
The Witch of Blackbird Pond	Elizabeth George Speare
The Snowy Day	Ezra Jack Keats
More Scary Stories to Tell in the Dark	Alvin Schwartz
And Leffe Was Instead of a Dad	Thorvall
Little Fellow	Winston

Table 9: Teacher Attendance in a Class Period Devoted to Intellectual Freedom

Response	f	%
Yes	135	37.1
No	229	62.9
Total	**364**	**100.0**

Table 10: Children's Literature Course Taken in Teacher Preparation Program

Response	f	%
One course	164	44.0
More than one course	197	52.8
None	12	3.2
Total	**373**	**100.0**

Table 11: Teachers' Current Reading in the Field of Children's Literature

Material Read	Yes f	Yes %	No f	No %
Children's books	367	98.1	7	1.9
Reviews of new children's books	285	77.7	82	22.3

Table 12: Extent to Which Teachers Read Children's Book Reviews in Professional Publications

Publication	Never f	Never %	Occasionally f	Occasionally %	Often f	Often %
Reading Teacher	139	37.7	183	49.6	47	12.7
Horn Book	287	79.7	66	18.3	7	1.9
School Library Journal	238	65.4	112	30.8	14	3.8
Special children's book editions of major newspapers	92	25.1	167	45.5	108	29.4
Other			7		15	

II Intellectual Freedom and the Curriculum

In part II, the focus of chapters addresses the impact of issues of intellectual freedom as they concern the curriculum. The articles in this section are basically divided into two parts. In the first four articles, the authors, Hugh Agee, Margaret Sacco, Jim Knippling, and Mary Ellen Van Camp, explore various aspects of censorship in the teaching and reading of literature in the classroom. In the first article, Hugh Agee discusses the concept of the free exchange of ideas in literature; whereas, Margaret Sacco focuses upon the role of young adult literature in the classroom. Jim Knippling focuses upon African American literature. Mary Ellen Van Camp discusses improving critical thinking by using literature. In her article, Margaret Sacco discusses the impact of censorship on realistic literature as a type of young adult literature that has gained popularity in the last twenty-five years. She also provides a discussion of sources for educators to use to prepare themselves for possible censorship. Jim Knippling examines the institutionalized censorship of books by African American writers. Mary Ellen Van Camp explores the significance of using literature as a means for improving critical thinking. She contends that literature can be used to explore uses of propaganda and persuasion to influence intellectual freedom.

The second section of part II looks at other aspects of the English language arts curriculum, the teaching of composition, the teaching of language, and the implementation of the principles of whole language in the classroom. In her article, Allison Wilson addresses the efforts to limit student inquiry by controlling the types of writing and topics for writing that students are able to explore in many composition courses. Additionally, she points out that the problem is often accentuated for students from outside the mainstream who are expected to do mindless grammar exercises, rather than have the opportunity to explore ideas through composing. Roy O'Donnell's chapter on censorship and language explores the historical conflict between freedom and societal restrictions. He discusses the changing contexts for language and their implications for censorship. Ellen Brinkley addresses the challenges to intellectual freedom from the Religious Right which confront the whole language movement. She frames her discussion within the context of controversy about the whole language movement and the challenges that its proponents regularly face from the Religious Right.

5 Literature, Intellectual Freedom, and the Ecology of the Imagination

Hugh Agee
University of Georgia

Recently, world leaders have begun to acknowledge with alarm the flagrant destruction of our natural environment and to consider steps to address this problem. While one must applaud this global environmental concern and support steps to meet this challenge, no less an effort must be made to preserve the intellectual environment of our nation's schools, wherein an increasing number of censorship cases threaten the ecology of the imagination. As Newbery Award-winning author Lloyd Alexander (1971) has observed: "The ecology of nature and the ecology of the imagination don't function in separate worlds. They'll stand or fall together. We can have no world of the imagination unless we have a real world to sustain it, and we won't have much of a real world unless we have the imagination to preserve and humanize it" (1). Implicit in Alexander's observation is the issue of stewardship. Imagination plays a role in all areas of learning, but most noticeably in school literature programs. Our stewardship challenge is to acknowledge the importance of intellectual freedom in schools and to take appropriate action to protect it from unreasonable assaults that threaten free access to that literature. Without intellectual freedom, there can be no ecology of the imagination.

To the uninformed, the concept of intellectual freedom may sound like an abstraction straight out of the ivory towers of academe, but in reality it is the backbone of free access to any materials and ideas in schools and libraries. Judith Krug (1972), director of the Office for Intellectual Freedom of the American Library Association, has defined the term as "the right of any person to believe what he wants on any subject and to express his beliefs orally or graphically, publicly or privately, as *he* deems appropriate. . . . the definition of intellectual freedom has a second integral part and that is total and complete freedom of access to all information and ideas regardless of the medium of communication used" (809–10). Krug cites numerous court cases that illustrate censors' beliefs that constitutional rights as they apply to children and teenagers should be monitored and at times restricted. The constitutional basis of these rights is discussed elsewhere in this book. However, Wayne Booth (1964) has offered a portrait of censors that is appropriate here:

> Most censors want to preserve some form of society in which they can exercise their own freedom; we can argue, following Mill and many others, that the kind of society the censor *really* wants cannot be maintained if his kind of censorship prevails. Similarly, most censors respect and seek to further the "truth" as they see it, and some of them can be shaken by arguing, with Milton and others, that truth flourishes best when ideas can compete freely. Or, again, many censors, irrational as they may seem to us, respect consistency and would like to think of themselves as reasonable; they can be shaken, sometimes, by showing the inevitable irrationalities and stupidities committed by any society that attempts to censor. (155–56)

With this in mind I shall look more closely at the role of imagination as it impacts on the study of literature in schools.

Traditionally, we think of literature as those creative efforts that fall within the categories of prose, poetry, and drama and the various subcategories of these. In our concern for the ecology of the imagination, Miller's (1969) definition is more to the point:

> Literature may be defined simply as the structured embodiment of the imagination in language. And the literary experience may be described as fundamentally an *imaginative* experience. When we read a work of literature, we somehow participate *imaginatively* in events, or acts, or thoughts, and this imaginative participation has many parallels to *actual* participation in real, as differentiated from imagined, experience. It is frequently assumed that by its very nature the actual experience is someway superior to the imaginative experience, and that therefore literature is a kind of frill or decoration and not a necessity of education. Simple reflection should confirm how narrow and restricted and confined one's life would be deprived of all imaginative experience, and should lead to the conclusion that literature is a basic necessity because it broadens, expands, and liberates—as all education should. (443)

Literature, then, offers through engagement and response a way of knowing not only the emotional and intellectual dimensions of the work within its own domain but also more about ourselves and the world that we are a part of.

Ecology by definition stresses relationships and interactions between organisms and their environment, on one hand, and those between humans and their environment, on the other. In the natural world we may not always be fully aware of the impact of disrupting relationships in ecosystems. The stewardship issue often posits divergent points of view. For instance, the effects of the continuing destruction of tropical rain forests may not be understood fully for some time as environmentalists look at global effects. Yet, those involved in clearing the land likely operate from the position of economic benefits to the region and beyond. This situation calls to mind a 1989 censorship incident in Laytonville, California, in which individuals loyal to the area's logging interests sought to have *The Lorax* by Dr. Suess removed from the required second-grade reading list because the book calls attention to environmental problems created by a greedy logger ("Lumber Backers," 1989, 4-D). A macrocosmic problem may easily overshadow the destruction of the habitat of some seemingly insignificant plant or animal in a microcosmic setting. One has only to turn to Ray Bradbury's short story "A Sound of Thunder" to contemplate the familiar "what if" question of the possible long-term effect of a time traveler's stepping on a butterfly while on a journey to the past to hunt a Tyrannosaurus Rex. Some readers may dismiss Bradbury's imaginative extrapolation as fantasy, but my students who have read this story are quick to recognize its point in light of ongoing reports of ecological mismanagement.

The same may be said of the possible impact of the repressive legislation of human individuality, as Kurt Vonnegut describes it in "Harrison Bergeron," a futuristic story of the results of hundreds of constitutional amendments by which everyone finally achieves "equality," which the government's Handicapper General rigidly enforces. Can we dismiss this product of the literary imagination when we contemplate its implications for the larger issue of human rights and the more focused issues of racism, sexism, ageism, etc.? Literary works that raise social issues may be considered too realistic or too depressing for some and lead to censorship challenges in school environments. However, if we accept a stewardship role in the ecology of the imagination, can we deny our students the right to read and to explore any literature developmentally appropriate for them in an atmosphere of free and responsible inquiry? When I consider the thorniness of such a question, I recall that *The American Heritage Dictionary of the English Language* (3rd ed., 1992) reminds me that the Indo-European root, *weik-*, from which the word *ecology* derives, also gives us the derivatives *village, villain, vicinity, diocese, economy,* and *parish* (2131). Villainy in matters of intellectual freedom as in matters of ecology is a matter of perspective, as we have seen in the example of *The Lorax* above. The treasured classics of some become for others despised works that corrupt and demean.

And what of imagination? Must it, too, be legislated? Why else would Plato ban poets? Yet imagination is actually essential to learning. In their discussion of the role of the imagination in the English classroom, Kutz and Roskelly (1991) contend that learning in any context "depends on the imagination for the making of new meaning" (220). For them, imagination "is the mind's ability and need to form by restructuring and formulating experience in terms of what it knows already and what it needs to know. Given what we're beginning to see now as its importance in learning, engaging the imagination should be a primary—maybe *the* primary—responsibility of teachers" (221). To underscore their position, Kutz and Roskelly turn to Alfred North Whitehead, who wrote: "The combination of imagination and learning requires some leisure, freedom from restraint, freedom from harassing worry, some variety of experiences, and the stimulation of other minds diverse in opinion and diverse in equipment" (Qtd. in Kutz and Roskelly 1991, 222). Whitehead's stance strongly supports the need for intellectual freedom in schools. Otherwise, no literate society can survive, much less flourish, without unrestricted freedom to read and to read widely.

Perhaps the most impressive illustration of the long-term role of imagination in human experience may be found in Daniel J. Boorstin's *The Creators* (1992), a rich and enlightening survey of the arts from ancient times to the present. A companion book to *The Discoverers* (1983), which Boorstin calls "a tale of man's search to know the world and himself" (1992, xv), *The Creators* stands as "a saga of Heroes of the Imagination." In his personal note to the reader, he writes:

> These creators, makers of the new, can never become obsolete, for in the arts there is no correct answer. The story of the discoverers could be told in simple chronological order, since the latest science replaces what went before. But the arts are another story—a story of infinite addition. We must find order in the random flexings of the imagination. . . . each of us alone must experience how the new adds to the old and how the old enriches the new, how Picasso enhances Leonardo and how Homer illuminates Joyce. (xv)

Through literature, readers also discover more about who they are and how they relate to the world in which they live and for which, as future stewards, they will have increasing responsibility.

So it is that literature in the school environment is the wellspring of the imagination. Alexander (1971) has drawn a fascinating parallel between the ecology of our external environment and the ecology of the imagination, that inner environment which, in his words, is "a household of emotions and attitudes; a complex balance of wishes, dreams, and hopes. . . . To keep it in good working order, this inner ecology needs all the resources of art and literature. To nourish our imaginations, we need the enrichments of all our creative modes and forms: poetry, drama, fiction, nonfiction, realism, fantasy—the whole spectrum of artistic experience" (2). To nourish our natural world, and in return to be nourished by it, we must cultivate sensitivity and responsibility; literature study can serve as a valuable ally in this process.

We should not overlook the role of the imagination as it relates both to the arts and to science. As Frye (1964) has described it:

> Science begins with the world we have to live in, accepting its data and trying to explain its laws. From there, it moves toward the imagination: it becomes a mental construct, a model of a possible way of interpreting experience. The further it goes in this direction, the more it tends to speak in the language of mathematics, which is really one of the languages of the imagination, along with literature and music. Art, on the other hand, begins with the world we construct, not with the world we see. It starts with the imagination, and then works toward ordinary experience: that is, it tries to make itself as convincing and recognizable as it can. (23)

Frye's observation offers us a model for exploring literature in the lives of children and young adults, an exploration that hinges on the vital role of the imagination in the realm of human experience.

We see in childhood an intense interest in the physical world which leads from observation to participation. As Frye suggests, the imagination moves the observer forward through participation toward understanding, allowing pauses for reflection and consolidation before the observer moves to new experiences and new understandings. Parents and teachers play important mentor roles in this process. Young observers create and re-create imaginative scenarios that have simple narrative lines. Their scenarios are often reflections of those they have observed or participated in, and they incorporate characters modeled after parents, siblings, teachers, friends, pets, storybook characters, imaginary characters, etc. The imagination shapes and reshapes these basic narratives in myriad ways and lays a foundation for children's imaginative entry into literature as represented by picture books, folk and fairy tales, mythology, biblical stories, and the like.

The role of language in this process cannot be overemphasized. Even before children begin speaking, they are enveloped in a world of language. As their language performance increases, children enjoy language play and engagement with those works in which authors play with sounds and manipulate words in clever ways. Countless children have delighted in the blending of verbal and visual artistry for pleasurable imaginative adventures. As children move into the teen years, many become more removed from the world of imagination they had experienced through literature. This is not to imply the demise of imagination. Rather, imaginative experiences take other nonliterary directions, particularly in the visual world of film and video. Nevertheless, the avid readers I have worked with or observed in secondary school and university settings are those who have had meaningful experiences with the world of narrative early in their lives. I have encountered students who have lost their enthusiasm for literature, but that often was a result either of their having little or no voice in the selection of the literature they had dealt with in their schooling or of their failure to have a positive experience with literature because of an overemphasis on critical analysis. In *Voices of Readers,* Carlsen and Sherrill (1988) identified positive experiences through which readers in their research came to love books. This study, and Appleyard's *Becoming a Reader* (1990), a developmental view of readers' growth from childhood to adulthood, would be valuable reading for any literature teacher in our schools.

How does all this relate to intellectual freedom and the ecology of the imagination? Any literary work is at risk in today's classrooms, including such classics as *The Scarlet Letter, The Adventures of Huckleberry Finn,* and *The Red Badge of Courage.* One parent (Muth 1986, 20-A) wrote of being asked to sign a permission slip to allow his daughter to read these works in her high school literature class. Thinking his daughter was "playing a clever joke" on him, he learned instead that parental veto power had become standard procedure in school reading selections but not in matters of compulsory school attendance or grade requirements for graduation. Muth's stance on this point warrants our attention:

> There is strong reason for enforcing the same kind of rules regarding a child's reading in school. Though dealing incidentally with adultery, *The Scarlet Letter* is really concerned with honesty and personal honor. Though I have been told that some blacks might find *Huckleberry Finn* objectionable, careful reading reveals it is a strong statement against segregation, one that was far ahead of its time. *The Red Badge of Courage* is a graphic and compelling argument against war, vividly depicting its horror and its carnage. Not only do I insist my daughter confront such literature, I argue that we are all better off if all children read these books in their formative years. (20-A)

What we lack here is the daughter's personal transactions with these works, but the point is that she was not denied the opportunity to extend her imaginative experiences through her engagement with them.

One basic point in the realm of intellectual freedom that must be acknowledged is that any person has the right to object to reading a particular literary work in a school setting, but that person should not have the right to block others from reading the work. No work is absolutely safe in the classroom, as many unsuspecting classroom teachers have discovered. We could identify a staggering lists of titles that have come under fire for a variety of reasons. School personnel often think of "the enemy" as those beyond the school environment, but censors are often within the educational establishment. Whoever the censors may be, they act according to what they consider right and good and appropriate, as Booth noted. Most cases can be resolved through negotiation. Others, unfortunately, become media events that create a negative atmosphere in which learning suffers. There are many excellent books and articles on censorship and intellectual freedom, but one valuable reference is *The Students' Right to Know* (1982). In this document Burress and Jenkinson remind us that the multicultural diversity of our society makes intellectual freedom necessary: "Intellectual freedom permits attention to the controversial issues that divide the nation, even in communities where a single point of view is dominant, though in the classroom neutrality is required concerning these issues" (4). Literature serves as a vehicle for coming to a better understanding not only of how people differ, but also of how they are alike as human beings, regardless of race, gender, ethnic background, etc. As Frye (1964) has said:

> Literature gives us an experience that stretches us vertically to the heights and depths of what the human mind can conceive, to what corresponds to the conceptions of heaven and hell in religion. In this perspective what I like or don't like disappears because there's nothing left of me as a separate person: as a reader of literature I exist only as a representative of humanity as a whole. (101)

For some this point of view may be too extreme, but barriers that distance individuals from one another cannot fall without dialogue, and good literature invites meaningful dialogue.

Robert Coles, in *The Call of Stories: Teaching and the Moral Imagination* (1989), has recounted how he came to value the vital connections between the "stories" of patients and the stories of literature as closely related moral journeys of the imagination. Coles's sense of the "moral imagination" no doubt evolved from the influence of his parents' intense interest in and reading (often aloud to each other) of many of the great novels of English, American, and Russian literature; from his studies of American literature in the Puritan tradition in college under Perry Miller; and from his intensive study of the works of two other physician/writers, Anton Chekhov and William Carlos Williams. It was his close association with Williams that led Coles to study medicine, and the literary achievements of Chekhov and Williams that inspired and sustained him in his career.

One of the case studies Coles shares in *The Call of Stories* is of a young man of fifteen, stricken with polio and facing the bleak reality that he would live the rest of his life without the use of his legs. Having lost both parents—his father killed in World War II and his mother killed in an automobile accident—Phil was understandably angry as Coles worked with him. However, a turning point occurred when Phil's English teacher from the previous year came to visit and left him a copy of *The Adventures of Huckleberry Finn*, a book he had read in this man's class but had no special affinity for. Yet after a couple of days he did start reading it and finished the whole book that night. Coles shares Phil's response:

> I can't tell you, I can't explain what happened; I know that my mind changed after I read *Huckleberry Finn*. I couldn't get my mind off the book. I forgot about myself—no, I didn't actually. I joined up with Huck and Jim; we became a trio. They were very nice to me. I explored the Mississippi with them on the boats and on the land. I had some good talks with them. I dreamed about them. I'd wake up, and I'd know I'd been out west, on the Mississippi. I talked with those guys, and they straightened me out. (35–36)

When Phil asked Coles if he had read a book that really made a difference for him, Coles spoke of William Carlos Williams's long poem, *Paterson*, and of Williams's effort to understand America's social history and moral values through his stories and poems that dealt largely with working-class people. Later, after Phil read J. D. Salinger's *The Catcher in the Rye*, he told Coles: "I've discovered a book that has a kid in it just like Huckleberry Finn" (37). From it, Coles reports, Phil could speak "on what it means to be honest and decent in a world full of 'phoniness'." Perhaps more important, "*The Catcher in the Rye* enabled him to return at least to the idea of school—to consider what kind of education he wanted, given his special difficulties" (38).

Coles also wrote about Ben, a Harvard undergraduate from eastern North Carolina, who "had for some time regarded himself as a failure; someone who seemed to fall between the cracks. He had been unable to imagine himself pursuing any pre-professional course of study, had even found it difficult to choose a field of concentration. He had also found himself ignored or rebuffed by those he liked" (68). Then the title of Ralph Ellison's *Invisible Man* caught his attention, and as the "invisible man" image grew in his thoughts, he decided to read the book:

> I'm a slow reader, and I had trouble at first getting into the novel, but I did, and once I was with Ellison, I stayed with him; I mean, I "connected" with the invisible man. I think, after a while, I began to see people the way he did: I watched people and tried to figure them out. I didn't want to be an outsider, but I was—the way black people are for us, for lots of us. The more I looked at people through my outsider's eyes, the more I felt alone and ignored; it was no fun—and it made me understand not only my own social problems, my trouble getting along with people, but how black people must feel in this world, especially when they come to a place like this. (69)

This literary experience was the beginning of Ben's escape from his "invisible man" status and of a continuing exploration of himself and his world through literature.

In concluding his book, Coles introduced Gordon, another Harvard student of comfortable means "who always asked a lot of himself" (199). Because he liked reading novels, Gordon became an English major:

> But I never liked the way the professors used the books—zeroing in on "the text," raking and raking, sifting and sifting it through narrower and narrower filters. I'm not against learning about symbols and images and metaphors, but there was something missing in those tutorials.... But I'd better stop blaming them. It was me. I don't have an abstract interest in literature. I love to read stories and get lost in them, and some of the characters—they become buddies of mine, friends, people I think of. (201–2).

Gordon changed his major to computer science and began tutoring students in a low-rent housing project where he shared literature with them, including some of Salinger's stories. He was concerned that he not be patronizing as he talked about literature with them, and he felt he did get some of them "hooked." Gordon said that in having to deal with major questions or moral issues, he remembered what his parents had said or what they might do in his situation, but also he found himself tuning in to characters he'd come to know through literature:

> Those folks, they're *people* for me. Nick Carraway or Jack Burden, they really speak to me—there's a lot of me in them, or vice versa. I don't know how to put it, but they're voices, and they help me make choices. I hope when I decide "the big ones" they'll be in there pitching. (203)

"So it goes," Coles concludes, "this immediacy that a story can possess, as it connects so persuasively with human experience. Dr. Williams and Dr. Chekhov and the needy children whom Gordon got to know as his tutees can offer their own kind of moral instruction.... All in all, not a bad start for someone trying to find a good way to live his life: a person's moral conduct responding to the moral imagination of writers and the moral imperative of fellow human beings in need" (204–5). Phil, Ben, and Gordon are not too far removed experientially from many high school students across this nation. Their case studies underscore the need in all schools for an atmosphere of intellectual freedom in which literature and the imagination can help students grow without the burden of repressive censorship.

In arguing for the need for transforming practice in the teaching of English, Kutz and Roskelly (1991) observed that "One of the reasons the disparate activities of literacy haven't been more fully integrated into the English classroom has been that teachers haven't seen how to connect those activities with any kind of real coherence" (219). The missing ingredient in the making of knowledge, in their judgment, is the power of the imagination, and literature offers a vital arena for exploring and developing that vital element. That arena will be limited if we allow censors to dictate how and with what resources we operate in our schools. It is commendable that a recent concern for *why* Johnny can't read gave us the worthy national goal of achieving literacy for every adult American by the year 2000. However, we must be equally concerned about *what* Johnny can't read, even if he is literate. This is a significant part of our stewardship obligation if the ecology of the imagination is to be a moving force in our society.

Works Cited

Alexander, Lloyd. 1971. Address. Third Annual Conference on Children's Literature in Elementary Education. The University of Georgia. Athens. 7 May.

The American Heritage Dictionary of the English Language. 1992. 3rd ed. Boston: Houghton-Mifflin.

Appleyard, J. A. 1990. *Becoming a Reader: The Experience of Fiction from Childhood to Adulthood.* Cambridge, MA: Cambridge University Press.

Boorstin, Daniel J. 1983. *The Discoverers.* New York: Random.

———. 1992. *The Creators.* New York: Random House.

Booth, Wayne C. 1964. "Censorship and the Values of Fiction." *English Journal* 53: 155–64.

Burress, Lee, and Edward B. Jenkinson. 1982. *The Students' Right to Know.* Urbana: National Council of Teachers of English.

Carlsen, G. Robert, and Anne Sherrill. 1988. *Voices of Readers: How We Come to Love Books.* Urbana: National Council of Teachers of English.

Coles, Robert. 1989. *The Call of Stories: Teaching and the Moral Imagination.* Boston: Houghton-Mifflin.

Frye, Northrop. 1964. *The Educated Imagination.* Bloomington: Indiana University Press.

Krug, Judith F. 1972. "Growing Pains: Intellectual Freedom and the Child." *English Journal* 61: 805–13.

Kutz, Eleanor, and Hephzibah Roskelly. 1991. *An Unquiet Pedagogy: Transforming Practice in the English Classroom.* Portsmouth, NH: Boynton/Cook-Heinemann.

"Lumber Backers Want to Ax Dr. Suess Book." 1989. *The Atlanta Constitution* (15 September): 4-D.

Miller, James E., Jr. 1969. "Literature as a Way of Knowing." *English Journal* 58: 443–45.

Muth, Richard F. 1986. Letter. *The Atlanta Constitution* (18 September): 20-A.

6 The Censorship of Young Adult Literature

Margaret T. Sacco
Miami University

Young adult literature is defined by Donelson and Nilsen (1989) as anything young readers between the ages of twelve and twenty choose to read. Burress (1986) summarized that censors generally attack books that are contemporary, written by American authors, and that treat their subjects realistically, which is the very essence of adolescent literature (Davis 1988). Since the 1930s there has been a tremendous growth in adolescent literature. Publishers added or expanded young adult divisions and promoted new authors. The advent of the available cheap paperbacks in the 1950s created a revolution. Teens could afford books and make a book they liked a bestseller. In 1967, a type of young adult literature, referred to as the "problem novel" or "new realism," emerged and became popular. Problem novels began dealing with the real-life problems and concerns of teenagers, problems which were taboo topics in the 1940s and 1950s, topics such as unwed pregnancy and early marriage, abortion, physical maturation, premarital sex, masturbation, neglectful or problem parents, teenage drinking and smoking, drug addiction, child abuse, divorce, death, racism, violence, homosexuality, alienation, poverty, teenage gangs, anti-Semitism, males and females in nontraditional roles, the questioning of authority and institutions, and so on. Some of these novels may contain offensive language or nonstandard English, may have unhappy endings, may have ethnic protagonists, may deal with several topics or situations, or may have all or several of the above. However, most of these novels support middle-class values and could not be considered obscene.

In the 1940s and 1950s, adolescent fiction usually did not deal with taboo subjects or contain offensive language. Protagonists in these junior novels were concerned with getting dates with the most popular male or female, using the family car, succeeding in sports, or being popular with their peers. These junior novels were read for escape or wish-fulfillment and generally had happy endings just like the romance novels of today.

Young adult novels have been made into popular movies and television shows. The literary quality of young adult novels has improved over the years, and these novels are taught and read in English classrooms. Teachers generally prefer to use the canon of great literature because they believe that one of their roles as educator is to expose students to the classics (Samuels 1982). English teachers who use young adult literature recognize that their classes are often filled with students who are neither affectively nor cognitively prepared for sophisticated adult literature. Sometimes these students are unable or unwilling to read the assigned classics (Samuels and Lowery-Moore 1987). However, the new realism genre relates better to the everyday life, problems, and experiences of adolescents than the classics. The popularity with teenagers of *Cliffs Notes* and plot outlines suggests that classical literature may not meet their interests and/or developmental needs, or that it may be beyond their level of comprehension. Those teachers who do not use young adult literature are either ignorant of its functions or fearful of censorship.

Any Book Can Be Banned

No book is safe in today's censorship climate, particularly those books that are taught as required reading for young adults. Since the emergence of the new realism in 1967, the number of censorship attacks on books has increased. However, Judy Blume, one of the most popular young adult novelists, agrees with censorship experts that since 1979, censorship problems have escalated (West 1988). Conservative groups saw Reagan's election as blanket approval to attack books and school curricula (West 1988). Required reading books of high literary quality and critical praise are among the most frequently attacked, books such as *The Scarlet Letter, Grapes of Wrath, Of Mice and Men, Brave New World, Flowers for Algernon, To Kill a Mockingbird, Lord of the Flies, The Chocolate War, The Catcher in the Rye* (perhaps the most censored book in America), *The Adventures of Huckleberry Finn, One Day in the Life of Ivan Denisovich, Animal Farm, A Separate Peace, 1984,* and so on. Of the aforementioned titles, *The Scarlet Letter* is probably the book most universally disliked by young adults. Nevertheless, the banning of these books suggests that censors do not have any concern for literary quality. Readers can find more titles by reading books about school censorship and censorship issues discussed in *The Newsletter on Intellectual Freedom*.

Brave New World, Romeo and Juliet

Donelson (1985), in his survey of censored books, noticed that there has been a marked decline in the number of protests of the following eight titles: *Soul on Ice, Catch-22, Manchild in the Promised Land, A Hero Ain't Nothing But a Sandwich, One Flew Over the Cuckoo's Nest, The Inner-City Mother Goose, Down These Mean Streets,* and *Black Boy.* He suggests that this decline is due to a return to the basics and a general decline in using anti-establishment and minority literature in the conservative climate of today's school.

On the other hand, powerful leftist censorship groups like The Council on Interracial Books for Children have criticized as racist those who have stocked or taught such books as Paula Fox's Newbery Award-winning *The Slave Dancer,* Ouida Sebestyen's *Words by Heart,* and Harper Lee's *To Kill a Mockingbird,* which are popular books with young adults.

Blacks and liberal censors have objected to the use of the word "nigger" in *The Adventures of Huckleberry Finn.* Additionally, fundamentalists complain that Huck's language and behavior are inappropriate for student reading. A young adult novel, *The Day They Came to Arrest the Book* (Hentoff 1982), revolves around an attempt to ban *Huckleberry Finn* from a high school reading list for being racist. The book is one of several that provides adolescent readers with a solid introduction to the philosophical and political underpinnings of the current censorship debate. Additionally, Avi's 1991 book *Nothing But the Truth* explores issues of freedom of speech and expression. Therefore, these books could be used effectively to teach young adults about the First Amendment.

Covert and Overt Censorship— Denying Students' Rights

Hidden or covert censorship is prevalent in schools and is usually the forte of self-censors. Teachers, administrators, school board members, librarians, selection committees, and curriculum supervisors are its most frequent players. Worst of all, covert censors believe they are not censoring books. Overt or open censorship is frequently reported in the media and is monitored by the *The Newsletter on Intellectual Freedom;* covert or hidden censorship is the most dangerous because individuals concerned with students' right to read and know cannot respond. Donelson (1985, 94), a known scholar of young adult literature and expert on censorship, has guessed that for every censorship attempt that is reported in the media, 50–100 incidents are "hush, hush" (see chapters 8 and 16, this volume).

Many teachers, librarians, curriculum supervisors, and book selection committees do not select books that they feel will cause problems and/ or expose young adults to unpleasant realities. These people insist that they are selecting quality books, however: "Selection's approach to the book is positive, seeking its value in the book as a book and in the book as a whole. Censorship's approach is negative, seeking for the vulnerable characteristics wherever they can be found—anywhere within the book, or even outside" (Jenkinson 1979, 72). Some people share Plato's belief that the reading materials of the young should be censored.

However, it is virtually impossible to select a book that at least one person will not find objectionable. Shakespeare's works and the Bible have been attacked and banned. In extreme cases, teachers have expurgated literature anthologies that the students purchased with their own funds. A school superintendent's wife removed magazines and young adult novels from a high school library and burned them. Both teachers and librarians have deleted offensive language from adolescent novels with magic markers and/or ripped off the covers of paperback books.

So-called educators have been known to scan media to identify which books are being challenged and remove those books from libraries and classrooms or put them on restrictive shelves. School librarians have "labeled" books by putting stars on the book pockets to restrict them to "seniors only." Public librarians have put controversial young adult titles in the adult collection and restricted their circulation to adults. School and public librarians who object to Judy Blume books have refused to put her books in libraries, though Blume is one of the most popular young adult authors and possibly the surrogate mother to many adolescents who want to learn about sex and growing up.

Both Judy Blume and Norma Klein write realistically about relationships and family living, which are subjects of great interest to teens. Judy Blume remains the most censored author according to the American Library Association's Office for Intellectual Freedom. Her books *Deenie* (1973), *Are You There God? It's Me, Margaret* (1970) and *Forever* (1975) deal realistically with the problems of growing up. Blume frankly and tastefully handles such teen anxieties as masturbation and physical maturation in *Are You There God? It's Me, Margaret* and *Deenie. Are You There God? It's Me, Margaret* has a depth of spirituality that is not usually found in young adult fiction and was one of the first novels for youth to discuss breast development and menstruation. *Forever* offended many censors with its specific descriptions of sexual acts and answers to the question, what does sex feel like the first time? Frank discussions of birth control, venereal disease, the responsibilities of both partners, and the fact that love affairs do not last a lifetime make *Forever* a worthwhile book for young adults. In *Forever* one of the heroine's friends has an abortion and is not punished for her unwed pregnancy by having to get married. Teens July and Bo Jo had to get married in the still controversial *Mr. & Mrs. Bo Jo Jones* (1967), which was also published by the adult division of a publishing house. Elaine and Buff in *Two and the Town* (1952) married too young in the first junior novel to deal with premarital sex. Louie Banks in Chris Crutcher's *Running Loose* (1983) decides that having a female as a friend is more important than sex. Felsen's *Two and the Town* was both didactic and preachy, but desperately needed. Young adults want to learn about the emotions and experiences of teens in love. *Two and the Town*, just as the Blume books, was censored and not put on library shelves.

The late Norma Klein, the second most censored author according to ALA's Office for Intellectual Freedom, was another writer who wrote frankly about sex. Her books have enjoyed wide readership and popularity among readers and have made book reviewers and librarians nervous. Klein's book *Mom, the Wolf Man and Me* (1972) was the first young adult novel to deal with an unmarried mother and her live-in lover. Also, Klein's books about homosexual teens and parents are usually not found in the classroom. However, teachers should use literature about people who are different to help teenagers develop compassion, understanding, and tolerance.

Blume, Klein, and other famous young adult novelists discuss how publishers and editors censor books in *Trust Your Children* (West 1988). Editors have suggested that authors tone down their stories and/or clean up the language. Authors who want to earn a living sometimes follow editors' suggestions to avoid possible censorship problems. Scholastic Press has bowdlerized language in paperback book club editions without the authors' permissions. Weiss (1988) reports that T. Ernesto Bethancourt was asked by an editor to make his heroine of the Doris Fein mysteries "less Jewish" and change her hair to blonde. Lines have been cut from Shakespeare's *Romeo and Juliet* by publishers who want to sell their books and are afraid of textbook censors. Robert Cormier's *The Chocolate War* was turned down by three publishers because he refused to give the novel an upbeat ending; *The Chocolate War* is considered by Donelson and Nilsen (1989) the best example of modern realism.

I Am the Cheese, After the First Death, The Bumblebee Flies Anyway, and *The Chocolate War* by Cormier all possess a high level of literary quality along with the author's skilled use of sophisticated literary devices. In the aforementioned titles, the protagonists champion nineteenth-century rugged individualism when they fight the corrupting evils of dehumanizing institutions. Ellis (1985) points out that it is ironic that censors who value individual rights over institutional rights attack Cormier's books. One of the most explosive censorship cases in recent years has taken place in Panama City, Florida. *I Am the Cheese* and Farley Mowat's *Never Cry Wolf* remain banned in schools there in spite of the fact that teachers offered alternative book choices for their students. Teachers defending the books received death threats, and a TV reporter covering the story had her apartment set afire. Cormier's defense of *I Am the Cheese* received a standing ovation. A lawsuit claiming that students' First Amendment rights had been violated was settled outside of court. The settlement restored *I Am the Cheese, About David,* and twenty-four other books that had been restricted since 1987 (Pipkin 1993, 36).

Parents genuinely have the right to censor what books their own child reads, but when they try to ban books so that other people's children cannot read them, this is wrong. People who censor what children read are trying to control teens. Many parents are afraid that their young adults are growing up too fast and may reject their values. Parents do not trust their teens with books that present points of view that differ from their own and/or books that present real life, for they think that they can protect adolescents from life. Very few parents can accept that their children are sexual human beings with normal desires and curiosity. Parents are fearful that they may be asked embarrassing questions. Some adults are uncomfortable with their own sexuality or think that sex is "dirty." When they see a word or passage in a book they consider offensive, it is easy for parents to go to a school and complain. As Cormier (West 1988, 38) points out, it is so much easier to get people to read nine words than a whole book.

Additionally, Henthorn (1986) suggests that censoring or banning a book will encourage students to read it. *Go Ask Alice,* written anonymously, is possibly the second most censored book today. It is a horrifying story of a middle-class girl's drug addiction and has remained popular since its publication. Some critics attribute its popularity to the censorship problems, rather than to interest in the book itself; however, teens have given testimonies that reading *Go Ask Alice* has stopped them from trying drugs. Teens have money to spend in bookstores and will buy the books that they want, regardless of what parents and teachers think.

In today's censorship climate parents can easily get the support of many sophisticated, organized groups that have either a conservative or liberal political agenda and that are trying to control or change public education. Often they will use charges of offensive language or accusations of ageism, racism, and sexism to get their foot in a school's door to gain power and authority. Generally, censors purport to know the truth while everyone else searches for it. An educator cannot teach literature without exploring values. Censors want their values taught; however, educators want to teach students to think critically and formulate their own values. Religious fundamentalists want to control the minds of students and save them from secular humanism, the school's religion. Conservative fundamentalists are crusaders for the back-to-basics movement, and they often do not trust or read books other than their own version of the Bible. Young adult problem novels work well with the whole language approach and response-based methodologies which empower students. Phyllis Schlafley's Eagle Forum fights student journal writing, role-playing, and values clarification because she feels these practices violate a student's privacy. However, English teachers usually suggest to pupils that student writing on intimate and personal topics belongs in personal diaries, not in school journals.

The Values of Young Adult Literature

Educators should know why they teach literature and why they teach what they teach to defend literature. In a classroom, daily teenage life can be discussed with adult supervision by using young adult novels. Adolescent literature is transitional, for it serves as a logical step between children's literature and adult literature. Young adult novels can serve as tools to prepare teens for the more complex classics by serving as models to teach literary conventions or as parallels to help young readers understand specific classics (Small 1977). Furthermore, young adults can gain vicarious experiences and discover the universality of adolescent experiences safely between the covers of a book with a teacher's guidance. Additionally, reading and discussing novels of teenage daily life with teachers and adults may have many benefits: It can give adolescents an opportunity to talk in third person about a problem that embarrasses them, and it can give readers confidence that they can solve problems, assuring young adults that they are not the only ones who have fears, doubts, and problems. It can also provide young adults with opportunities to explore being different and to play various roles. It can give teens an understanding of the world and the way people find their places in it. Finally it can help young adults gain insight into their own behavior and possible consequences.

In conclusion, young adult literature is here to stay as long as our nation has an economy and a mentality that allows it to exist. B. Dalton, in 1979, was the first bookstore chain to establish a young adult section. Now their shelves are filled with "happily ever after" series formula books and some publishers are responding to the new conservatism with "squeaky clean" books for young adults. At present, censors are frantically attacking fantasy and other literature in the *Impressions* elementary reading series, and attacks on young adult fantasy, occult fiction and nonfiction, and young adult horror will probably be increased.

As Carlsen (1974) reminds us, we are literature-consuming and literature-creating animals. Young adults have found literature satisfying and valuable in their lives: "Neither war, social revolution, depression, imprisonment, nor a materialistic culture seem to deter readers" (24). However, in the future it is possible that teachers may have to use only books from state-mandated reading lists in the classroom. The following questions remain: Will authors be silenced? Will editors publish books that contain controversial topics and/or language? Will young adults have the freedom to read books of their choice and think for themselves? Will teachers have the right to teach students to think critically and choose books to help students think critically? The answers to these questions depend partly on the actions of teachers, librarians, administrators, parents, and concerned citizens and on their commitment to intellectual freedom.

English educators should educate other educators, administrators, and parents about the psychological and developmental values of young adult literature, its literary quality, and its usefulness as models or tools to teach classic literature. Furthermore, they should clarify the teaching methods they employ. In addition, English teachers and librarians should build library collections on censorship and learn all they can about censorship so they can become informed and involved in dealing with censorship issues with administrators, other teachers, parents, students, and concerned citizens. *Censorship: Managing the Controversy* (1989) should be read by all educators, for it does the following: explains all sides of censorship issues, identifies censorship organizations and their philosophies, gives reasons for censorship, and explains school policies and strategies to combat it. A well-written book selection policy and a policy for handling censorship complaints should be established. English departments may want to send letters to parents explaining reasons for teaching from certain books and the department's teaching philosophy and methods. Some teachers may want to get parental permission slips signed to give students permission to read certain books. However, the letters and/or permission slips should be sent through the post office. Provisions should also be made so that parents can examine the books used. A written rationale should be prepared for each book that is required reading. *Censored Books: Critical Viewpoints* (Karolides, Burress, and Kean 1993), *Celebrating Censored Books!* (Karolides and Burress 1985), and Shugert's *Rationales for Commonly Challenged Taught Books* (1983) contain rationales for the most challenged books and should be available in each school to serve as models to help teachers write their own rationales. Written book rationales should identify what age level the book is appropriate for, with citations to the reviews, as well as attached copies of reviews. English teachers should build coalitions with librarians, museum personnel, media personnel, professional education organizations, and anti-censorship groups (see chapters 12, 15, and 18, this volume). These coalitions should work together to get an intellectual freedom law passed in their states to give students and teachers academic freedom. Additionally, English teachers should join the Assembly on Literature for Adolescents (ALAN) and receive *The ALAN Review* for useful articles and to keep up with the field of young adult literature. English teachers should support other teachers who have censorship problems (wherever they are) and write letters of support. Additionally, teachers should try to obtain an academic freedom clause in their collective bargaining contract. If a censorship problem occurs, English teachers should remain calm and follow procedures established by written school policies (Davis 1988).

Works Cited

Burress, Lee. 1986. "Are School Censorship Pressures Increasing?" *Virginia English Bulletin* 36(1): 72–82.

Carlsen, G. Robert. 1974. "Literature IS." *English Journal* 63(2): 23–27.

Censorship: Managing the Controversy. 1989. Alexandria, VA: National School Boards Association. (1680 Duke St., Alexandria, VA 22314, $20; $16 members & $3.50 postage and handling.)

Davis, James E. 1988. "Censorship and the YA Book: A New Column: Beyond Weather Reports: ALAN's Role in the Current Censorship Storms." *The ALAN Review* 15(3): 62–64.

Donelson, Kenneth L. 1985. "Almost 13 Years of Book Protests—Now What?" *School Library Journal* 31(7): 92–98.

———, and Alleen Pace Nilsen, eds. 1989. *Literature for Today's Young Adult.* 3rd ed. Glenview, IL: Scott, Foresman.

Ellis, W. Geiger. 1985. "'Dare We Disturb . . . ?' A Defense of Robert Cormier's Novels." In Karolides and Burress, 29–31.

Henthorn, Karla S. 1986. "Censorship: The ****** Solution." *Virginia English Bulletin* 36(1): 28–29.

Hentoff, Nat. 1982. *The Day They Came to Arrest the Book.* New York: Dell.

Jenkinson, Edward B. 1979. *Censors in the Classroom: The Mind Benders.* Carbondale: Southern Illinois University Press.

Karolides, Nicholas J., and Lee Burress, eds. 1985. *Celebrating Censored Books!* Racine: Wisconsin Council of Teachers of English.

———, ———, and John Kean, eds. 1993. *Censored Books: Critical Viewpoints.* Metuchen, NJ: Scarecrow Press.

Pipkin, Gloria Treadwell. 1993. "Challenging the Conventional Wisdom on Censorship." *The ALAN Review* 20(2): 35–37.

Shugert, Diane, ed. 1983. *Rationales for Commonly Challenged Taught Books.* Enfield: Connecticut Council of Teachers of English.

Samuels, Barbara. 1982. A National Survey of the Uses of Adolescent Literature in the Secondary Classroom: Grades 7–12. Unpubl. Doct. Diss. University of Houston, University Park.

———, and H. Lowery-Moore. 1987. "YA Books in the Classroom: Bridging the Basics: The Young Adult Novel in a Back-to-Basics Society." *The ALAN Review* 14(2): 42–44+.

Small, Robert C. 1977. "The Junior Novel and the Art of Literature." *English Journal* 66(7): 56–59.

Weiss, M. Jerry. 1988. "Censorship and the YA Book: A New Column: A Dangerous Subject: Censorship." *The ALAN Review* 15(3): 59–61.

West, Mark. 1988. *Trust Your Children: Voices against Censorship in Children's Literature.* New York: Neal-Schuman.

7 Censorship and African American Literature

Jim Knippling
University of Nebraska–Lincoln

In many written histories of African American literature, censorship is something of a missing *topoi*, a conspicuous absence which has something to teach us about the operations of dominant culture and ideology. While more than a few symptomatic instances of the blatant and contestable banning or the violent editing of African American literary productions are too individually complex and too numerous to document here, what becomes crucial to consider are the multifarious inhibitive pressures historically brought to bear upon Black literary writing, pressures which overlap and conflict with one another in such a dense thicket of considerations that out-and-out censorship can often become almost beside the point in some senses.

This is not to say that the question of censorship really is irrelevant within the context of African American literature; it is anything but. As a subtopic within a literature, though, it must be approached with a certain skepticism regarding its boundaries and its historical identifiability. A preoccupation with censorship as an evil in itself—rather than as a phenomenon symptomatic of an entire range of oppressive circumstances—can at worst become a rather indulgent and naïve consideration, a way of localizing and demonizing a locus of interference within what must otherwise be presumed as an irreproachable literary "superhighway" of unproblematically communicable experiences. Where does censorship begin or end?

In March of 1973, Clarence Major published an open letter to June Jordan on the question of censorship. Jordan's novel, *His Own Where*, had just been banned in Maryland because its use of Black English was seen as a potentially detrimental influence upon Black children. Major commiserates with Jordan and proceeds to update her on his own run-ins with censorship, adding that "if we let things slide, the ones against freedom of expression may have their way." In December of 1972, Major and Jane Delynn had taped a reading of their published creative writing for WNYC radio, but the program never aired because of "dirty" language in both works. As Major put it to Jordan, "Both Delynn and I said words like 'fuck' and 'shit' just as they appeared in our work" (Major 1974, 153). Major's focus on the question of a suppressed vernacular signals one of the crucial political stakes in the struggle against censorship: what versions of the natural, the everyday, the familiar, and the acceptable are allowed public expression?

Consider the case of *Native Son*, which marks, if not a turning point in the course of African American writing, then at least a certain line of demarcation. Shortly after the novel's publication and successful reception in the spring of 1940, Richard Wright (1908–1960) finished composing a lecture/essay while vacationing in Mexico. This famous text, "How 'Bigger' Was Born," would be included in most subsequent editions of the book; it recounts the author's boyhood acquaintance with five defiant Southern rebels, five "Biggers," whose memory had fueled Wright's earliest conception of the novel in particular ways. Wright recalls the creative stage at which he had arrived at a compelling vision of his protagonist as "a figure who would hold within him the prophesy of our future" (Wright 1991, 866). The author's imaginative absorption in his material is conveyed as convincingly as are Bigger's most pressing emotional hungers and obsessions—but in the early stages of Wright's planning a certain paralysis occurs. "Like Bigger himself," Wright recounts, " I felt a mental censor—product of the fears which a Negro feels from living in America—standing over me, draped in white, warning me not to write" (Wright 1991, 867).

The warnings of this spectral censor are various: beware the likely reaction of white racist readers who will see in Bigger a confirmation of their own unenlightened notions of young Black men as murderous rapists; beware the rejection of comrades in the Communist Party who will object to the nuanced depiction of Bigger's subjectivity as an overly individualized and insufficiently politicized or collective approach to questions of oppression; and beware the repulsion of respectable African American professionals who will consider themselves misrepresented and besmirched by the novel's unflinching saturation in sordid elements of Black American life. Wright's mastery over his "mental censor" is negotiated through his relationship to his protagonist, for he decides that submitting to the mental censor would mean "reacting as Bigger himself reacted: that is, I'd be acting out of *fear* if I let what I thought whites would say constrict and paralyze me." In overcoming the fear implied by this internalized self-censorship, Wright seems to find his very impetus for writing the book: "I said to myself, 'I must write this novel, not only for others to read, but to free *myself* of this sense of shame and fear'" (Wright 1991, 868).

The power generated by this combustible struggle resounded immediately among readers. Offered by the Book-of-the-Month Club as one of
its two main selections, *Native Son* sold over 250,000 copies in its first
three weeks of publication. Of course, Wright had had to bargain with
actual censors as well as spectral ones. Wright's publisher, Harper and
Brothers, had sent page proofs to the Book-of-the-Month Club in August
of 1939, and the planned fall publication had been delayed as the club
considered the manuscript. Arnold Rampersad (1991) has documented
the processes by which the book club requested considerable alteration
of the manuscript. Edward Aswell, Wright's editor at Harper and Brothers, relayed the objections of the book club to Wright in a letter: "And
incidentally the Book Club wants to know whether, if they do choose
Native Son, you would be willing to make some changes in that scene
early in the book where Bigger and his friends are sitting in the moving
picture theatre. I think you will recognize the scene I mean and will
understand why the Book Club finds it objectionable" (Rampersad 1991,
912). Wright complied with the request, rewriting the entire scene. The
Library of America's 1991 edition of the novel included in Wright's *Early
Works* has restored the original text.

The objectionable scene, which occurs in Book One, within the novel's
first thirty pages, may seem on the surface a trivial matter, but Wright's
revision grows into a considerable alteration of the text. In the original
theatre scene, Bigger and Jack slump in their seats and masturbate while
waiting for the film to begin: "'I'm polishing my nightstick,'" Bigger says
(Wright 1991, 472). The scene is rendered predominantly in dialogue, as
Bigger and Jack taunt one another, brag about their virility, remark on
passing women, giggle, and race one another to climax. Afterwards they
change seats: "'I don't know where to put my feet now,' Bigger said,
laughing" (Wright 1991, 473). This passage was extensively revised by
Wright for the published 1940 edition, with Bigger and Jack simply
resuming a discussion begun earlier, concerning their planned robbery
of Blum's Delicatessen.

Prior to the theatre scene, Bigger's position as a petty outlaw has been
"racialized" in clear ways by this planned robbery; though his gang has
already executed a few heists, Blum was to be their first white victim.
What the original theatre scene tends to do is to "sexualize" Bigger for the
first time, with overtones of the illicit, and with a special connection to
Mary Dalton. For in rewriting the theatre scene, Wright also eliminated
an extended description of a newsreel depicting wealthy young debu-
tantes cavorting on a Florida beach and featuring Mary Dalton especially.
Mary is shown in closeup in the company of Jan Erlone, with the
newsreel's narrator remarking leeringly upon the relationship: "*Mary
Dalton, daughter of Chicago's Henry Dalton, 4605 Drexel Boulevard, shocks*

society by spurning the boys of La Salle Street and the Gold Coast and accepting
the attentions of a well-known radical while on her recent winter vacation in
Florida" (Wright 1991, 474).

Bigger recognizes Mary's address as the one where he is to report that
very night for his new job. It is possible that Wright, having been effectively deprived the masturbation scene which occurs in close proximity
to the newsreel scene, and thereby deprived the suggestive juxtaposi-
tion, no longer felt motivated to stage such a rare coincidence. But the
elimination of the newsreel scene also dilutes one of Wright's apparently
key intentions regarding the depiction of Mary. For the newsreel under-
scores the extraordinarily inviolable "legitimacy" of Mary; she is posi-
tioned as a legitimate object of desire in spite of her daring forays into the
realm of otherness and leftism. Bigger is titillated while watching the
closeup of Mary's legs being chased by Jan's legs, as the voice-over
continues:

> *Ha! He's after her! There! He's got her! Oh, boy, don't you wish you were*
> *down here in Florida?* The close-up faded and another came, showing
> two pairs of legs standing close together. *Oh, boy!* said the voice.
> Slowly, the girl's legs strained upward until only the tips of her toes
> touched the sand. *Ah, the naughty rich!* There was a slow fade-out,
> while the commentator's voice ran on: *Shortly after a scene like this,*
> *shocked Mama and Papa Dalton summoned Mary home by wire from her*
> *winter vacation and denounced her Communist friend.* (Wright 1991, 475)

Mary's flaunted capacity to flirt with difference and danger while
remaining fundamentally safe and inviolable all the while is, in the
original, a fairly crucial component of the dynamic entered by Bigger.
Many of the later scenes in which Mary appears in person were also
edited to eliminate Bigger's more overt sexual impulses in her presence.
A line describing the "glimpse of white thigh" spotted by Bigger in the
rearview mirror as he drives Mary and Jan through the park was cut by
Wright, as was the account of Bigger's response: "He sighed and sat up
straight, fighting off the stiffening feeling in his loins" (Wright 1991, 518).
Also deleted was a passage which renders explicit Bigger's state as he
carries Mary's semi-conscious body toward her bed, just prior to her
death:

> He tightened his arms and his lips pressed tightly against hers and
> he felt her body moving strongly. The thought and conviction that
> Jan had had her a lot flashed through his mind. He kissed her again
> and felt the sharp bones of her hips move in a hard and veritable
> grind. Her mouth was open and her breath came slow and deep.
> (Wright 1991, 524)

Keneth Kinnamon has documented Aswell's note in the margin of this
latter passage, a note reading "'suggest cutting this'" (Kinnamon 1991,

14). Clearly Wright felt compelled to soften his daring treatment of what Calvin Hernton has called the "scarlet equation" of American fiction, the ultimate taboo: sexual impulses, energies, or activities between African American males and European American females. As is the case with so much African American literature, though, it is impossible to pinpoint who the censor is, or even whom the censor is hiding behind. Kinnamon has hypothesized convincingly upon the cutting of these later scenes, but even the textual scholar is confined to speculation:

> As Aswell knew, and as he must have argued to Wright, to retain such highly charged sexual scenes would risk censorship and thus prevent the larger political message from being conveyed, or at best undercut that message by diverting the salacious reader's intention. For whatever reason, the changes were made, resulting in a softened, less threatening, more victimized Bigger. . . . (Kinnamon 1991, 14–15)

Chester Himes (1909–1984), a friend and associate of Wright, experienced similar difficulties in attempting to deal with the "scarlet equation" in fiction. His 1955 novel, *The Primitive,* described by Langston Hughes in private correspondence as "a really sickening interracial passion tale," was drastically altered by its publisher, New American Library (Hughes 1980, 350). Himes made a special trip from Paris to New York to argue about editorial revisions, and almost got into a fistfight: "Not only did NAL want to change the title but also to delete all controversial assertions. I contended they might as well throw away the book for it was all controversial and intended to be so" (Himes 1977, 19).

But Himes's career also demonstrates the elusiveness of censorship as a force, the indistinguishable boundary between spectral censors, de facto censorship, and more overt literary oppression. Like Wright with "How Bigger was Born," Himes produced a speech/essay concerning the various visible and invisible forces of censorship impinging on creative work; entitled "Dilemma of the Negro Novelist in the United States," the lecture was delivered at the University of Chicago during the summer of 1948 (see Himes 1966). It delineates various conflicts and hurdles within the intellectual crusades of the African American writers, and claims that "various factors of American life and American culture will be raised to stay his pen" (Himes 1966, 54). Himes elaborated a sense of the multifarious inhibitive forces lying in wait for the Black author, and characterized the author's struggle against these forces as a perpetual challenge on every level:

> The urge to submit to the pattern prescribed by oppression will be powerful. The appeal to retrench, equivocate, compromise, will be issued by friend and foe alike. The temptations to accede will be tempting, the rewards coercive. The oppressor pays, and sometimes well, for the submission of the oppressed. (Himes 1966, 53)

Himes's speech categorizes several types of publishers and describes the potential conflicts between the author and each type. Those publishers motivated strictly by commercial interests (the majority) will be uninterested in "honest" novels by Black writers because such writing is generally considered a poor business venture. Those rare publishers who will occasionally set aside the consideration of profit in order to accept a novel on principle are often "liberal white people" who consider themselves authorities on the subject of race—based often upon their contact with middle-class Black people—and who will therefore erect "the barrier of preconception," expecting comforting illusions from the fiction. And then there is the overtly racist publisher: "But there will be no conflict between the Negro writer and this publisher; it will never begin" (Himes 1966, 54).

The speech was received in stony silence at the University of Chicago; nobody clapped. Himes stayed on for the following week, drinking heavily in a state of despair—over not only the speech but also the state of his writing career, due predominantly to the reception of *Lonely Crusade* (1947). The novel had expressed the skepticism of a wartime union organizer toward the several ideologues who would like to recruit him: union leaders, Communist Party members, and captains of industry who offer to buy him out. Himes's protagonist falters in virtually all of his assigned ideological roles:

> [T]here were times such as this when he was more Negro than Communist, and his American instincts were diametrically opposed to the ruthless nonconformity of revolutionary maneuvering; when the long list of his acts as an executive of the Communist Party judged themselves in the light of Christian reason; when the voice of his Baptist mother could be heard in the night of his soul; when virtues such as honesty, loyalty, courage, and kindness, charity, and fair play had meaning and value; when his mind rebelled and could not follow the merciless contradictions of reality. (Himes 1947, 254)

In 1972, Himes told various interviewers that the Communist Party launched a campaign against his book in New York by having people go into bookstores and break the bindings, or buy the book and demand their money back because it was trash. Blanche Knopf had overseen the novel's publication, and had lined up for Himes a series of radio interviews and book signings, all of which were inexplicably canceled at the last minute. The novel received a critical stoning which traumatized and effectively silenced Himes, the otherwise prolific author of seventeen novels, for five years. The *Daily Worker* likened *Lonely Crusade* to the "foul words that came from the cantankerous mouth of Bilbo."

Bilbo was a notoriously racist U.S. Senator from Mississippi who, ironically, had served as governor of that state during Himes's childhood there. Himes wrote in the manuscript of his 1972 autobiography *The Quality of Hurt* about his family's acquisition of a noisy car: "We got into so many controversies with the cracker farmers of the county by frightening their mule teams that Governor Bilbo, who was to become a senator, dismissed my father from the school and drove him from the state" (Himes 1972, 77). The sentence was edited by Doubleday, rendered in passive voice so as to delete Bilbo's name. In fact, the autobiography was heavily edited throughout. Himes's disclosures regarding his first marriage (that he slept with his wife-to-be on the first night of meeting her and that he smoked marijuana with her) were cut. His line about amorous activities in college—"I was still fucking Rose because she was a whore and I probably caught the clap from her"—was edited to read, "I preferred older, amoral women" (Himes 1972, 114).

While it becomes evident that censorship is in some sense everywhere, refusing to hold still as an issue particularly in connection with African American literature, it is equally clear that the often invisible forces of censorship have been dealt permanently resounding blows. In a 1969 interview, Himes acknowledges that the processes of censorship are often naturalized and "automatic," but he remains optimistic anyway:

> [T]he American publishers have . . . a conspiracy of censorship where they don't even need to be in contact with one another to know what they are going to censor; there are certain things that they just automatically know they are going to censor, and they all will work in the same way. Yes, it's true that this automatic and unspoken conspiracy of censorship among white publishers works against the black man. He has an absolute wall against him, but in the course of time this will break down. (Williams 1969, 70)

Works Cited

Himes, Chester. 1947. *Lonely Crusade*. New York: Knopf.

———. 1966. "Dilemma of the Negro Novelist in the United States." In *Beyond the Angry Black*, edited by John A. Williams, 52–58. New York: Cooper Square.

———. 1972. *The Quality of Hurt*. [Manuscript]. Beinecke Library, Yale University.

———. 1977. *My Life of Absurdity*. New York: Doubleday.

Hughes, Langston. 1980. *Arna Bontemps—Langston Hughes: Letters*. New York: Dodd, Mead.

Kinnamon, Keneth. 1991. "Introduction." In *New Essays on Native Son,* edited by
    Keneth Kinnamon, 1–34. Cambridge, MA: Cambridge University Press.

Major, Clarence. 1974. *The Dark and Feeling.* New York: The Third Press.

Rampersad, Arnold. 1991. "Notes on the Texts." In *Richard Wright: Early Works,*
    909–915. New York: Library of America.

Williams, John A. 1969. "My Man Himes." [Interview]. *Amistad* 1: 25–93.

Wright, Richard. 1991. *Early Works.* New York: Library of America. [Includes
    "How Bigger was Born" and *Native Son.*]

8 Intellectual Freedom and the Student: Using Literature to Teach Differentiation of Propaganda and Persuasion

Mary Ellen Van Camp
Ball State University

Recent articles in professional journals and the popular press, as well as televised documentary reports, indicate that censorship persists as a problem in many communities and school districts around the country. For many teachers this raises the question of how to deal with frequently censored materials in the classroom. The question is valid, especially when one realizes that textbook publishers have generally dealt with the censorship issue by removing virtually all controversial material from their publications intended for classroom use. Thus, in classrooms where study is limited to basal textbooks, students may not be taught the critical-thinking strategies which are required when reading controversial material beyond the classroom.

As a part of their efforts to teach critical thinking, many elementary and secondary classroom teachers have long tried to raise students' consciousness about the use of propaganda in the mass media, especially as it relates to advertising and the political campaign rhetoric. Certainly this is an important topic for classroom study. As a result of this instruction, students learn propaganda terminology and are often able to identify obvious examples of the various propaganda techniques. They recognize the use of the testimonial when they see movie and sports personalities selling cars or other items on television, and they can identify the bandwagon technique when an advertiser says, "Join with the thousands who have already tried our product." But one wonders if students are able to make the finer distinctions between these propaganda techniques and the other persuasive devices as they are used by speakers and writers in everyday life situations. For example, can students identify the various and more subtle persuasive devices used by politicians at either election time or when a critical issue is coming to a vote? Can students recognize in newspapers and magazines the uses of factual material to convey a persuasive message? The question here is whether students are being given enough or the right kind of information and exposure to a variety of contexts in which propaganda techniques and other persuasive devices are actually used, in order to make critical evaluations of the speaker's or the writer's message and motives.

One wonders further if most students are able to apply the critical-thinking strategies which would help them to distinguish between deceptive propagandistic material and other material which might be categorized as legitimate persuasion. Perhaps not, according to available information on reading achievement in *The Reading Report Card: Progress toward Excellence in Our Schools* (1985). The report, prepared by the Educational Testing Service and based on the National Assessment of Educational Progress, summarizes four national assessments of reading achievement from 1971 to 1984. The data indicate that while "there has been at least a leveling off in the previous downward trend," many students still lack inferential comprehension and inferential reading skills (29). Thus, one would tend to believe that many students also would have difficulty making the distinctions between propaganda and persuasion suggested here.

The problem is not one of limited application, but rather one that covers a broad spectrum of spoken and printed messages. Not only students but nearly everyone in our society is bombarded daily with many propaganda and persuasive messages via newspapers, magazines, books, direct-mail advertising, radio, television, and telephone. If it is true that many students lack the critical-thinking strategies which are necessary in order to make such distinctions when reading or listening, then what can be done to teach these essential life skills?

In order to deal with the topic in more detail, it is necessary to define the terms propaganda and persuasion as they are being used here. Propaganda is defined as messages which are intended to encourage or reinforce some sort of action or belief, but which also involve some sort of deception. The deception in propaganda often derives from how the language is used or manipulated, or from some deliberate masking of intention. Persuasion, on the other hand, is used to indicate carefully constructed messages which are intended (1) to encourage an action; (2) to convince or influence thinking about a belief; or (3) to reinforce an already existing belief. The primary difference here is that persuasion does not contain any deliberate deception intended by the author or speaker.

In a democratic society, an enlightened citizenry is a basic political requirement. As our society has become more complex, an enlightened citizenry has become necessary for economic, social, and aesthetic reasons as well. But if the citizenry falls short of the requirement of being enlightened, then propaganda can become a menace to the public, and all forms of persuasion become suspect. Consequently, it is up to the public schools and, specifically, to classroom teachers to do their part in creating a citizenry that is enlightened and thus able to distinguish propaganda from material which qualifies as a legitimate form of persuasion. The question is how this is to be done.

One possible answer to the question is to create adults who are critical thinkers and who possess the skills, strategies, and abilities of mature critical readers. As Willavene Wolf, Charlotte Huck, and Martha King indicated in their book *Critical Reading Abilities of Elementary School Children*, published by the Ohio State University Research Foundation in 1967, one of the important abilities of mature critical readers is the "ability to identify and analyze the devices authors sometimes use to persuade or influence the reader" (134). Wolf, Huck, and King go on to identify commonly used propaganda techniques such as glittering generalities, testimonial, bandwagon, card stacking, and so forth. These techniques are widely used in diverse forms by many authors for a variety of purposes, so it is important to teach students to recognize them in whatever form an author might use them. Teaching about propaganda is useful to students, and at the same time, differentiating propaganda from material which utilizes some form of legitimate persuasion as a contrast. One important issue here is that classroom teachers must create meaningful contexts to carry out what Wolf, Huck, and King have suggested.

One means for creating meaningful context is to encourage and allow students to read widely in self-selected books. Students must read both fiction and nonfiction, and they must become immersed in a great variety of literature. In so doing, they will encounter propaganda and persuasion in many forms. Thus, they can learn to identify propaganda techniques and persuasive devices in actual books and experience meaningful literary contexts for evaluating authors' uses of propaganda or persuasion and responding to it accordingly.

I am suggesting here that propaganda and persuasion can be specifically differentiated, but generally may not be differentiated sufficiently in classroom instruction to provide students with strategies applicable to real-world contexts. Many teachers cover units with their students in which they teach about propaganda techniques. Many textbooks in social studies, in language arts, and in speech communication, in fact, have brief sections devoted to propaganda techniques or devices. Unfortunately, they generally fail to distinguish the propaganda techniques from persuasive techniques which are legitimate forms for the presentation of a point of view in speaking or writing. Because teachers may not explain about the differences between propaganda and persuasion, students may only memorize the textbook information in order to identify it on some later test without seeing its further significance. Thus, propaganda techniques may be taught without a meaningful real-world context.

In a well-developed language arts program that is soundly based in the study of literature, including a variety of fiction and nonfiction, the context would be provided. In fact, there would be an endless number of contexts and a variety of perspectives from which the propaganda and the persuasion might be viewed, discussed, and evaluated.

In order to clarify what is meant by differentiating between propaganda techniques and legitimate persuasion, it will be useful to look at some commonly identified propaganda techniques and then specify their counterparts within the realm of persuasion. The listing which follows will be helpful in making some comparisons and contrasts.

Propaganda Techniques	*Persuasive Devices*
1. Testimonial—A prominent person recommends an action or provides an endorsement for a product or service.	1. Authoritative opinion expressed by someone in a position to know because of research, professional service or personal experience.
2. Claiming a cause-effect relationship where none exists.	2. Showing a legitimate cause-effect relationship.
3. Bandwagon—Suggests taking an action because others are taking it.	3. Suggests taking an action because it is right, just, ethical, or appropriate.
4. Glittering Generality—uses language deceptively to mask the intention and create the appearance of truth.	4. Presenting a generalization drawn from several independent and reliable sources.
5. Plain Folks—making reference to nonexistent bonds of ordinary or common relationship.	5. Making reference to human bonds which are legitimate, universal, and clearly related to the topic.
6. Card-Stacking—Attempting to deceive by omitting important facts.	6. Presenting all of the arguments in support of one side of an issue with regard for moral and ethical use of evidence.
7. Encouraging action out of unreasonable guilt or fear.	7. Encouraging an action based on personal and social responsibility.

A few literary examples will help to develop the perspective presented here. In a series of integrated language arts and social studies lessons, a middle school or junior high class might take up the topic of nuclear war. Classrooms could be supplied with a few copies of the following books:

> *Children of the Dust* by Louise Lawrence
> *Wolf of Shadows* by Whitley Strieber
> *Warday* by Whitley Strieber and James Kunetka
> *Return to Hiroshima* by Betty Jean Lifton
> *Hiroshima No Pika* by Toshi Maruki
> *When the Wind Blows* by Raymond Briggs

Each of these books provides a different perspective on the topic of nuclear war and could be used to develop students' critical-thinking strategies for reading persuasive or propagandistic material. *Children of the Dust* is variously categorized as science fiction and science fantasy. It portrays life among two related groups of people after a nuclear attack and describes a vision of the nuclear winter and the human mutations which result from the radiation. *Wolf of Shadows* by Whitley Strieber provides an interesting contrast to the Lawrence book. Strieber's book is primarily a science fantasy, but it also portrays the effects of nuclear winter on the survivors of a nuclear attack.

To develop students' critical-thinking strategies still further, they might read Strieber and Kunetka's *Warday*. The novel portrays two journalists who travel around the United States and describe the effects of nuclear attack on the country and the people. The novel takes on a sense of realism because of its journalistic elements and its references to real cities such as New York, Washington, D.C., and San Antonio. Because of its vocabulary and general reading level, the novel might be most appropriate for students twelve years of age and up.

Betty Jean Lifton's *Return to Hiroshima* provides still another perspective on nuclear war to develop students' thinking about persuasion and propaganda. The book uses a combination of photographs and artwork to portray the effects of the nuclear attack on Hiroshima. The book would be especially useful for helping students understand how actual information can be used for persuasive purposes. Students might also be asked to consider and evaluate the impact of the book's message as it moves from actual Hiroshima photographs to artwork and then back to actual photographs.

For purposes of contrast and comparison, students might next read *Hiroshima No Pika* by Toshi Maruki. This award-winning book describes and illustrates the effects of the bombing of Hiroshima on the community, on a particular family, and on an individual child. It is an especially good book for developing students' thinking about the impact of artwork and illustrations in the presentation of a persuasive message. Students might be asked to evaluate the focus of individual illustrations and the artist's use of color as a part of creating a persuasive message.

The final literary example for this topic is Raymond Briggs's *When the Wind Blows.* This book uses cartoon art and impressionistic paintings to present a provocative and devastating message about the effects of nuclear war on an elderly British couple. The couple lived through the bombings of London in World War II, and they believe they can survive the impending nuclear attack if they prepare sufficiently. This is decidedly a picture book for students twelve and up. In developing their persuasive-thinking strategies, students might be asked to evaluate how both the cartoon art and dialogue are used to develop the book's persuasive message and how the impressionistic paintings contribute to the book's total impact. Finally, students might be asked to consider the effect of the black end pages on the reader's response to the book's persuasive message.

After the students have had some time to read some or all of these books, the teacher could set up a series of small-group discussions in which students could compare and contrast the books in several respects. The teacher might provide the students with a list of questions to get the group discussions started. The list could include questions like:

- What are some of the similarities and differences in the views of nuclear war that these books present?
- What methods do the authors use to present their views?
- With the appropriate books, how do the illustrations contribute to the impact of the books?
- What facts do the books present and where do they deviate from factual presentations?
- Cite examples from our study of propaganda techniques and persuasive devices to show which techniques or devices the authors have used to present their views.
- What were your responses to each of the books?
- How did your responses vary as you read each of the books?

It is questions such as these that are likely to stimulate both careful and critical reading strategies as well as the higher-level critical-thinking strategies that are so important. In addition, with each of the books

identified for use with the nuclear war topic at the middle school or junior
high school level, there are opportunities for extending students' reading
and thinking to other topics as well. It is this element of using quality
literature which tends to promote wide reading and thus enables students to become independent critical thinkers.

One of the key elements in this sort of instruction is to allow the
students to discover their own perspectives as the discussion moves
along. At the same time, it is the teacher's responsibility to ask the right
questions so that the small-group discussions have some guidelines for
both their direction and their purpose. As more than one teacher has
discovered, "How to tell students what to look for without telling them
what to see is the dilemma of teaching" (Grugeon and Walden 1978, 224).

Another combination of books which a teacher might use with a class
in order for students to analyze how a nontraditional, persuasive point
of view is presented is *William's Doll* by Charlotte Zolotow and *Max* by
Rachel Isadora. Both books present a boy who in some way differs from
the traditional role model for little boys. William has many traditional
male toys that he enjoys, but he wants a doll; Max is a little league baseball
player who comes to enjoy dancing with his sister's ballet class. (Students
might be asked to compare and contrast the books in relation to the
persuasive devices used by the authors to present their nontraditional
views.) Again, as in the previous example, the teacher needs to ask the
right questions in order to stimulate students' thinking and to develop
the students' critical-reading strategies.

Another topic that might be studied through a variety of literature
focusing on the author's use of persuasive devices is appreciation of
cultural diversity. With this topic there are many outstanding works of
fiction that the teacher might make available for students to read, but for
the purpose of discussion here, a focus on just a few books will make the
point. Students might be asked to compare and contrast Barbara Cohen's
books *Molly's Pilgrim* and *Gooseberries to Oranges*. Both books deal with
similar thematic concerns of the immigrant experience, but their stories
and modes of presentation are very different. *Molly's Pilgrim* is the story
of a young immigrant girl who is not accepted by her classmates simply
because she is different. Later, through a Thanksgiving class project, the
girl gains acceptance from her schoolmates as all of the children learn
what it means to be a pilgrim. *Gooseberries to Oranges* is the story of an
eight-year-old Russian girl who comes to America to live with her
immigrant father after the deaths of her mother, an aunt, and a cousin.
The title is symbolic of the gooseberries that the little girl enjoyed eating
in Russia and the happiness she felt in her native village, while the
oranges represent the new fruit she comes to enjoy in California and the

happiness she finds living with her father in a new country. After reading these stories, students could again be asked a series of questions or given a list of questions around which to focus their discussion. For example, the list might include questions like the following:

> What persuasive methods or devices does the author use to present her views?
>
> What elements of the books make the characters seem realistic?
>
> How does the sense of reality within the stories contribute to the persuasion?
>
> How do the illustrations contribute to the impact of the books?
>
> How do the immigrants seem different and how do they seem very much like the Americans in the books?

As teachers work with their students, they will have opportunities to develop many other questions which will extend students' thinking about these books and others that they may choose to read.

For further development of the appreciation of the cultural diversity topic, students might also ready Gloria Skurzynski's book *The Tempering*. In this book students will read about a variety of ethnic groups living in one town and struggling against the forces which many immigrants faced during the early 1900s in this country. The book is also a good one for students to read because it brings in other topics which might interest students, such as the rise of unions in the United States, and which might stimulate students' interest in reading other books on related topics.

For teachers who may wish to implement some of the ideas presented here and who may also be looking for other activities for developing students critical-thinking strategies, some recent NCTE publications may be helpful. The *Thinking through Language* series by Barbara Dodds Stanford and Gene Stanford (1985) has a variety of suggested activities which teachers at the junior high and senior high levels may find quite adaptable to their students. Book One of this series emphasizes perception and nonverbal thinking, while Book Two emphasizes analytical and verbal thinking. Another NCTE publication, entitled *Activities to Promote Critical Thinking* (Rudasill 1986), contains a series of activities for teaching and developing students' critical and creative thinking in connection with composition and speaking and listening, as well as through the study of literature.

An outstanding school curriculum might be defined as one that uses each school day to teach students as much as possible in the time available. That means teaching more than one topic or skill at a time, and it means making full use of the available resources. Literature provides the richest resource for achieving that kind of a curriculum. The lessons suggested here for teaching about propaganda techniques and persuasive devices are examples of trying to teach more than just a list of techniques and devices which are to be memorized by students. Instead of memorization, the goal is to create mature critical readers through wide reading in actual books. Thus, students will see propaganda and persuasion as they are actually used by authors in order to present a variety of ideas and concepts. Within the framework of wide reading and a curriculum in which teachers ask appropriate questions to stimulate critical reading and critical thinking, students will learn to distinguish between deceptive propaganda and legitimate persuasion. With this sort of classroom curriculum in place, students would have the best chance possible for becoming mature critical readers who are able to make valid judgments as they evaluate the quality and merit of the ideas they find in the media and in all forms of print.

Works Cited

Professional References

Grugeon, Elizabeth, and Peter Walden, eds. 1978. *Literature and Learning*. Philadelphia: Open University Press.

The Reading Report Card: Progress toward Excellence in Our Schools: Trends in Reading over Four National Assessments, 1971–1984. 1985. Princeton, NJ: Educational Testing Service.

Rudasill, Leah. 1986. "Advertising Gimmicks: Teaching Critical Thinking." In *Activities to Promote Critical Thinking*, edited by Jeffrey N. Golub, 127–29. Urbana: National Council of Teachers of English.

Stanford, Barbara Dodds, and Gene Stanford. 1985. *Thinking through Language*. Urbana: National Council of Teachers of English.

Wolf, Willavene, Charlotte Huck, and Martha King. 1967. *Critical Reading Abilities of Elementary School Children*. Project No. 5-1040. Contract No. OE- 4-1-187. Columbus, OH: The Ohio State University Research Foundation.

Children's and Adolescent Literature

Briggs, Raymond. 1982. *When the Wind Blows*. Illustrated by Raymond Briggs. New York: Schocken.

Cohen, Barbara. 1982. *Gooseberries to Oranges*. Illustrated by Beverly Brodsky. New York: Lothrop, Lee, & Shepard.

———. 1983. *Molly's Pilgrim*. Illustrated by Michael J. Deraney. New York: Lothrop, Lee, & Shepard.

Isadora, Rachel. 1976. *Max*. Illustrated by Rachel Isadora. New York: Collier/ Macmillan.

Lawrence, Louise. 1985. *Children of the Dust*. New York: Harper and Row.

Lifton, Betty Jean. 1970. *Return to Hiroshima*. Photographs by Eikoh Hosoe. New York: Atheneum.

Maruki, Toshi. 1980. *Hiroshima No Pika*. Illustrated by Toshi Maruki. New York: Lothrop, Lee, & Shepard.

Skurzynski, Gloria. 1983. *The Tempering*. New York: Clarion/Houghton-Mifflin.

Strieber, Whitley. 1985. *Wolf of Shadows*. New York: Alfred Knopf/Sierra Club.

———, and James Kunetka. 1983. *Warday*. New York: Warner.

Zolotow, Charlotte. 1972. *William's Doll*. Illustrated by William Pene DuBois. New York: Harper & Row.

9 Censorship and the Teaching of Composition

Allison Wilson
Jackson State University

Few issues have excited greater controversy in American society than has the age-old battle between personal freedom and group conformity. Thus, when an "offensive" book is removed from library shelves or from an institution's curriculum, representatives of the media, brandishing notebooks and microphones, are likely to rush headlong into the fray, creating a situation in which responsible adults are forced to align themselves with one faction or the other. English teachers, in particular, cannot remain aloof from such an emotional conflict, since many of the works under attack (especially works of fiction) fall squarely within their instructional domain.

It seems to me, however, that another brand of censorship also has profound implications for the English classroom, a brand of censorship so subtle that it is misunderstood by educators and undetected by community leaders and media representatives. The censorship I have in mind—which might best be described as the counterproductive removal of all intellectual content from the teaching of composition—is difficult to recognize both because it is altruistically motivated and because it appears on the surface to be a logical response to the "academic short-comings" of today's student population.

This brand of censorship is also camouflaged by the various guises in which it appears; for the reasoning behind the removal of stimulating subject matter from writing activities—whether a clearly articulated statement contained in official documents or, more often, simply an unspoken or even unconscious assumption—sometimes varies according to the background and culture of the relevant student population. If students come from disadvantaged backgrounds and lack fluency in standard English, the reasoning most often goes something like this:

> Students cannot write essays until they can write paragraphs; they cannot write paragraphs until they can write sentences; they cannot write sentences until they memorize the rules of grammar. Students

must, in short, master standard English in isolation before they are equipped to produce content.

If, on the other hand, students come from middle-class backgrounds and are fluent in standard English, the most popular arguments against significant intellectual involvement often take one of the following forms:

> Because students have little experience with life in the "real" world and can relate only to the immediate environment, they should not be asked to examine or analyze the ideas of others until they have learned to articulate their own thoughts. Thus, writing assignments should be personal and emotive, never requiring students to look beyond themselves.

> Because students lack moral judgment and do not possess a fully articulated value system, they should not be encouraged or even permitted to adopt nonmainstream (anti-Christian, anti-capitalist, etc.) viewpoints. Writing activities, then, should remain on "safe," tried ground and should never stimulate "dangerous" trains of thought that might lead to any form of logical or ethical questioning of the status quo.

Obviously, all three arguments, though quite different, abridge personal freedom in similar ways, thus resulting in similar types of intellectual sterility, since teachers subscribing to any of these theories must design writing activities that discourage innovation and creativity while rewarding superficiality in both form and content.

In my experience, the major types of inhibitive activities—many of which are so firmly entrenched in English curricula as to remain unquestioned by even the most renegade of teachers—are the following:

1. the substitution of any type of activity (the completion of isolated grammatical/mechanical exercises, the memorization and recitation of rules, the analysis of model essays, for example) for actual writing;

2. the use of preliminary grammatical/mechanical exercises, especially when these (a) are not directly related to actual student writing performance and/or (b) occupy more instructional time than does actual writing;

3. the exclusive use of personal writing topics requiring no knowledge of larger issues or contrasting viewpoints and therefore no outside reading or other research; and

4. grading or marking practices (a) that focus only on "correct" surface features and arbitrary, predetermined patterns of organization or (b) that reward only that content that conforms to the teacher's/school's point of view.

Below, I offer detailed explanations, based on my own experiences and those of other educators, as to why these particular types of activities represent a form of censorship that abridges or totally eliminates the opportunity for productive intellectual involvement and that is ultimately devastating to the individual growth of student writers.

Preparing to Write versus Writing

It is obvious that young children, when functioning in a natural learning environment, do not acquire any skill by memorizing preliminary lists and rules. They learn by jumping headlong into the task at hand. The process of formal education, however, seems firmly grounded in the belief that human beings must spend a great deal of time preparing to perform rather than performing; and nowhere are the results of this belief so evident as in the teaching of composition. In the case of mainstream populations, students are often drilled, year after year, in "the basics of writing," during which time they fill in blanks, memorize rules, and analyze artificial fragments of isolated prose in an effort to learn *exactly* what *every* piece of writing *must* contain. Bogel and Hjortshoj (1984) call this the "orthodox method" and provide this succinct description:

> ... among all its variations you will find an almost exclusive concern with writing as a finished product, and with the varieties of form, logic, and purpose—along with standards of "correctness"—that these finished products should represent. (3)

The logical flaw in this approach is obvious, as is the subtle censorship: Students are not only misled by the naïve assumption that such a personal act as writing can be governed by a finite set of unambiguous, all-purpose laws but also, due to the amount of time and energy that must be devoted to learning these "laws," have only minimal opportunity to discover what the act of writing really entails. Furthermore, since English teachers themselves are easily misled by an approach that seems so neat and logical, they are apt to devote more time—often far more time—to the study of these "rules" than was originally intended, thus leaving less time for the production of any written ideas at all, let alone ideas that are personally significant.

Where nonmainstream populations are concerned, the censored environment is even more inhibitive of personal growth; for it is often presumed that these students must internalize certain "basic mainstream knowledge," ranging from social behavior (e.g., taking turns and raising one's hand to be recognized) to linguistic performance (e.g., reciting the parts of speech and recognizing sentence types) before they

are equipped even to talk about writing. Farr and Daniels (1986) describe
the situation this way:

> When schools serve many students from economic, social, or
> linguistic minorities, the curriculum is often reorganized to make
> learning more segmented, subdivided, and decontextualized; this is
> called "skill-building." The assumption is that if students do not
> bring middle-class language and learning styles with them to the
> classroom, the presumed subcomponents of these "skills" need to be
> taught to the children first, before anything else can be learned. In
> practice, this means that students spend a good deal of time working
> on oral drills and workbook pages that have no immediate meaning
> or application. (52)

Furthermore, in my own experience, I have discovered that it is unlikely
that these students will ever be allowed to make the anticipated transi-
tion from "preliminary" drills to genuine writing activities, primarily
because most, due to boredom or lack of purpose, will never perform
isolated tasks to the satisfaction of teachers raised and/or educated in the
mainstream tradition. Once again, therefore, students are robbed of their
individuality by a brand of censorship that smothers youthful curiosity
and enthusiasm in a mountain of "preliminaries," while abridging or
totally usurping the amount of time available for genuine intellectual
involvement.

Studying Grammar versus Using Grammar

One particular type of preliminary writing activity that seems particularly inhibitive to students from all backgrounds and cultures is the
formal study of grammar, in that young writers are apt to assume, either
consciously or unconsciously, that the choice of specific words and
patterns is the first step in a writing process as well as the most important
aspect of the final written product. But it appears to me that these
assumptions only guide students away from productive intellectual
pathways and into repeated dead ends. As Lindemann (1987) has pointed
out,

> although traditional grammar claims to study the sentence, the
> approach focuses on taking language apart, not on putting it together.
> Students analyze and dissect sentences by diagramming them or
> labeling each word as a part of speech. Generally, they are someone
> else's sentences, not the student's. As a result, students may learn
> terminology and doubtless some principles of editing, but they
> haven't learned how to *create* discourse, only to label, diagram, or
> analyze it. Since the traditional approach doesn't encourage stu-

dents to apply grammatical principles to the composing process, teachers must. If grammar is taught at all, it should be tied to writing instruction. The student's own prose, not the chapter-by-chapter arrangement of a text, should determine which grammatical principles offer workable solutions to writing problems. (110)

And Strong (1986) has concluded that even sentence-combining exercises, which are obviously far more likely to influence students positively than are traditional rules and parsing, are themselves not as productive as an inquiry approach (12), an approach that seems to me the direct opposite of the censored, intellectually sterile procedure necessitated by preliminary grammar study.

For students from standard-English-speaking backgrounds, who are often given a yearly prewriting dose of grammatical and mechanical "review," premature focus on surface correctness can be harmful enough, in that an instruction-imposed fear of dangling, splitting, and splicing can lead to oversimplification of both ideas and presentation. For young writers from nonstandard-speaking backgrounds—those who are labeled or at least thought of as "remedial"—the "grammatical fallacy" is much more harmful and can be so devastating as to bring about a complete rift between student and school, thus ending all intellectual involvement. It would seem, research aside, that common sense would, by this time, have led experienced writing teachers to the conclusion that this approach is not only ineffective in improving writing performance but can actually be harmful. This is not the case, however; for "remedial" students are subjected to such a procedure with shocking frequency, as Wiener (1981) discovered:

> After examining countless syllabi for beginning writers over the country, I have found that remedial students suffer daily doses of run-ons and apostrophes as the program of cure for sick writers. With rare exceptions almost every syllabus I studied worked from a heart of grammar and mechanics, each day's toil a new effort at labels and definitions and a new attempt to apply them through underlining and circling and connecting subjects and verbs and commas and adverbial clauses. In only some cases was frequent writing demanded of the student. (6–7)

In short, students are forced to study grammar but are rarely encouraged or even allowed to use it for expressing their own ideas and reactions.

Spontaneous Reaction versus Analytic Response

During my first year of teaching writing, during which time, despite my own experience as a writer, I diligently attempted to follow the product-

based "common" syllabi used in my department, one of my students
wrote the following on an end-of-semester teacher-evaluation form:

> I sooooo tired of writin in every class about being Black and poor and
> how my past effect me. Why couldn't we of read some stories and
> discussed

This criticism struck me as significant for two reasons. First and most
obviously, it pointed up the fact, all too clearly, that the preliminary and
ongoing study of isolated textbook grammar dictated by the common
syllabi had not improved this student's written language. Less obviously, but certainly more important, it emphasized the student's frustration with the intellectually sterile environment that had been repeatedly
imposed upon him, presumably because of race and linguistic difference—a frustration I soon learned he shared with many of his classmates
at the predominantly black institution he attended. For it seems that on
the rare occasions when minority students are finally allowed to concen-
trate on something more substantial than noun plurals and verb tenses,
they are rarely allowed to advance beyond the redundant emotive topics
with which many writing instructors begin every semester of every
school year. It seems to me, then, that such an approach not only stunts
intellectual growth by censoring the writing environment to conform to
the educational establishment's concept of these students' mental capa-
bilities, but also becomes a self-fulfilling prophecy by anchoring
nonmainstream students to the most simplistic level of inquiry. How, for
example, are basic writers ever to advance beyond what Shaughnessy
(1977) has described as "the [egocentristic] assumption that the reader
understands what is going on in the writer's mind and needs therefore
no introductions or transitions or explanations" (240) if they are never
given an opportunity to examine diverse concerns from diverse viewpoints? And how, after writing what, in effect, is the same essay from
elementary school through the first year of college, can these students be
motivated to engage "the reader" when they themselves have long since
lost interest? As Rose (1988) has indicated,

> Creating simple topics to aid in the correction of error . . . might be
> a less successful strategy than we think—error cannot be isolated
> and removed. . . . Furthermore, we might be demoralizing our [basic
> writing] students by giving them the same kind of topic they have
> been writing on for so many years. (323)

Judging from what I myself have witnessed, I would say that Rose's
observations are accurate indeed, even if a bit understated. What is more,
mainstream, "nonremedial" students seem to fare little better where
intellectual stimulation is concerned: The widespread practice of
beginning with emotive, noncritical topics often leads teachers to devote

an inordinate amount of time to the compilation of soul-searching narratives that, though supposedly nonfictional in nature, are more akin to short story writing than to the kinds of academic prose typical of disciplines with "real" subject matter.

Conformity versus Individuality

The field of composition research and theory has grown so rapidly over the past several decades that phrases like "invention strategies," "making meaning," and "discovering form" are dropped regularly and casually into the conversation whenever two or more English teachers get together. And it is quite obvious that at least some of these teachers do indeed incorporate such concepts into classroom activities, thus emphasizing the importance of meaningful content and inherent patterns of organization. It is surprising, then, how many student essays are still returned to their authors with copious red-inked surface minutiae but minimal comment concerning the more substantial aspects of a piece of writing. Once, for example, I was assigned a composition class previously taught by another faculty member, who turned over to me copies of her assignments and of all the work the students had completed up until that time. I was greatly impressed by the interesting assignments she had constructed but equally depressed by her grading practices. She had covered the essays with grammatical and mechanical corrections but had responded in no way to either the shockingly original and/or the shockingly illogical statements that appeared in most of the papers, thus perpetuating the kind of inhibited writing environment described so perfectly (more than two decades ago) by Jenkinson and Seybold's (1970) hypothetical student writer:

> Confused and angry, he stared at the red marks on his paper. He had awked again. And he had fragged. He always awked and fragged. On every theme, a couple of awks and a frag or two. And the inevitable puncs and sp's. (3)

As a coordinator of freshman composition, I was repeatedly troubled by the frequency with which I saw this type of "grading." I am still troubled by the large numbers of my former students who come to me in panic because their present teachers insist on "five-paragraph, three-point" essays or who assign "opinion" topics, then penalize young writers for expressing any opinion (the questioning of Biblical "truth," for instance) that does not correspond to community mores. Jenkinson and Seybold's frustrated student writer encountered similar censorship whenever he attempted to express himself:

> The teacher didn't like what he said [about people not really caring for their fellow man] . . . and wrote in the margin: "How can you believe this? I disagree with you. See me after class." He didn't show up. He didn't want another phony lecture on the brotherhood of man.
>
> That wasn't the only time a teacher disagreed with what he wrote. One even sent him to the principal's office for writing about his most embarrassing moment even though she had assigned the topic. She told the principal he was trying to embarrass her. But all he did was write about his most embarrassing moment, just as she had told him to. And it was a gas. (5)

So much for the making of meaning!

But how can a writing teacher avoid the above forms of intellectual censorship and create an environment conducive to, not restrictive of, the production of meaningful written ideas? Obviously, any teacher can learn to reject preliminary drills, irrelevant grammatical principles, emotive topics, and arbitrary grading practices in favor of idea-based prewriting assignments and context-based revision activities. The major change, however, must be a change in teachers' attitudes; for it seems to me that teachers will never be able to release the full intellectual potential of the young writer until they are able to put themselves in that young writer's place, until they are able to see themselves, not as all-knowing, all-wise receptacles of knowledge, but as fellow thinkers and explorers. In *Writing without Teachers*, Elbow (1973) describes the kind of give-and-take environment I have in mind:

> Can [a writing class] have a teacher? Yes and no. I find I can set up a teacherless writing class in my own class *as long as I follow all the same procedures as everyone else:* I too must put in my piece of writing each week; I too must get everyone's responses and reactions to it; I too must give my own reactions to other pieces of writing. . . . When I succeed at this I help break the ice and encourage them to share their reactions and responses even if they don't trust them. In short, I can only set up something like the teacherless class in my own class if I adopt more the role of a learner and less the role of a teacher. (ix)

True, the concept of a "teacherless" environment *per se* may not be appropriate for all classrooms or for all student populations at all times: Some young writers *do* seem to need a more structured environment; and some teachers may prefer to stay active as writers, not by completing the same assignments given the students, but by engaging in their own purposeful writing activities (professional articles, curricular materials, departmental reports, etc.). But there is no doubt that a shift *in the general direction* of this concept—a shift in the direction of a student-teacher partnership—would alleviate much of the intellectual censorship that has often made a mockery of writing instruction.

Works Cited

Bogel, Fredric V., and Keith Hjortshoj. 1984. "Composition Theory and the Curriculum." In *Teaching Prose: A Guide for Writing Instructors,* edited by Fredric V. Bogel and Katherine K. Gottschalk, 1–19. New York: Norton.

Elbow, Peter. 1973. *Writing without Teachers.* New York: Oxford University Press.

Farr, Marcia, and Harvey Daniels. 1986. *Language Diversity and Writing Instruction.* Urbana: National Council of Teachers of English.

Jenkinson, Edward B., and Donald A. Seybold. 1970. *Writing as a Process of Discovery: Some Structured Theme Assignments for Grades Five through Twelve.* Bloomington: Indiana University Press.

Lindemann, Erika. 1987. *A Rhetoric for Writing Teachers.* 2nd ed. New York: Oxford.

Rose, Mike. 1988. "Remedial Writing Courses: A Critique and a Proposal." In *The Writing Teacher's Sourcebook.* 2nd ed., edited by Gary Tate and Edward P.J. Corbett, 318–37. New York: Oxford University Press.

Shaughnessy, Mina P. 1977. *Errors and Expectations.* New York: Oxford University Press.

Strong, William. 1986. *Creative Approaches to Sentence Combining.* Urbana: National Council of Teachers of English.

Wiener, Harvey S. 1981. *The Writing Room: A Resource Book for Teachers of English.* New York: Oxford University Press.

10 Freedom and Restrictions in Language Use

Roy C. O'Donnell
University of Georgia

Because freedom of thought and expression is essential in a democracy, censorship of language is rightly regarded as a threat to all other freedoms. Freedom of speech is truly the cornerstone of a democratic society, but the basic concept of organized society is incompatible with absolute freedom of the individual. When the interests and desires of individual members of society come in conflict with those of other members or the group as a whole, then the larger society imposes restrictions. Since language underlies or impinges on practically every aspect of human experience, it is inevitable that certain restrictions will from time to time be imposed on the language we use.

The restrictions society places on language use may be considered under two broad categories: restrictions that have the force of law, and restrictions that have the force of social disapproval. The areas of endeavor in which language is restricted vary, but they usually include religion, and they often include biological functions and social relationships. The language thus restricted can be classified variously as profanity, obscenity and vulgarity, and insults and falsehoods.

Two of the Ten Commandments given in Exodus 22 are concerned with restrictions on language: "You shall not make wrong use of the name of the Lord your God" (v. 7), and "You shall not give false evidence against your neighbor" (v. 16). These restrictions are subsequently expanded: "You shall not revile God, nor curse a chief of your own people" (v. 28), and "You shall not spread a baseless rumor. You shall not make common cause with a wicked man by giving malicious evidence" (23.1). Twentieth-century secular laws against slander, libel, and perjury impose similar restrictions in our society. Among the ancient Hebrews, fear of using God's name in vain led to their avoiding entirely the utterance of the sacred name. The penalty for reviling God (blasphemy) was death by stoning, and the only sin Jesus pronounced unforgivable was slander spoken against the Holy Spirit (Matthew 12: 31–32).

Since Biblical times penalties for profane or blasphemous utterances have varied greatly in their severity. Rawson (1989) quotes from a summary of Spanish laws issued in New Orleans in 1769 as follows: "He who shall revile our Savior or His Mother the Holy Virgin Mary, shall have his tongue cut out, and his property shall be confiscated, applicable one-half to the public treasury and the other half to the informer" (7). He cites another law less general in scope and less severe in penalty which was passed by Parliament in 1606, making it a crime "for anyone in any theatrical production to jestingly or profanely speak or use the Holy name of God, or of Christ Jesus, or of the Holy Ghost, or of the Trinity, which are not to be spoken but with fear and reverence" (5). The penalty for violation of this law was a fine of ten pounds. Similarly restricting profanity, as well as obscenity, was a clause in the Hollywood Production Code of 1930: "Pointed profanity (this includes the words *God, Lord, Jesus Christ*—unless used reverently—*hell, s.o.b., damn, Gawd*), or every other profane or vulgar expression, however used, is forbidden" (5). Another specific restriction on the use of profane language cited by Rawson is George Washington's General Order to the Continental Army of July 1776: "The General is sorry to be informed that the foolish and wicked practice of profane cursing and swearing, a vice hitherto little known in an American army is growing into fashion. He hopes the officers will, by example as well as influence, endeavor to check it, and that both they and the men will reflect that we can have little hope of the blessing of Heaven on our arms if we insult it by our impiety and folly" (5–6).

While the severity of penalties for irreverent language has been greatly diminished in English-speaking societies, strict penalties are still enforced in some parts of the world. A current example is the reaction of some Islamic leaders to Salman Rushdie's *Satanic Verses*, which they regard as profanely insulting to their religion. Rushdie has so far avoided having the death penalty carried out by going into hiding, but some of his translators have been less fortunate.

The tendency to use profane language seems to be well-established as a part of human behavior, and it manifests itself in various ways. What Robertson and Cassidy (1954) call "minced forms" result "when the human impulse to swear is held in check by religious or social prohibitions" (248). These minced forms of words or phrases suggest the forbidden item rather than state it outright. *Gad* is substituted for *God*, *darn* for *damn*, and *dodburned* for *God-damned*. Examples of further distortions of the sacred name are *goodness, gosh, gorry, Godfrey*, and *golly*. "Jesus is suggested by the Elizabethan *Gis* (now *Jeez*), and by the modern *Gee Whiz, Jerusalem*, and 'for *Pete's* sake'; Christ is alluded to in *cripes*, 'for the love of Mike,' the otherwise meaningless 'O for *crying* out loud'; *Jiminy*

Crickets and the more recent *Jeepers Creepers* attempt to combine the two. A curious exhibition indeed, of the human desire to sin combined with a want of courage" (248).

While the use of profane language has long been severely restricted, it was only in relatively recent times that obscene and vulgar language became a matter of great public concern among speakers of English. Rawson (1989) points out the fact that "neither England nor the United States had any anti-obscenity statutes until the nineteenth century, when improvements in public education combined with developments in printing technology to create a popular demand for the kind of literary works that previously had circulated without restriction among society's elite" (7). Before the development of mass production printing, books were too expensive for people of ordinary means, and the reading public was composed mainly of those who were economically privileged. Although various forms of censorship affected religion and politics, people were allowed considerable latitude in setting their own standards of decency in language use.

With wider dissemination of books, certain kinds of material came to be regarded as a threat to public morals. In 1708, a printer named James Read was arrested for having published *The Fifteen Plagues of a Maidenhead.* According to Rawson, the judge dismissed the indictment, finding that the work did indeed tend "to the corruption of good manners," but that there was no law to punish its publisher (7). Subsequently, judges began to take a sterner view of such offenses, and a printer named John Wilkes was put in jail for publishing *An Essay on Women* in 1763. It is possible that his sentence might have been less severe if he had not also been accused of certain political offenses.

While standards of decency in language may not have caused much public concern before the nineteenth century, it does not follow that there were no restraints. Over the centuries, many Christian believers have been influenced by the Apostle Paul's admonition in his letter to the Ephesians (4:29): "No bad language must pass your lips, but only what is good and helpful to the occasion, so that it brings a blessing to those who hear it." The Wesleyan revival of religion in the eighteenth century increased public awareness of Biblical standards of conduct and contributed to the development of a more clearly defined sense of middle-class morality.

Incidentally, a comparison of translations of the Bible itself illustrates that what is regarded as vulgar language varies over time: the King James version includes the words *dung, piss,* and *whore,* which in later times were on the prohibited list. The fact that standards of taste in the use of language change over time is further illustrated in a letter written by Sir

Walter Scott (cited in Rawson 1989). Scott relates how his grand-aunt had asked him in the 1790s to procure for her some books by Aphra Behn, which she remembered from her youth. Scott told her he did not think she would approve of "either the manners, or the language, which approached too near that of Charles II's time to be quite proper reading." Having reluctantly complied with his grand-aunt's request, Scott reported:

> The next time I saw her afterwards, she gave me back Aphra, properly wrapped up, with nearly these words: "Take back your bonny Mrs. Behn, and if you will take my advice, put her in the fire, for I have found it impossible to get through the very first novel. But is it not," she added, "a very odd thing that I, an old woman of eighty and upwards, sitting alone, feel ashamed to read a book which sixty years ago, I have heard read aloud for the amusement of large circles, consisting of the finest and most credible society of London?" (9–10)

Efforts to eliminate vulgarity in language in the early nineteenth century are seen in Henrietta and Thomas Bowdler's *Family Shakespeare*, published in 1807, and in Noah Webster's edition of the Bible, published in 1833. Both works substituted words for those that had come to be regarded as offensive. Organized group efforts to stamp out obscenity were made by the Boston Watch and Ward Society, the New York Society for the Suppression of Vice, and in England, the Organization for the Reformation of Manners. These groups initiated private suits charging obscenity and indecency under the common law and worked for formal statutes to require government enforcement of their moral standards.

Efforts to criminalize "indecent" materials resulted in the Obscene Publications Act of 1857 in Great Britain, and the Comstock Postal Act of 1873 in the United States. Rigorous enforcement of these laws went so far as to inhibit the use of certain words even in scholarly works and to exclude them from dictionaries. Concerning the Comstock Act, Mencken (1963) says, "Once that amazing law was upon the statute books and Comstock himself was given the inquisitorial powers of a post-office inspector, it became positively dangerous to print certain ancient and essentially decent English words" (358). Partridge (1961) notes that a four-letter word for the female pudendum in one form or another dates from the Middle English period. He substitutes an asterisk for a vowel in his spelling of the word and notes that "owing to its powerful sexuality, the term has since C. 15, been avoided in written and spoken English" (198). Partridge goes on to say: "Had the late Sir James Murray courageously included the word, and spelt it in full, in the great *O(xford) E(nglish) D(ictionary)*, the situation would be different; as it is, neither the *Universal Dict(ionary) of English* (1937) nor the *S(horter) O(xford) D(ic-*

tionary) (1933) had the courage to include it" (198). Partridge also omits the vowel from the word denoting "an act of sexual connexion." Both of these words spelled in full are included in several recently published dictionaries.

Victorian social delicacy required the use of many euphemisms for parts and functions of the human body. Various ways of avoiding Anglo-Saxon words referring to sexual union and the organs involved had already been developed, but the need to substitute *bosom* and *stomach* for *breast* and *belly*, for example, is associated with Victorian sensibility. Such delicacy of expression extended beyond references to the human body. Pieces of chicken were referred to as *drum sticks* and *white meat* instead of *legs* and *breasts*.

Euphemism was sometimes far reaching in its application to established words. *Cock* came to have such strong sexual overtones that the name of the barnyard fowl was changed to *rooster*, and *cockroaches* became simply *roaches*. Other words that contained syllables sounding like the offending word were replaced. Rawson (1989, 85) gives as examples *haystacks* and *weather vanes* as replacements for *haycocks* and *weather cocks*. Extending even further, *bull* was another term that was avoided because of its sexual potency. Substitutes included *cow brute, cow critter, top cow*, and *seed ox*. Other words with varying degrees of proximity to taboo topics were also changed. *Harlot*, a synonym for the harsher word *whore*, became *fallen woman; stockings* became *hose;* and *arse* became *backside* or *seat*. *Ass*, homonymous with *arse*, was replaced by *donkey* or *jack*. Excretory functions were performed under the guise of *washing one's hands* or *excusing oneself;* and the place where these functions were performed was known variously as the *privy, water closet (W.C.), toilet, bathroom*, and various other names as the substitutes themselves became "soiled" with use.

Some of the laws passed in the Victorian era are still on the statute books. The state of Georgia passed a law in 1865, which was re-enacted in 1983 (State Law 16-11-39-2), prohibiting the use of "obscene, vulgar or profane language" in the presence of anyone under fourteen years of age, if such language threatens "a breach of peace." The *Atlanta Constitution*, on May 15, 1991, reported that a shoe salesman had been arrested in Clayton County for violation of this law. A customer, accompanied by her fifteen-month-old daughter, went to a shoe store in Riverdale to return a pair of shoes she had previously purchased. When the sales clerk told her she would need to come back later since he had insufficient cash on hand to give her a refund, she complained about the inconvenience. According to the newspaper report, the sales clerk responded by shrugging his shoulders and saying, "Lady, sh— happens." The offended customer went to the police and signed a criminal warrant, resulting in the arrest of the clerk. The maximum penalty he faced was a fine of $1,000 and a year in prison, but he was spared the penalty when the charge was subsequently dropped. Apparently the law is far from dormant, however; the news item states that it is not unusual for solicitors in the Metropolitan Atlanta area to use it "a couple of times a year," usually when someone is offended by being called "an obscene name."

The Victorian concern over vulgar, indecent, and obscene language apparently did not extend to uncomplimentary names for members of ethnic groups. Terms of opprobrium have probably been in use as long as groups of people have seen other groups as being different from themselves, and the tendency to use them seems to be as well-established as the tendency to swear. Apparently, such terms were used rather freely in the nineteenth century, and in fact some that have had wide currency since then found their way into the English language during that period.

Frog, referring to a Frenchman, came into use in England about 1870, according to Partridge (1961, 303). *Wop* is traced by Mencken to *guappo*, (1963, 372) a Neapolitan term denoting a showy, pretentious fellow; Italian immigrants brought the latter term with them to America about 1885, and within a decade *wop* came to signify an Italian. *Dago*, from Diego, was first used in the 1830s to designate a Spaniard. It was probably transferred to Italians in the 1880s. *Greaser* as a term for Mexicans and other Spanish Americans became common during the war with Mexico. Mencken (374) cites an early example of its use in a letter written in Texas in 1836. *Wetback*, suggesting the illegal method of entry of some Mexican immigrants, is of more recent origin. *Irish* as a derogatory prefix was used in England as early as the seventeenth century, and subsequently in the United States. Mencken cites the following compounds from the nineteenth century: *Irish dividend*, an assessment on stock, 1881; *Irish spoon*, a spade, 1862; and *Irish pennant*, a loose end of rope, 1840. "In the days of the great Irish immigration," says Mencken, "the American designation of almost anything unpleasant was hung with the adjective and it was converted into a noun to signify a quick temper" (372). Both the Irish and the Germans, often referred to as *Dutch* (Deutsch), are viewed negatively in the following folk rhyme quoted by Rawson (1989, 210):

> The dirty, dirty Dutch
> They don't amount to much
> But they're a damned sight better than the Irish.

Both *Irish* and *Dutch* can now be used without offense.

Jew as a synonym for *usurer* goes back at least to the early seventeenth century. Its conversion into a verb seems to have occurred in America in the early nineteenth century. Rawson says, "A curious effect of the long and largely successful campaign of Jews in the first half of the [twentieth] century to eliminate the use of *Jew* as a verb was that many people, including numerous Jews, started to avoid using the word in any sense at all" (220). Mencken, writing prior to World War II, said: "Certain American Jews carry on a continuous campaign against the use of *Jew*, and American newspapers, in order to get rid of their clamor, often use *Hebrew* instead. The very word *Jew* appears to be offensive to American Jews, and they commonly avoid it by using *Jewish* with a noun" (377). Rawson notes that the word *Jew* is no longer shunned to the degree it formerly was, "But even so, careful speakers are more likely to say 'He is Jewish' than 'He is a Jew'" (220).

The appropriate word for designating people of African descent has long been the subject of disagreement, and many of the words that have been used have at one time or another had negative connotations. Mencken cites an article on this subject which appeared in the May 1937 issue of *Opportunity*, the organ of the National Urban League. The article, written by Dean Kelly Miller of Howard University, traced the history of common American designations of persons of Miller's race. Mencken's summary is as follows:

> In the first days of slavery, they were called *blacks*, and even after interbreeding lightened their color the term continued in use. Then came *African*, which was accepted by the race "in the early years, after it first came to self-consciousness," and still survives in the titles of some of its religious organizations. A bit later *darky* or *darkey* began to be used and "at first carried no invidious implication." Then came *Africo-American* (1835 or thereabout), but it was too clumsy to be adopted. After the Civil War the wartime coinage freedman was in wide use, but it began to die out before the 70's. In 1880 . . . *Afro-American* was invented by T. Thomas Fortune, editor of the *New York Age* . . . At some undetermined time after 1900, Sir Harry Johnston, the English African explorer and colonial administrator, shortened *Afro-American* to *Aframerican*, but the latter has had little vogue. (380–381)

Negro, from Latin *niger*, is the Spanish and Portugese word for *black*; it was borrowed by the English during the sixteenth century. Mencken notes that one objection to its use was that it frequently was pronounced as *nigger*, a word that came to be bitterly resented by persons so designated. The *Oxford English Dictionary*'s earliest example of *nigger* comes from a poem by Robert Burns published in 1786. The *Dictionary of American English* traces *nigger boy* to 1825 and *nigger talk* to 1866. Rawson notes that in its early use *nigger* was not necessarily pejorative, and in fact was sometimes used without contempt well into the twentieth century.

Hayakawa (1949) relates an account of a distinguished Negro sociologist who in his adolescence was hitchhiking in an area where Negroes were seldom seen. He was befriended by a kindly white couple who gave him food and a place to sleep in their home. He was grateful for their kindness, but he was profoundly upset by the fact that they kept calling him "little nigger." He finally got up courage enough to ask the man not to call him by that "insulting" name. Hayakawa gives the ensuing dialogue:

"Who's insultin' you, son?"
"You are, sir—that name you're always calling me."
"I ain't callin' you no names, son."
"I mean your calling me 'nigger.'"
"Well, what's insultin' about that? You are a nigger, ain't you?" (90)

Resistance to the hated word intensified during the 1930s. When Agatha Christie's 1939 play *Ten Little Niggers* was published in the United States, it had to be retitled *Ten Little Indians* (it was later changed to *Then There Were None*). Racial integration in the 1950s and 1960s intensified concern over appropriate ways to designate ethnic origin, a concern which continues to manifest itself in various ways.

The *Atlanta Constitution* on May 3, 1991, reported that the play *Coup/Clucks*, by Kentucky writer Jane Martin, had opened the previous week in Gainesville, Georgia, and was drawing fire both from members of the black community and from members of the Ku Klux Klan. Black critics had complained about the use of derogatory terms for blacks in the dialogue. On the other hand, a black actor in the play stated that it accurately portrays racism and the Klan, and that it is "not so much anti-black or anti-white as anti-bigotry." The business manager of the Theater Alliance said the play "addresses racism and bigotry head-on. It makes a statement through comedy and laughter." But the humor was obviously lost on some black citizens and Klan members alike. An NAACP official was quoted as saying: "I really didn't appreciate it, and I didn't find it funny. . . ." Klan members reacted by carrying signs on opening night with this message: "This play contains profanity and sexual suggestions."

In the latter half of the twentieth century, as the American public in general has become decreasingly sensitive about the use of profane, obscene, and vulgar language, there has been a growing sensitivity to the need to avoid potentially offensive words referring to all kinds of minority groups. Evidence of this sensitivity is widespread. A news item in the *Atlanta Constitution* on July 14, 1991, reported that a man in Hollywood, Florida, was sentenced to serve three months in federal prison and three years on probation for shouting racial slurs and making threats to keep a black woman from moving into the neighborhood. The man was also ordered to perform 100 hours of community service. *The Las Vegas Review Journal* on May 11, 1991, carried an editorial comment on the report that a U.S. Immigration and Naturalization official in Miami had earlier that week met with a group of twenty angry Chinese Americans to apologize for using the word *Chinaman* in reference to Chinese detainees. As a gesture of conciliation the official agreed to hire three Chinese interpreters for an INS camp near Miami and to name a liaison to speed the release of Chinese refugees. The opening sentence of the item was: "Credit the Politically Correct with securing booty as a result of their self-righteous attacks," a statement which reflects a growing countersensitivity.

The *Atlanta Constitution* on January 14, 1991, reported that Fulton County education officials had drafted a proposed anti-bigotry policy that prohibits racial, ethnic, religious, or gender-related slurs that "tend to provoke violent resentment." One official indicated that the proposed policy was aimed more at adult visitors than at students. The proposed policy is reported to be similar to policies in other school systems across the country, including some in Michigan, Ohio, Colorado, Maryland, and the state of Washington. Without listing specific words or acts, the proposed Fulton policy refers to "fighting words" that are abusive and provoke resentment. The policy statement echoes a state law that, without referring to bigotry, makes the use of "fighting words" a misdemeanor. Students who violated the policy would be subject to "appropriate disciplinary action" that could include suspension from school. Visitors who violated the policy would be asked to leave and would be subject to arrest if they did not comply.

The same news article reports the implementation of a policy in Tacoma, Washington, schools against derogatory remarks, acts, pictures, and gestures. The policy, in effect since 1986, was recently amended to include jokes referring to any ethnic, racial, or sexual group. The article goes on to report that a black teacher in Tacoma was recently given a verbal reprimand for violating the policy. Her offense was that of commenting to her class that black students have to work twice as hard to succeed because "it's a white world run by blue-eyed people." The white students in the class took offense, although the teacher reportedly did not mean to be derogatory.

An item in the January 11 issue of the same paper reported that the proposed policy was unanimously adopted by the Fulton County Board. It also stated that Emory University has had a similar policy in effect since 1988.

In the January 14 issue, a *Constitution* editorial writer refers approvingly to the Fulton County Board's action. He begins his column by saying, "A lot of folks are starting to get sensitive about sensitivity," and he refers to complaints about the "sensitivity police" on the prowl these days, "making sure that only politically correct thought is given voice." He notes the argument that this is the new censorship, which stifles debate and leaves no room for disagreement about the accepted party line. He cites several examples of what he regards as examples of "over sensitivity" reactions, and says, "I think sensitivity to the feelings of others is a good thing, and I believe there are circumstances when it should not only be encouraged but mandated." He concludes by saying, "The (Fulton County) policy doesn't require that people not be bigots. It does require that while on school property they at least be civil about it. In the school setting, that level of sensitivity is, I think, quite appropriate."

Many public figures who were not "appropriately sensitive" have found themselves the objects of wrath when they have carelessly, and possibly unwittingly, used recently proscribed words. Their reaction to the pressure to use politically correct language is reflected in President Bush's 1991 commencement address at the University of Michigan. A May 4 *New York Times* news release reported that the President attacked what he called the notion of "political correctness," saying it had led to "inquisition," "censorship," and "bullying" on some college campuses. The news report identified the speech as part of a growing political backlash against the idea that free speech should be subordinated to the civil rights of women and members of minority groups. "Ironically," the President said, "on the 200th anniversary of the Bill of Rights, we find free speech under assault throughout the United States, including on some college campuses."

Garry Trudeau in his "Doonesbury" comic strip for May 19, 1991, satirized the "new appropriateness" in language on college campuses. He portrays a commencement speaker delivering an address with the following complete text:

> Graduating seniors, parents and friends—Let me begin by reassuring you that my remarks today will stand up to the most stringent requirements of the new appropriateness. The intra-college sensitivity advisory committee has vetted the text of even trace amounts of subconscious racism, sexism, and classism. Moreover, a faculty panel of deconstructionists have reconfigured the rhetorical components within a post-structuralist framework, so as to expunge any offensive elements of Western rationalism and linear logic. Finally, all references flowing from a white male, Eurocentric perspective have been eliminated, as have any other ruminations

deemed denigrating to the political consensus of the moment. Thank
you and good luck.

The efforts of advocates of politically correct language demonstrate
that people with liberal leanings may have as much interest in restricting
language use under certain circumstances as do those of a more conservative persuasion. Part of the difference between them lies in what they
think needs to be restricted. Their efforts probably also lend support to
the conclusion that some sort of restriction on language in any society is
inevitable. What must be guarded against is any sort of restriction that
will interfere with the freedom of expression and the free flow of ideas
that are essential to the health, and indeed the continuing existence, of a
democratic society. We must somehow maintain a balance between
necessary restrictions and freedom.

Works Cited

Hayakawa, S. I. 1949. *Language in Thought and Action*. New York: Harcourt, Brace.
Mencken, H. L. 1963. *The American Language*. 4th ed. New York: Alfred A. Knopf.
Partridge, Eric. 1961. *A Dictionary of Slang and Unconventional English*. New York:
     Macmillan.
Rawson, Hugh. 1989. *Wicked Words*. New York: Crown.
Robertson, Stuart, and Frederic G. Cassidy. 1954. *The Development of Modern
     English*. 2nd ed. New York: Prentice-Hall.

11 Intellectual Freedom and the Theological Dimensions of Whole Language

Ellen H. Brinkley
Western Michigan University

Even as enthusiasm for whole language spreads, whole language advocates are finding their beliefs and practices challenged on a variety of fronts. In such cases it is tempting to dismiss the attacks of extremists but wise to take the charges against whole language seriously and to find out what motivates such charges.

Some of the protesters seem simply misinformed—for example, those who link whole language with a whole-word or "look-say" method of teaching reading. Whole language teachers argue that the whole-word approach to teaching reading, as well as the phonics-first approach, represents a view contradictory to whole language, for both begin by working with bits of language in isolation rather than within the context of authentic texts (see Weaver 1988).

Other protesters, however, hold more philosophical differences with the tenets of whole language, as conceptualized by a variety of theorists. Many challenges related to whole language are motivated by theologically based concerns expressed by parents and other advocates of the Religious Right. While most whole language activists take a strong social-constructivist theoretical stance, few explicitly address the broader philosophical and theological dimensions of whole language theory and practice. Whole language classroom teachers and leaders can benefit from clarifying their own philosophical stance as they seek to understand and address the concerns of the protesters. This chapter, then, will consider varying worldviews that provoke attacks on whole language, highlight particular classroom experiences most often subject to attack, and explore the edges of whole language classroom practices.

The responses by Carle Henson and Constance Weaver to an earlier draft provided theological and whole language insights, respectively, which created a rich dialogue—though they never met—that is partially revealed in this chapter.

I once characterized a part of the conflict of worldviews by using as a conference presentation title, "Shirley MacLaine and Charles Colson in the Whole Language Classroom." I chose these particular persons because of the differing worldviews they hold and because both have written as "evangelists" eager to persuade readers to embrace their particular perspective. MacLaine, a well-known actress, has written several books about her spiritual experiences (e.g., *Going Within*) and seems to reflect the perspective commonly *referred* to as "New Age." Colson, best known as an advisor to former President Richard Nixon who went to prison after Watergate, has written several books (e.g., *Kingdoms in Conflict*) about his own religious conversion experience and seems to reflect a new right, Christian fundamentalist perspective.[1]

A visit to a neighborhood Christian bookstore revealed not fewer than twenty different titles devoted to exposing the evils of the New Age philosophy. Several of these texts have chapters devoted to the effects of New Age that are perceived to exist in the classroom. While some of the accusations are not leveled at whole language teachers in particular, the pedagogical theories and classroom practices identified are often those associated with whole language. For example, within the pages of these texts appear long lists of terms and topics that vigilant readers are urged to watch for as they guard against the evils of New Age. A partial list (see Cumbey 1985; Martin 1989; Rowe 1985) includes:

holism, whole	human potential
multicultural education	self-esteem
intuition	possibility thinking
self-awareness	unity
guided visualization	global studies

Admittedly, it is difficult not to oversimplify, but there are identifiable tenets that allow for comparison between the fundamentalist and the New Age worldviews. For example, to the fundamentalist, reality and truth are perceived as absolute, though human nature is thought to limit what can be known about reality and truth. To the New-Ager, reality and truth are seldom perceived as absolute, but instead are thought of as relative, created and constructed by individuals who perceive them from individual perspectives. To the fundamentalist, the human condition is perceived as basically sinful, though God can forgive and remove sin. To the New-Ager, the human condition is seen as oneness with that which is divine, though persons can become alienated from the unity of the "God-self." To the fundamentalist, the remedy for the sinful human condition is said to be repentance and faith in God, who can transform the sinner and empower the faithful. To the New-Ager, unlimited potential is perceived as already available to those who seek within themselves the divinity that exists there.

Clearly whole language teachers and theorists personally possess a wide range of philosophical and theological perspectives that may or may not resemble either fundamentalism or New Age. Many whole language advocates may consciously identify with neither of the worldviews just described. However, as whole language teachers are expected, as professionals, to make more decisions themselves about curricular materials and classroom experiences and as they share more of themselves as co-learners with their students, they will benefit from consciously considering and naming their own perspective and beliefs.

Holism and Multiculturalism

The term "whole language" itself creates a problem for some. Those who embrace "whole" language know that the term originates with the emphasis on whole texts rather than on isolated parts as a way to develop reading and writing. Fundamentalists, however, have been warned to reject anything labeled "holistic" or "whole." Parents who might hear a description of their son or daughter's whole language classroom one day might be warned the next day, in a book called *Unmasking the New Age*, that

> The root idea of the New Age is oneness, unity and wholeness—the one for all. The controlling metaphor for the "old paradigm" was the machine. The earth, the state and humanity were seen as assemblages of individual parts (atoms as it were) isolated and insulated from each other. New Age politics seeks to replace this atomism with a holism that sees the planet as an interrelated system—an organism rather than a machine. (Groothuis 1986, 114–15)

Given such texts, whole language advocates may find it difficult to enlist the support of parents who believe that "individual parts" are somehow better kept separated.

Another fear associated with "holism" is the belief that it suggests a single world government and religion. While whole language teachers accept and value cultural diversity and encourage an understanding of a variety of cultures, fundamentalists have been warned to reject and to fear multiculturalism and religious pluralism. Indeed, the Christian is said to "grieve for the Hindu, the Buddhist, the atheist, the Satan worshipper and men and women of all religions and all creeds who have not yet accepted Jesus Christ as their personal Lord and savior" (Marrs

1987, 127). Any notion of multiculturalism, then, might be viewed with suspicion, for "globalism taught in the classroom is dangerous because it is based on a monist worldview that espouses not only the unity of all mankind but a unity of all religious beliefs too" (Martin 1989, 58–59).

Interestingly, with Eastern European countries breaking up into smaller sectarian states and with racial conflict re-emerging in the United States, fundamentalists show signs of reversing their earlier thinking about unity and diversity. In fact, a 1992 NACE/CEE (National Association of Christian Educators/Citizens for Excellence in Education) newsletter warned that

> Multiculturalism emphasizes diversity among races rather than our commonalities ("created equally") and thus breeds prejudice. . . . Parents have begged our schools to stop multiculturalism before it breeds racial violence—only to be called "elitist bigots." (Simonds 1992, 1)

Unity now seems to be considered more desirable to such groups, while diversity and multiculturalism continue to be rejected. What fundamentalists advocate instead of multiculturalism is "Americanism" (Simonds 1992), however that might be defined.

In response to such views, whole language advocates surely will not abandon their holistic emphasis or multicultural materials and activities. Classroom teachers who teach multicultural student populations and who acknowledge a shrinking world of interdependent ethnic groups and nations cannot in good conscience focus solely on a dominant culture, even one labeled "Americanism." Whole language teachers can reject the kind of paranoia that reflects fear of any perspective other than one's own. Beyond that, whole language teachers can affirm the rich variety of unique persons, places, and experiences. They can affirm within a Christian perspective that "Creation is not a homogeneous soup of undifferentiated unity but a created plurality" (Groothuis 1986, 20). They can explain carefully the tenets of teaching whole language so that it is clear that teaching about other cultures is not advocating cultural, political, or religious revolution.

Empowered Language Learners

Whole language teachers do, however, believe in empowering students and make no apologies for nudging students to rely on themselves. Having read Graves, Harste, Freire, and others, they have learned new respect for their students and for students' potential and have designed student-centered classrooms in which students help make decisions about curriculum and learning experiences. They want students who are self-confident of their abilities to handle well a variety of literacy tasks.

Such self-reliance makes fundamentalists uncomfortable, however, for they are reminded daily of their own shortcomings and the limits of human potential when they cite verses such as "All have sinned and come short of the glory of God" (Romans 3: 23). They question where "student-centered" stops and where indulgent "self-centeredness" begins. They may have let Mr. Rogers's affirmation slide by unnoticed—"I like you just the way you are"—even though it suggests a positive view of human nature. They have rejected, however, the views of Shirley MacLaine and the New-Agers, who claim considerably more for human potential as they use as mantras such expressions as "I am God in light."

Such words are blasphemy to fundamentalists, who find human nature basically sinful and who preach the need for being "transformed" by God's grace, since the human condition does not allow for "saving" oneself. Fundamentalist parents, then, sometimes resist a school focus on self-esteem or on student empowerment and shudder to hear warnings by fundamentalist authors that "The New Age Movement . . . is teaching our children that they are gods, and that the only authority they need follow is the 'inner light' of their Higher self" (Hunt 1983, 33).

In response to this challenge, whole language teachers will need to think through carefully their own view of human nature and to acknowledge that there are limits to self-sufficiency and to human powers. Most of us, for example, do not believe that we can will ourselves to float bodily into the next room, though some New-Agers argue otherwise. Whole language theorists can agree or disagree about the human capacity for good and evil, but classroom teachers surely must respect the best self that each student brings into the classroom and must build on that. There is no other choice. Their purpose is not to make students feel unworthy or in need of repentance but to encourage students, as would most parents, to fashion the best "self" they can.

Whole language teachers might even remind fundamentalist parents that their own faith ultimately presents a positive view of human potential, as expressed in the verse so many recite, "I can do all things through Christ who strengthens me" (Phillipians 4:13). The question is, of course, whether one is thought to be capable of empowering oneself or whether power comes only from submission to God. Unquestionably, however, one of the most appealing elements of whole language is that it nudges both teachers and students to become empowered, to cast off the old limits, and to explore uncharted language learning possibilities. Whether the power is thought to be produced by God or by self, for the sake of students from varying worldviews,

> One generation of teachers has somehow got to bring through one
> generation of students who will have thoughts we have not had
> before. It is clear the nation's and the planet's problems cannot be
> solved by just thinking along the lines we do now according to our
> heritage. (Moffett 1989, 86)

This is not to reject any currently held religious views or to disregard what we already know about addressing needs but rather to recognize that the magnitude of today's problems call for profound insights and solutions intended not to repeat the mistakes of the past. Whole language teachers can respect the perspective of God-fearing fundamentalists who emphasize human inadequacy, but they must create classrooms not constrained by these limits. As they establish classroom learning communities, they encourage a pooling of personal resources but respect individual students' rights to achieve all that they humanly can.

Writing and Reading as Meaning-Making Processes

Critics of whole language have focused relatively little attention thus far on writing, and few particular links have been made between writing and New Age. Protesters are, however, resisting the expressive writing encouraged by whole language teachers, who urge students to write about topics that matter to them. Widely distributed materials encourage parents to challenge classroom activities such as logs, autobiographical writing, and personal journals (Jones 1990, 192).

Although such items are generally regarded by the protesters as invasions of student and family privacy, fundamentalists may also believe that students' reflective writing is a waste of time or perhaps thought to be too focused on self. At any rate, James Moffett predicts that "the next swing of censorship will concern student writing" (1988, 229) as students experience the satisfaction to be gained from writing about their experiences, their attitudes, and their learning. Parents who seek to control what their children read might similarly try to restrict what their children write and think. The problem for such parents, as Moffett sees it, is that "students who really author outgrow just being somebody's children" (229). In fact, some home-schooling materials seem to lend support to Moffett's assertion, since they often prescribe heavy doses of penmanship drills rather than encourage composing meaning. Home-schooling advocate Blumenfeld, for example, insists that "cursive writing is one of the indispensable tools of literacy, and it should be taught to every child thoroughly and systematically from grade one onward" (cited by Jasper 1987, 51).

As whole language teachers plan classroom writing assignments and experiences, they will surely want to reconsider asking students to "write about a time your parents embarrassed you" (Jenkinson 1990, 40). Further, they will want to think through carefully journal writing guidelines (e.g., suggesting that pages of "private" entries be folded over) and to discuss with students what is and what might not be appropriate for a school log or journal. They will want to continue, however, to encourage students to give voice to their thoughts and to use writing to discover and to construct meaning for themselves.

Critics of whole language have focused primarily on reading, especially as it has been redefined through research as a meaning-constructing process occurring as readers "transact" with texts. This definition of reading, however, poses a potential dilemma for fundamentalists. If, as whole language theorists believe, meaning is constructed by an active reader, then meaning is a relative thing and is not entirely contained in the text, for every reader constructs at least a slightly different meaning. This logic is important to understanding the fundamentalist's perspective because of the significance placed on comprehending biblical texts. For those who believe in a literal reading of the Bible, to suggest that meaning does not exist in the text reduces the impact of the Bible as the "Word of God." To suggest that readers can construct their own meaning of the Word of God allows for a variety of interpretations that fundamentalists reject (see Hudson 1992).

Such discussions ultimately lead to the question of what is absolute and what is relative, what is real and what is not, what is right and what is wrong. Fundamentalists flatly reject MacLaine's (1989) assertion that "reality is basically that which each of us perceives it to be" (45) and that "the objective reality shifts according to our subjective perception of it" (213). Colson (1987), in fact, links the issue to school content and, as if in response to MacLaine, regrets that while "once the object of learning had been the discovery of truth, now each student must be allowed to decide truth for himself" (213).

The issue of what is absolute and what is relative has further implications for whole language and for the teaching of reading and writing. When a beginning reader "miscues," for example, should the deviation from the original text be considered absolutely inaccurate? Interestingly, fundamentalists reject the notion of accepting "pony" for "horse." Rather than recognizing that the young reader who makes such a substitution surely is comprehending what is being read, they insist that because such substitutions look and sound different, they reflect sloppy reading and an "undisciplined mind" (Lowe n.d.). To those who read texts literally, precise word identification and definition are paramount, even for beginning readers. Likewise, to fundamentalists the functional or invented spellings of beginning writers are seen as inaccuracies to be corrected, though whole language teachers regard such spellings as an indication of developing skill in using what young writers know to compose messages of importance to them. On a less conscious level, fundamentalist parents may find the notion of error so distasteful as to link it with the concept of wrongdoing or sin. If so, then to say—as whole language teachers do—that error is welcome when it is a sign of risk taking and growth, might be thought to further blur in students' minds the line between the absolute and the relative, between right and wrong.

Parents who press for correctness in word identification and in spelling are likely to prefer a phonics-first approach to their children's literacy learning. Moffett (1988) believes that those who advocate a phonics-first approach and those who emphasize grammar study for older students have more serious motives:

> those who see themselves as God's spokespeople prefer phonics, precisely, I think, because it shuts out content and focuses the child on particles of language too small to have any meaning. In other words, what phonics amounts to for those who are sure they have a corner on God's mind but are very unsure of being able to hold their children's minds is *another way to censor books* (unconsciously, of course) *by nipping literacy in the bud*. (226)

Moffett's indictment is surely an overstatement for many fundamentalist parents, most of whom genuinely want their children able to "rightly divine the word of truth" (II Timothy 2:15). Whole language teachers must be prepared, however, to respond to these issues as well. They can point out to parents, for example, the part *error* plays in a variety of learning situations, such as learning to ride a bicycle. There are always a number of failed attempts or "errors" that occur naturally on the way to success. They may have greater difficulty in persuading parents that an early overemphasis on phonics often impedes rather than expedites the reading process, but whole language teachers must give parents the benefit of the doubt that they want the best reading instruction available for their children. They must recognize how reasonable the letters-to-phonics-to-words approach appears to parents who may recall similar methods from their own school days. Whole language teachers, then, will make great efforts to explain via parent newsletters and classroom visits the reasons for whole language.

What Whole Language Teachers Can Do

Whole language teachers must realize the scrutiny with which they are being observed. As they contemplate such scrutiny, they might respond by worrying themselves into longing for the old days when someone else made curricular decisions for them. Or they might decide to self-censor their own teaching practices before others get the chance, avoiding any classroom experience or material that might prompt any possible objection. Nothing would please the protesters more. Fortunately, there are several positive alternatives.

Whole language teachers can build on the professional strength that so many have developed already—the strength developed from learning why and how whole language works and the strength developed from learning how to articulate whole language to parents, administrators, and the community. They can also support each other, networking with other whole language teachers and leaders through TAWL (Teachers Applying Whole Language). They can call the CELT (Center for the Expansion of Language and Thinking) Hotline for materials and specific advice if their meaning-centered and student-centered classroom practices are challenged. They can provide special support to evolving whole language teachers as they cast off old ways and reconceptualize literacy learning and how it can be implemented in a whole language classroom.

Whole language teachers and leaders must be politically astute as well. They must act responsibly and not dismiss as absurd the charges against them or their program. When they are tempted to react in "that's ridiculous" amazement, they must instead take each charge seriously and respect both the perspective and the potential power of their challengers. Whole language teachers can tell their own success stories in the pages of professional publications and at professional conferences, and they can write their own letters to editors and to politicians. At each step they can decide where best to focus their time and energy—recognizing that those at the most extreme edges philosophically will not change their minds but that support is more likely to be forthcoming from those who are undecided or perhaps mildly hostile to a whole language perspective.

Whole language theorists and teachers might go further yet and seek to avoid self-censoring out of curricula all mention of religion. Some student textbooks have already been so censored, as in cases where Pilgrims are defined as "people who make long trips" and Christmas is defined as "a warm time for special foods" (cited by Shanker 1990). Whole language teachers must be careful, of course, to distinguish between *teaching about* religion and *promoting* religion, but they need not deny the existence of a spiritual dimension to personal and societal life. Adrian Peetoom (1989), in fact, encourages whole language teachers to "seek to have children from Bible homes share their insights in the same way as they seek to have . . . Hindi stories and Polish folktales become part of the classroom *curriculum*" (322). As Peetoom points out, such actions are "messy" ones fraught with the possibility of criticism, but if a whole language view of language learners is indeed holistic, then "as we value the narratives of our own lives, so we must value the narratives of others" (322).

Although whole language leaders must be ready to confront their attackers when intellectual freedom is threatened, they must, it seems to me, use extreme care in describing and defining whole language. I worry when I hear Donald Graves call whole language a "worldview" and when Jerome Harste claims further that "a whole language worldview empowers a new set of learners and creates a new social order" (cited by Goodman et al. 1991, 377). Surely such statements represent the edges of what whole language can claim. Perhaps the designation of whole language as a worldview goes too far, even though whole language seems to reflect a particular worldview. Though not as apt to spark fervent zeal, perhaps the designation of whole language as a "dynamic philosophy of education" ("WLU," 1989) more closely reflects its relevance to teaching and to learning and ultimately renders whole language more defensible.

Without doubt, the discussion of these issues raises at least as many questions as it answers. But the threats to whole language—and to the kind of education it promises—are real, and politics and religion are at the heart of the threats. Extremists from a variety of perspectives threaten to impose their own agendas. One New Age writer has said,

> The classroom must and will become an arena of conflict between the old and the new—[on the one side] the rotting corpse of Christianity, together with all its adjacent evils and misery, and [on the other side] the new faith . . . resplendent in its promise. (Dunphy 1983, 26)

Meanwhile, Jerry Falwell has said, "I hope I live to see the day, when as in the early days in our country, we won't have any public schools. The churches will have taken them over again and Christians will be running them. What a happy day that will be" (cited in Beane 1990, 87). Because whole language is threatened by both extremes, whole language leaders must continue to explore the edges of whole language and be vigilant to protect what is too good to lose.

Although whole language advocates have seldom discussed the links between pedagogy and theology, whole language educators and parents of many faiths—including some fundamentalists—see their philosophical and theological perspectives as entirely consistent with whole language classroom praxis. Surely it is time to hear from people of faith who hold less extreme views as we respond to deep parental concerns and protect intellectual freedom.

Note

1. The following distinctions, provided by Provenzo (1990, 99), are instructive: Evangelicals can be described as American Protestants who "stress conservative doctrines and morality, together with a traditional or literal interpretation of the Bible" and who emphasize "an individual commitment to Jesus Christ" and "missionizing." Fundamentalists can be described as conservative Evangelicals who "hold to the inerrency of the Scriptures" and who "keep their churches strictly separate from Christians with different religious points of view, including moderate Evangelicals." Provenzo prefers the term "ultra-fundamentalists" to describe those who most often challenge teachers and schools—that is, those who combine a new right political agenda with a fundamentalist Christian belief system. I find the "ultra" label misleading, however, since it suggests an extreme or excessive fundamentalism rather than link the political and religious perspectives. Thus, I have opted to use "fundamentalists" to refer to new right Christian fundamentalists, though I recognize its limitations.

Works Cited

Beane, James A. 1990. *Affect in the Curriculum*. New York: Teachers College Press.

Center for the Expansion of Language and Thinking. 325 E. Southern, Tempe, Arizona.

Colson, Charles. 1987. *Kingdoms in Conflict*. New York: William Morrow; Grand Rapids, MI: Zondervan.

Cumbey, Constance E. 1985. *A Planned Deception*. East Detroit, MI: Pointe Publishers.

Dunphy, John. 1983. "A Religion for a New Age." *The Humanist* (January/February): 23–26.

Goodman, Kenneth S., Lois Bridges Bird, and Yetta M. Goodman. 1991. *The Whole Language Catalog*. Santa Rosa, CA: American School Publishers.

Graves, Donald H. 1990. Keynote Speech. Whole Day of Whole Language. Annual Convention of the National Council of Teachers of English. Atlanta, Georgia. 19 November.

Groothuis, Douglas R. 1986. *Unmasking the New Age*. Downers Grove, IL: InterVarsity Press.

Hudson, Kathi. 1992. *Reinventing America's Schools*. Vol. 2. Costa Mesa, CA: National Association of Christian Educators/Citizens for Excellence in Education. 3 vols.

Hunt, David. 1983. *Understanding the New Age Movement*. Eugene, OR: Harvest House.

Jasper, William F. 1987. "Basic Training: Learning to Read Needn't Be Like Boot Camp." *The New American* (16 March): 51.

Jenkinson, Edward B. 1990. *Student Privacy in the Classroom*. Bloomington, IN: Phi Delta Kappa Educational Foundation.

Jones, Janet L. 1990. *What's Left after the Right?* Portland, OR: Washington Education Association.

Lowe, Helen R. [n.d.]. "Solomon or Salami." *The Reading Reform Foundation Basic Information and Catalog.* Tacoma, WA: Rpt. from *The Atlantic Monthly,* November 1959.

MacLaine, Shirley. 1989. *Going Within.* New York: Bantam.

Marrs, Texe. 1987. *Dark Secrets of the New Age.* Westchester, IL: Crossway.

———. 1989. *Ravaged by the New Age.* Austin, TX: Living Truth.

Martin, Walter. 1989. *The New Age Cult.* Minneapolis: Bethany House.

Moffett, James. 1988. *Storm in the Mountains.* Carbondale: Southern Illinois University Press.

———. 1989. "Censorship and Spiritual Education." *English Education* 21: 70–87.

Peetoom, Adrian. 1989. "Whole Language and the Bible." *Language Arts* 66: 318–22.

Provenzo, Eugene F., Jr. 1990. *Religious Fundamentalism and American Education.* Albany: State University of New York Press.

Rowe, Ed. 1985. *New Age Globalism.* Herndon, VA: Growth.

Shanker, Albert. 1990. "Teaching about Religion." *New York Times* (23 September): E7.

Simonds, Robert. 1992. "President's Report." National Association of Christian Educators/Citizens for Excellence in Education. Costa Mesa, California. June.

Weaver, Constance. 1988. *Reading Process and Practice.* Portsmouth, NH: Heinemann.

"WLU: Nature & Purpose." 1989 (Fall). *Whole Language Umbrella.* [Newsletter]. Berkley, Michigan.

III Providing Support for Teachers

In this section, the authors explore the censorship issues that confront teachers today. The four chapters explore different ways that teachers can prepare and protect themselves from attacks on their intellectual freedom as professionals. In the first chapter, Jean Brown and Elaine Stephens advocate establishing an intellectual freedom group in each school to help teachers and librarians handle censorship problems. This chapter introduces a number of issues that will be explored in the remaining chapters of the section. In his chapter, John Kean explores the type of situations that may confront a high school teacher when there are challenges to teaching materials. Additionally, he provides general guidelines for developing policies in any school. Adrienne May and Paul Slayton approach the issue of censorship from the perspective of what can be done for in-service teachers when challenges occur. They provide a detailed series of steps to minimize the potential problems of censorship. In the concluding chapter of the section, Bob Small and Jerry Weiss use actual letters from censors as illustrative potential problems. They then offer suggestions of organizations and sources of support when teachers confront censorship problems. They also include suggestions for reading.

12 Being Proactive, Not Waiting for the Censor

Jean E. Brown
Saginaw Valley State University

Elaine C. Stephens
Saginaw Valley State University

A censorship challenge does not happen to just one teacher or one librarian. When a challenge occurs, it happens to everyone in that school, to everyone who uses that library, to everyone in that community. The reaction of those who have had firsthand experiences with censorship is often a combination of intense emotions such as anger, intimidation, shame, frustration, and fear. An inevitable by-product of these attacks is that teachers, librarians, and administrators are frequently changed by the experience. They may become overly cautious and create an atmosphere of nervous concern that inhibits their best professional judgment. When this happens, educators and librarians abdicate their professional responsibility and give the critical decision making about the free exchange of ideas to the censors. As teachers and librarians lose control over their jobs, there is an air of oppression that has an impact on everyone in the environment. This response is not surprising. Using the term "challenge" when we talk about censoring is significant because of its confrontational connotation. It implies that teachers or librarians have used inappropriate or even dangerous or irresponsible professional judgment and that they need to be chastised.

One mistake that often occurs at the time of a challenge is that teachers try to "tough it out" alone without seeking support from others. This tendency reflects the shock that they experience when their competence, professionalism, and in some cases, values and morals are called into question by those who challenge materials, teaching methods, or classroom processes. We have found that teachers actually feel that the challenge is an assault on them personally; they are ashamed and embarrassed and don't talk about what has happened to them. The teacher or teachers directly involved, the administrator in charge of "solving the problem," and possibly the school librarian are often the only ones who are even aware that there is a problem. This reluctance among teachers to present their position and to rally the forces behind them appears to the censors to imply that the teacher and the school have something to hide. It may even appear to be an admission of guilt. It also gives the censors the power of "dividing and conquering." Certainly, those who have raised the challenge are benefitted by silence on the school's side. Frequently what happens is that while the school remains quiet, the opponents are recruiting their supporters. The opponents are well organized, and if teachers have remained silent, then they have not prepared for the battle.

Frequently the initial reaction of teachers, librarians, or administrators who are encountering censorship is that of shock, shock that this type of action could be happening against their school. Too often this shock is the combined result of never having been threatened with censorship before and a basic belief that "Censorship can't happen here." The reality is that no community, no school, and no classroom is exempt from the possibility of challenge to instructional materials (both print and nonprint), teaching methods, and classroom practices. No one is immune from possible attack. Challenges to instructional materials can come from a wide range of sources, all along the spectrum from the reactionary right to the radical left. While some challenges are the result of organized campaigns of special-interest groups, often challenges are the result of the objections of the parents of one student. Parents certainly have the responsibility to make judgments about what their child is reading or viewing; however, the problem arises when they seek to impose their views on all students. Whatever the source of these challenges, schools need to be prepared to take action in support of intellectual freedom. While there are no absolute ways to prevent censorship challenges, those schools who have neither material selections policies nor procedures to address challenges are at a serious disadvantage when censors make their charges. As in every aspect of teaching, preparation is crucial. On the most fundamental level, preparation begins with a realistic perception about who "the Censors" are. As long as teachers conjure up images of censors as wild-eyed reactionaries who burn books, they are going to be ill-prepared to deal with the average censor, who might be any member of their community:

> Historically, we know that ignoring potential censors is a self-defeating action. Censors do not go away, nor are they often satisfied with small victories. Many censors are like addicts, propelled by an ever-expanding desire to have their will prevail. (Brown 1992, 3)

Educators need to achieve a sense of balance between being aware that attempts to control the curriculum or classroom practices can take place anywhere and falling into the trap of a siege mentality in which they conjure up imaginary foes. Preparation is not synonymous with paranoia. It is, however, the best defense against potential complaints.

Guarding against Self-Censorship

At the most fundamental level, schools need to be totally committed to the principle that teachers are the instructional experts who have the knowledge, expertise, responsibility, and professionalism to select print and nonprint instructional materials for their students. A commitment of this type would eliminate one of the most pervasive, yet subtle, types of censorship: self-censorship. In an address at the 1992 Annual Convention of the National Council of Teachers of English in Louisville, Kentucky, Madeleine L'Engle identified self-censorship as perhaps our biggest censorship problem. As the number of challenges increases, teachers become increasingly intimidated. If they lack confidence in their administration to support them, they are likely to make their material selection decisions based upon achieving a sense of safety. Self-censorship happens when teachers "select" instructional materials based upon fear of challenges rather than on the merit and instructional value of the materials. For instance, a teacher may avoid a particular author who has a reputation for being controversial. Or teachers may feel that they cannot use certain instructional materials due to a lack of administrative support without ever actually seeking support from the administration. In a supportive environment which values teachers' professionalism and decision making, decisions are based upon establishing solid rationales and meeting well-defined criteria. Teachers also have the security of clearly defined procedures giving them support and guidance in the event of a challenge. We must recognize that the possibility of censorship from external groups or individuals is a reality in any school. While this prospect may appear to be daunting, it should serve, in fact, as a call for action. (Kathie Krieger Cerra explores self-censorship in greater detail in chapter 4 of this volume.)

Where to Begin

Preparedness is essential. In 1991 at the Annual Convention of the National Council of Teachers of English in Seattle, Washington, the issue of how schools can be prepared was explored as part of the SLATE workshop. The following reflects the organization and compilation of suggested actions articulated by the participants. We believe that these suggestions provide an overview of preparedness and an introduction to a number of ideas that are explored in greater depth in the remaining chapters in this section. We have grouped the suggestions of the workshop participants into three major categories. The first grouping reflects concerns about the roles and responsibilities of teachers; the second category deals with establishing policies and procedures to protect against challenges; and the final category addresses school and community relations.

Building Bridges: Cooperation between Teachers and Librarians

One of the easiest ways to combat feelings of isolation is by building cooperation among the professionals in schools. The cooperation among teachers, librarians, and administrators is an initial step in being prepared before censorship problems arise. To that end, we suggest that schools establish an Intellectual Freedom Group (IFG; Brown and Stephens 1993). This group should be chaired by the school librarian or media coordinator, and the membership should be composed of teachers, students, administrators, and parents. Membership in the group should be determined by interest; for example, until recently, few censorship challenges were made in content areas other than English, but now censorship is a potential problem in social studies, science, health and physical education, among others. For this reason, the Intellectual Freedom Group may be of interest to a wider representation of the faculty than in previous years, when issues of censorship were frequently only addressed by English teachers and librarians. The group serves as the first line of defense because it provides several functions. Forming a group of this type will focus on the potential problem of censorship in an academic way, devoid of the emotionalism that accompanies a challenge.

An initial action that an IFG should undertake is either to examine any existing policy statements on intellectual freedom and on the selection of instructional materials and procedures having to do with requests for reconsideration of materials or to develop these policies and procedures if they are not in place. Existing policies and procedures should be reviewed regularly to make sure that they address current conditions and circumstances. The IFG provides a valuable service in coordinating these types of efforts; it can also serve to oversee developing rationales for instructional materials, collecting background materials about authors, materials, and books, and establishing files of reviews.

While an IFG should spend most of its time involved in preventative efforts, it can also serve as the review committee when there is a challenge. Because it is composed of teachers, librarians, administrators, parents, and students, the IFG has the breadth to address challenges based on the work that it has previously done with policies, procedures, and collecting materials. When a challenge is made, a representative or representatives of the person filing the challenge should be added to the IFG until that challenge is resolved.

Whether or not there is an IFG in the school, teachers, librarians, and administrators need to establish selection criteria and apply them consistently to all print as well as nonprint instructional materials. The first responsibility of the teacher is to provide students with varied and quality learning experiences. They must be able to do this without living under a constant cloud of fear. Teachers also need to be reflective about their curricular choices in order to guard against self-censorship. Schools should plan staff development experiences for teachers and administrators so that they become informed about how to handle challenges. In a 1990 survey conducted at the fall conference of the Michigan Council of Teachers of English, 91 percent of the respondents indicated that they were personally aware of challenges which they or their colleagues had experienced. Additionally, over one-third of the respondents indicated that they did not know if their school had a policy to address challenges to curricular materials, while only 17 percent indicated that their schools had made any attempt to educate teachers about the policies and procedures. Certainly, these figures indicate that at the very least, schools should institute staff development experiences to inform and prepare their teachers in case a challenge arises. This need demonstrates another area in which an Intellectual Freedom Group could be effectively used.

In a related matter, teachers sometimes make the mistake of not taking censors seriously enough. Regardless of how absurd a challenge may seem to an informed person, those making the complaints are usually earnest and dedicated to their point of view.

> One danger in the charges that would-be censors make is that frequently they seem so absurd and uninformed that teachers too often fail to take the charges seriously unless they are specifically affected. Until teachers either experience censorship directly or witness it firsthand, it is an unpleasant abstraction at best. Unfortunately, we have learned that no place is immune, nor is any book, video, or teaching practice. Teachers can be challenged for teaching a book that they have used for years or for introducing a new teaching method. We cannot anticipate what will incur the wrath of the censors, nor can we be too well-prepared to meet any challenge. (Brown 1992, 3)

All schools should seriously consider the following actions:

- Develop specific rationales for all instructional materials;
- Make sure that all materials selected are consistent with the educational objectives of the class;
- Be sensitive to the potential concerns of the community;
- Educate and seek support from colleagues, administrators, media, and members of the community;
- Have an IFG actively involved before there is a challenge;
- Communicate to students the importance of and the need for the open exchange of information and ideas; and
- Provide staff development for all teachers on censorship and conflict resolution.

Having a visible Intellectual Freedom Group in a school before there is a problem will provide teachers who face a challenge with an open, obvious support system. An IFG is a positive way to combat a sense of fear and isolation that both teachers and librarians experience when there is a challenge.

Establishing Policies and Procedures

There are systematic procedures that schools can adopt to safeguard against censorship challenges. Schools need to have policies and procedures in place that address both the selection of print and nonprint materials and also the action to be taken when challenges or complaints occur. Additionally, schools should develop or collect rationales for all print and nonprint materials that have been adopted for classroom use. The policies, procedures, and rationales should be on file in the school and available to everyone. Schools should have a designated review committee that reflects both the school composition with teachers, administrators, and students, and the community as a whole, including providing a spot for a designee of the person or group who has initiated the challenge. The single most important point is that policies and procedures need to be in place before a challenge is ever made.

The following list states policies and procedures that all schools should have:

- Clear, public adoption policy for curriculum and books;
- Systemwide policies and procedures to address challenges. The application of policies must be consistent in all cases and proce-

dures followed rigorously. Allow involvement from a wide social spectrum; don't attempt to isolate any group, including the radical right;

- Appropriate timelines to facilitate the timely resolution of issues and challenges. Involve the complainants in the process;
- Permanent intellectual freedom committees at both the building and system levels;
- Provisions for reevaluating materials;
- Qualifications for the professionals who then make the decisions about selection of books and materials, including library materials;
- Clear and articulated roles and responsibilities for the school board who makes the final decisions;
- Open-door policy that includes encouraging parents and other concerned adults to visit classrooms regularly; and
- Open-door policy that includes provisions for dissenters to visit classrooms to see how the materials are being taught, providing that they are there only as observers without the right to interfere with the class or students.

School and Community Relations

The relationship between the schools and the communities in which they exist is a crucial one. While the central mission of the schools is to educate students, too often we fail to seize the opportunity to educate the community about the positive things that are happening in the schools. Additionally, administrators should provide opportunities for community involvement in the schools. Inviting visitors to the school, having review materials available to the public, and allowing open membership on committees are examples of ways in which schools can demonstrate that they welcome involvement from the community. Inherent in this type of openness is the message that the school has nothing to hide.

School and community relations can be strengthened through:

- An aggressive and positive public relations program;
- Parent advisory committees that work with faculty and meet on a regular basis, not only when there has been a challenge;
- Special programs that involve students and community members in a variety of ways; and
- Active media promotion and support.

Looking Ahead

The next two chapters, "The Secondary English Teacher and Censorship," by John M. Kean, and "Keeping Abreast in the Trenches: In-Service Censorship Education," by Adrienne C. May and Paul Slayton, examine many of these issues in greater detail. Chapter 15 in this book, "What Do I Do Now? Where to Turn When You Face a Censor," by Bob Small and Jerry Weiss, provides specific information about organizations and publications that will help anyone confronted by a challenge. Margaret Sacco's chapter, "Using Media to Combat Censorship," also examines the role of the library media specialist. Additionally, the National Council of Teachers of English publishes several pamphlets that should be available in every school. They include: "The Students' Right To Know," "The Students' Right To Read, " "Common Ground," and "Censorship: Don't Let It Become An Issue in Your Schools." "Common Ground," a joint publication of the National Council of Teachers of English and the International Reading Association, is a source of many helpful suggestions for schools facing censorship.

The process of being aware of potential problems and having strategies to address them is the best way to ensure that intellectual freedom is protected in all schools.

Works Cited

Brown, Jean E. 1991. "What You Don't Know Can Hurt You: Censorship in Michigan." *The Michigan English Teacher* 41.4 (March/April): 4–5.

———. 1992. "Michigan Teachers Explore Experiences with Censorship." *SLATE Newsletter* 17(1): 3–4.

———. 1993. "It Can Happen Anywhere." *The Michigan English Teacher* 43(3): 5

———, and Elaine C. Stephens. 1993. "Being Prepared *Before* the Censor Comes." Paper presented at the Michigan Association of Media Educators. Kalamazoo, Michigan. October.

13 The Secondary English Teacher and Censorship

John M. Kean
University of Wisconsin–Madison

Attempts to censor both instructional materials and teaching practice have increased rapidly during the last decade. Although secondary English teachers may never face a challenge to their teaching material, teaching procedures, or classroom curriculum, they should prepare themselves for such a challenge. English teachers try to teach students how to think—creatively, logically, and critically. They teach language, literature, and communication skills—reading, writing, speaking, listening, and using media. They should help their students understand, respect, and appreciate the diversity and pluralistic nature of human motives, conflicts, and values. They help students learn to make judgments and to act on them. They do this through literature that they choose to teach, the lens that they help students create for viewing the world, the writing that they have them do for publication, and the questions that they ask about literature. It is theoretically possible to do all of the above and not to offend anybody, but this is highly unlikely.

English teachers need to be informed not only about their subject, but about current affairs and current conflicts concerning the function of education in American society. Issues related to race, class, gender, and religious affiliation are directly related to curriculum decisions that are made in English classrooms. They are also related to the political context in which those decisions are made. What literature shall be taught? What alternatives shall be available when parents object to their sons' and daughters' required reading? Should students be required to keep journals? If so, what kind? Should students write autobiographies? Should students give personal responses to literature? What should be the approach to language that might be sexist, racist, disparaging toward the physically challenged, vulgar, sexual, or in a vernacular other than edited American standard English? What should be the approach to fantasy or realistic fiction that includes violence, sexual imagery, witchcraft, unflattering views of particular religions, authority figures, parents, or presents homosexuality at all or in a positive portrayal? How shall student expression, written or oral, be controlled? Should it be controlled at all? Edward Jenkinson (1990), who has been studying censorship for almost twenty years, notes "that nearly every aspect of public education has incurred the wrath of some individual or group" (15). Jenkinson presents a long list of materials and practices that have been challenged across the curriculum—health, science, social studies, and English, but I am still shocked by the number of times the challenges are within the humanities and particularly the English curriculum. Given this state of affairs it behooves English teachers not only to know their craft, their materials, and their objectives but to know also what they must do in the event that their decisions of what and how to teach are challenged by people outside the profession, by administrators, and even by their colleagues (see chapters 6, 14, and 15, this volume).

Most challenges do come from outside, from parents or other individuals who are sincerely concerned about what the schools are teaching their own children and those of the rest of the community. Sometimes the challenges come from parents who have had the occasion to examine materials that their children bring home. At other times they come from parents who have been alerted by an organized group about practices or materials which they believe are a danger to children or to an established way of viewing the world and how it has or should operate. At other times the challenges will come from other professionals within the school system who typically have the same motivations as those outside the system—the protection of children or an established worldview. Consequently, there is no one, simple procedure that teachers can take to defend their own decisions or those of their colleagues with whom they have cooperatively developed curriculum. There are a number of steps that are appropriate and can mitigate the effects of these attacks on academic freedom for English teachers.

English teachers should know their school district's policy on the selection of instructional materials and the policy for the reconsideration of those materials. That policy should include objectives, a list of those persons responsible for selection, criteria for selection, procedures for selection, a statement on controversial materials and procedures for reconsideration and the handling of complaints.[1] Typically such policies state that materials are selected by the school district to *implement, enrich,* and *support* its *educational programs,* to *provide for a wide range of abilities,* and to respect the *diversity of many differing points of view.* It is important to attend to all of the key words in the above sentence when one selects materials. The relevance of the material to the curriculum is supposed to be reasonably clear to an educated person. Unfortunately, this is not always the case, particularly when someone not party to the original selection does not take into account the many variables that the teacher might be using. These include but are not limited to such variables as the number of students, pupil characteristics, theories of learning, theories about curriculum, prescribed curriculum, local school community, state guidelines, classroom management strategies, current social and political events, and evaluation procedures.[2]

Because there are so many variables involved in selection, it becomes important to have written records that document the reasons why the material has been selected. Although this is particularly important when newly published (or available) curriculum is introduced, it is becoming increasingly important to review long-used standard materials as well. Recent challenges to secondary English materials have involved not only contemporary fiction such as *The Color Purple,* but work which has been included in the curriculum for many years, such as *Manchild in the Promised Land* and *To Kill a Mockingbird.*

Most policies spell out who is responsible for selecting the material to be used. Typically at the secondary level, the responsibility is delegated to a department faculty or a textbook evaluation committee under authority from the school administration and ultimately the board of education. In most school districts, teachers are also permitted to select materials individually for occasional use in the classroom. If the material is to be used on a regular basis, however, it must be reviewed and approved by the committees established for that purpose. A major benefit of the committee process is the review by other professional staff and sometimes community members who can support the teacher when a work is challenged. A major drawback is, of course, the potential for stifling innovation and responding to the "teachable moment" in the classroom. Although most districts are able to strike a balance between the need for control and spontaneity, some districts, because of more frequent challenges and the increasing confusion over the availability of material that is perceived as more controversial, are limiting the teacher's freedom to select materials without committee review.

Such policies are restrictive but tolerable when applied to ordinary curriculum material such as textbooks or literature anthologies. They are regressive and stifling when applied to material where timeliness is a major factor—magazines, newspapers, collections of contemporary poetry, story stories, or contemporary young adult fiction which are included in the curriculum not only for their literary or artistic qualities but because of their interest to students and their relevance to issues which we want them to think about. As the school curriculum and our teaching strategies have become more responsive to the pluralistic nature of

American society and to the cultural diversity of its students, the shock to the sensibilities of those who are culturally hegemonic has produced more frequent challenges regarding the appropriateness of these materials and practices.

Most policies, although they may seem clear at the general level, do not always seem so at the implementation level when the theme of the short story, the language used by the poet, or the recommendations of the editorialist move beyond the alleged bounds of propriety in a particular community. To cover this problem, most policies also include statements about controversial materials, typically referenced to the American Library Association's Library Bill of Rights.[3] This policy speaks directly to what should be in the library but not what should be in the classroom collection or what should be read, discussed, debated, and written about in the classroom.

Thus the teacher needs to know what the district's goals are and what the expectations are for the English curriculum. The teacher's goals to teach literature as a mirror of human experience, reflecting human motives, conflicts, and values, come into direct conflict with some people's understanding of the school's primary role as that of inculcating community values. With the first set of goals, the teacher chooses literature to stimulate thinking, to provide the marketplace atmosphere where ideas are problematic, where questions are asked to discover, to evaluate, to make judgments. With the second, a teacher eschews the marketplace and chooses literature to lead to a particular point of view and ultimately to teach that literature has no connection to life.

Most policies related to controversial materials in the classroom and most goal statements should be reviewed and reworked to reflect an ever-increasing complex cultural, social, political, religious, and technological society where indeed there are competing and perhaps mutually exclusive views of what is moral, what is correct, what is defensible, what is normal, what is necessary, and what is unnecessary.[4]

All of the above leads to the question of what criteria will be used to evaluate curriculum material and teaching practice. Most policies have lists of criteria that require not only the professional knowledge of local staff but the collected wisdom of professional peers who review material for instructional uses. These criteria include, among many others, educational significance, contributions the subject matter makes to the curriculum, favorable reviews in standard selection sources, favorable review based on preview and examination of materials by professional personnel, reputation and significance of author, producer, and publisher, the contribution material makes to breadth of representative viewpoints on controversial issues, high artistic quality, and/or literary style.[5] This clearly means (as noted before) that English teachers should always think about the educational significance of material that they are going to use on a regular basis. This obviously does not need to apply to every piece of poetry which the teacher decides to read to students, but it clearly does apply when the topic, theme, or language of the poetry is likely to be controversial, and could be deemed to be so by a prudent person who understands the values of the community in which he or she is teaching. Note, I am not recommending that teachers don't use a particular poem, but that they apply these criteria before using it. The issues become somewhat more complex, incidentally, when the poetry is produced by students.

The student's right to free speech has always been in limbo, and school district policies across the country have reflected this confusion. The most recent Supreme Court decision (*Hazelwood School District v. Kuhlmeier* 1988) has given school districts, in the absence of any state law to the contrary, discretion to censor student expression if there is "reasonable" educational justification. At the risk of oversimplification, any student expression produced as part of schoolwork or assisted by the teacher is subject to restriction. Clearly, English teachers should become familiar with state law and school district policy in this area.

Something may be educationally significant but still be somewhat problematic as it relates to the curriculum. As teachers move away from using anthologies and emphasize writing, speaking, listening, and reading across the curriculum, we find literature teachers using historical accounts, math teachers and science teachers using fiction and biography, and all teachers attempting to tie their curriculum to the needs of culturally diverse students. Such integration needs to be encouraged, but it places even more responsibilities on the teachers to justify curricular choices. The material may encourage role-playing, simulations, or other activities that some censors believe have the potential to alienate students from their parents, their religion, and civic responsibility by putting them into psychologically dangerous situations. Teachers clearly need to be aware of these concerns and use such techniques in ways that do not threaten students or subject them to ridicule.

Teachers should be familiar with a wide range of review media and use them when selecting material. These include for the English teacher such standard sources as the *English Journal, The ALAN Review, Your Reading: A Booklist for Junior High and Middle School Students, Books for You: A Booklist for Senior High Students* (all NCTE publications) and *SIGNAL* (an IRA publication). There are of course many occasional publications from professional organizations and methods textbooks which regularly review material that is used in the English program. Most of these should be available in the professional collections in the local school district, state education agency, or college or university that has a teacher-education program.

Equally important is the professional appraisal of the local materials selection committee. Material should always be carefully examined by professionals who will be expected to use them. The professional review media are used to support local evaluation, not to replace it. Librarians, because of the nature of their work, often must rely on the review media, but teachers should use the review media to find out about material and to support their own independent examination. This forces the teacher to think about how the material fits the local curriculum and ensures the artistic integrity of the material. Independent examination has become increasingly important to do when examining literature, particularly anthologies of literature, because publishers' editors have bowdlerized authors' work to avoid controversy.

Attending to the balance of views on controversial issues may seem more appropriate to the health curriculum (sex education), science curriculum (evolution), social studies curriculum (political and economic education), but since the English teacher is concerned with moral and values education through the study of literature, and may also be responsible for drama, forensics, student publications, and in some schools, media education as well, examining the curriculum materials to achieve balance on controversial issues becomes critical.

The last criterion to be discussed is artistic or literary quality. Although quality issues may not seem to be related to censorship issues, they often are, for what the professional literary critic may judge as meritorious is seen as trash by people whose social agendas outweigh all other criteria. For this reason, *Huckleberry Finn* has been censored because it offends African American sensibilities, while *To Kill a Mockingbird* has been censored because it is favorable to African Americans.

The application of these criteria typically operates so that the more of them that apply, the more likely that one can successfully defend the chosen material, but even overwhelming professional support based on the most careful interpretation of criteria will not succeed in all cases. Some material will be censored in some fashion. In the final analysis, the local school district board of education does have the authority to decide what material will be used in the classroom. Even this authority, however, can be challenged in the courts. But such challenges in the legal system have ended in mixed results. In the absence of any compelling reason not to, the courts have refused to usurp the authority of the school board.

Every school district should have a reconsideration policy to go along with its selection policy. Typically such policies spell out who is to be involved in reconsideration decisions, how decisions should be made, and how complaints should be handled. Most policies specify that some mix of administrators, teachers, librarians, and community representatives should be involved in making decisions. They are typically empowered to take testimony, and to make recommendations concerning how the material should be handled. The range of recommendations include

1. keeping the material as is in the curriculum;
2. keeping it in the curriculum but requiring parental permission for students to use the material;
3. keeping it in the curriculum but making it optional by student choice;
4. taking the material itself out of the curriculum but permitting discussion of it;
5. moving the material to another grade level deemed more appropriate;
6. removing it from the curriculum but making it available in the library;
7. making it available in the library but to a restricted age or grade level; and
8. removing it from the library as well as the curriculum.

There are, of course, permutations on these options.

The procedures discussed above may seem difficult to undertake, but they are designed to ensure that material selection committees are properly judicious in selecting material and that the process for choosing and challenging materials is orderly and fair. Although such policies will not prevent challenges, they will ensure that professional judgment issues and intellectual freedom issues are dealt with. When districts either do not follow the policies that they have or do not have policies, they run a greater risk that teachers, students, and the materials will not be treated fairly and honestly.

Now that we have discussed formal school district policies and procedures, we can turn to personal alternatives that teachers should be aware of if they are to successfully negotiate challenges to their material, their curriculum, or their teaching procedures.

Every censorship attempt has a different scenario but there are some general guidelines that might help:

1. When a parent, other community member, or school district personnel asks for a justification for some assignment or material, assume that the parent simply wants to know what is going on. Always treat the question fairly; remember that the person asking the question is unlikely to have had the same workshop, methods course, or have read the curriculum that provided the stimulus for you to be doing what you are. Do not assume a common frame of reference. Be very thorough in your oral or written response.

2. When you receive a formal letter from a representative of a group or read about a public concern with your curriculum, consult with your principal, who should in turn work within the appropriate school guidelines as discussed above. You should also inform your educational association or union representative.

3. When a member of the school board or an administrator complains orally or in writing about your program or the material that you use which appears to question your committee's or your own professional judgment, inform your educational association or union representative.

4. For items 2 and 3 in this list, you should consider contacting your local or state NCTE affiliate representative and the English consultant at your state department of education. This action benefits both you and the profession. They can provide help directly or refer you to other appropriate groups that might assist. Your contact also alerts them to potential problems for your colleagues in other districts or allows them to better understand a pattern that may be developing across the state. At the same time your union or association representative should have contacted a mid-level service unit of the association or union, or the state organization directly for assistance.

5. At the same time, your colleagues and you should begin to gather all of the information that you can related to the material or technique under question, anticipating that at the least you will need to present this material to an administrator and more likely to the reconsideration committee in support of your own statement. Such material should contain copies of the particular goals and objectives that the material or activity is related to, a description of the material or activity that may be contained in the school's written English curriculum, professional references which recommend and/or review the material or activity positively, and, if possible, testimonials from experts who know the English curriculum. If you locate negative reviews of the material, you should also include

them with your own counterstatements as to why the material is appropriate for use in your classes.

6. If you anticipate that some aspect of your program or material has the potential for controversy, discuss it with colleagues and administrators to ensure that they understand what you are doing or using and why you are using it. Although it is possible to invite trouble by such consultation, it forces you to think through your own curriculum carefully and is likely to lead to a more supportive environment in which to work.

7. Keep yourself informed about the current issues related to censorship by reading the American Library Association's *Newsletter on Intellectual Freedom*, attending to the work of the National Council of Teachers of English's Standing Committee against Censorship, the work of your state affiliate's committee against censorship, and the work of the many national and state coalitions and organizations that are working to promote the freedom of students to read and to learn and of teachers to teach.[6]

Notes

1. For model policies, consult Reichman 1988 and Ochoa 1990.

2. These variables are taken from a list of twenty-two educational design variables suggested by Beatrice Naff Cain (1990).

3. Although the ALA Bill of Rights may be found in many publications, one useful source which also contains statements from other organizations both for and against censorship is the National School Boards Association's *Censorship: Managing the Controversy* (1989).

4. For an overview of the English teacher's responsibilities, see "Essentials of English," a statement approved by the Executive Committee of the National Council of Teachers of English (October 1982) and published as a pamphlet by NCTE in 1982. See also Burress and Jenkinson (1982).

5. For a more complete listing of criteria see Reichman (1988).

6. These guidelines are adapted from ones I wrote for *Dealing with Selection and Censorship: A Brief Handbook for Wisconsin Schools* (Wisconsin Department of Public Instruction 1991).

Works Cited

Burress, Lee, and Edward Jenkinson, eds. 1982. *The Students' Right to Know.* Urbana: National Council of Teachers of English.

Cain, Beatrice Naff. 1990. "Toward a Creative Educational Design Model." Paper presented at the Annual Meeting of the National Conference for Research in English. Atlanta, Georgia. 18 November.

"Essentials of English." 1982. Urbana: National Council of Teachers of English.

Jenkinson, Edward B. 1990. "Child Abuse in the Hate Factory." In Ochoa, 15.

National School Boards Association. 1989. *Censorship: Managing the Controversy.* Washington, D.C.: NSBA.

Ochoa, Anna S., ed. 1990. *Academic Freedom to Teach and Learn: Every Teacher's Issue.* Washington, D.C.: National Education Association.

Reichman, Henry. 1988. *Censorship and Selection: Issues and Answers for Schools.* Arlington, VA: American Association of School Administrators and American Library Association.

Wisconsin Department of Public Instruction. 1991. *Dealing with Selection and Censorship: A Brief Handbook for Wisconsin Schools.* Madison, WI: WDPI.

14 Keeping Abreast in the Trenches: In-Service Censorship Education

Adrienne C. May
Mary Washington College

Paul Slayton
Mary Washington College

The ongoing battle over the right to know is not a nice and neat conflict between the censors and the anti-censors. Contenders do not wear uniforms or badges denoting their allegiances. Shining white armor does not distinguish the "good folk"; nor do the villains come equipped with black helmets. The battleground is totally unlike Gettysburg or the battle for Normandy beach on D-Day during World II. On those battlefields, banners and uniformed battalions clearly define where stood the opposing combatants. The censorship war is more akin to the guerrilla actions of the Vietnam conflict with its fluid, indeterminant battlelines and the lack of a clearly identifiable enemy. The would-be censor may be a friend or a parent seeking to prevent a child from knowing about a specific evil, for example, vulgar expressions, or a professional colleague who is a pacifist wishing to remove, from the library stacks or the classroom, any book which glorifies war. In at least one respect censors and anti-censors operate from identical motives: each wishes to protect young people, seeking to protect youth from perceived evils. Those supporting censorship would do so by denying youth the opportunity to know of the evils lurking; those opposing censorship would do so by protecting youth from the many vicissitudes of life by helping them learn of the myriad pitfalls awaiting in a less than perfect world.

Preservice "basic" training of teachers only prepares them for the generalities of the struggle over censorship. Preservice programs characteristically expose future teachers to (1) the confusing and slippery legal foundations of the student's right to learn; (2) the structures of educational policymaking (especially state and local guidelines); (3) the impact on curricular choice of textbook publishers and textbook adoption procedures; (4) the support role of professional organizations available to the teacher facing a censorship crisis; and (5) the teacher's role in curricular decision making (see chapters 12, 13, 15, and 16, this volume). Having explored these areas, the beginning teacher should come to that first classroom setting aware but undaunted by the cloud of censorship— aware that censorship attempts may come from any quarter; aware that no piece of material, classic or contemporary, can be so innocuous that someone, somewhere, cannot find objectionable qualities in it; and aware that the territory being contested in the censorship conflict is the curriculum and the curricular materials of the schools. This "basic" training should raise not the combative spirit of the teacher but the level of teacher preparedness, the ability to make and defend sound, professional curricular choices.

Although absolutely essential, "basic" training in censorship is not sufficient. Schools, academic departments, and individual teachers must be prepared to defend their curricular decisions at the local level where the generalities of "basic" censorship training will not fully serve the individual teacher, especially in the current climate of educational reform. In the absence of national or even explicit statewide curricula, curricula and curricular materials differ even between schools within a local school district. This will become increasingly true in an era of not only district-based but even school-based management in which teachers will play a more decisive role in curricular matters and will undoubtedly become even more accountable for their choices. Culturally and linguistically, the student population has never been more diverse. Academically, the field of English literature and composition studies has never been more theoretically fractured. Politically and socially, teachers and schools are being called upon to do more than ever before with, as usual, too few resources. Given this current educational climate, no school's curriculum is a static entity; thus, arming oneself and the school for the censorship fray is never in the past tense. As teachers must continually prepare themselves to make better choices in their planning for learning, so too must they be capable of defending their curricular choices wisely and professionally. The general preparedness teachers achieve through preservice "basic" censorship training must be augmented by a strong, locally specific in-service program.

Since the ultimate decision concerning any act of censorship rests at the local district level, with the superintendent and the school board, each school district should establish a dependable, written censorship policy. But since most censorship attempts focus on the particular curricular materials in a specific school and are precipitated by a disgruntled parent or community member, school districts should take a "grassroots," departmental approach to developing the district policy. Individual departments within each district school should develop anti-censorship strategies which can then be refined, revised, and renegotiated into a district-level policy. This grass-roots departmental approach ensures teacher support and the optimal use of local teaching professionals—those best acquainted with the attitudes and mores of the community, the abilities and interests of local students, the available curricular materials, and the local social sensibilities most likely to evoke censorial ire.

Any successful censorship in-service program must address three sets of departmental practices:

- practices which discourage potential censorship,
- practices during ongoing censorship attempts, and
- practices which strengthen the profession and discourage future attempts at censorship.

In-servicing should encourage teachers to consider each of these sets of practices in a positive, constructive manner. When teachers develop, first as departments and then as a school district, coherent strategies for combatting censorship attacks deleterious to the students' right to know, each individual teacher will possess both the professional knowledge and the personal self-confidence needed to counter wisely any threat to her own and her departmental and district curricula.

Practices Which Discourage Potential Censorship

Teachers, as departments and as members of school districts, must take the initiative concerning potential censorship by establishing a sensible, supportable strategy which is more offensive than defensive. They must win over the local community's trust and confidence before would-be censors can undermine public trust. English teachers must ask, and answer, for themselves several key questions.

Do we, as an English department, know what our curricular goals are? Do we know how these English goals relate to other district departments? Each department, in cooperation with other district departments, should reach consensus concerning realistic curricular goals, with particular attention to the educational (intellectual, social, emotional) needs of the students they serve. This would involve not only refining the general state-curricular goals but also integrating their curricular choices, as much as possible, into an interdisciplinary curricular vision. Curricular choices within English studies that reflect a knowledgeable familiarity with the curricular goals of other academic departments are more defensible than those that are narrowly focused within the realm of English studies alone. Such an interdisciplinary focus only strengthens the arguments of curricular choice and potentially gains allies from other disciplines for English teachers on occasions of censorial attacks.

Does this department have a policy encouraging the use of supplemental texts and the students' right to read and to write? English teachers should encourage one another to be responsibly innovative in the classroom. Frequent, professionally well-reasoned forays beyond the "standard" textbook should be promoted, but adequate departmental support for such instructional diversity should be a matter of policy. Students have an educational right to read broadly and to write honestly and expressively in their own voices. Departments should have a *written policy* endorsing (1) the teachers' right and responsibility to find and use the most appropriate texts and curricular materials for their courses; (2) the students' right to read independently from selections in the school's and local public library's collections; and (3) the students' right to write in their own vocabularies from their own experiences and understandings of themselves and the world. Furthermore, the department should create a *supplemental text rationale* form, such as the one endorsed by NCTE, which each teacher would be required to complete and the department would be required to endorse before the teacher taught the supplemental text. The endorsement of these rationales could also be solicited from the building principal, thus involving the administration in the curricular choices of the department. Departmental and administrative endorsement of these rationales ensures that the teacher is properly interpreting the stated English curricular goals and further guarantees that no teacher is left without her colleagues' and the administration's support in times of censorship attacks.

Does the department have an established, written grievance procedure for potential censors? Prior to the onslaught of a censorship attack, English teachers should enact, in cooperation with their administration, a clearly stated procedure to be followed on occasions of censorship attempts, including a "request for reconsideration" form to be completed by the would-be censor. The responsibilities of all parties—the censor, the English department, the school librarian, the administrator—should be clearly delineated (see chapters 11, 17, and 18).

Does the department know about recent censorship attempts? English teachers need to keep abreast of current trends (and outcomes) of attempts at censorship, through the NCTE, ALAN, and ALA publications. Another excellent source is the People for the American Way's report entitled *Attacks on the Freedom to Learn*, published biennially. State and local professional organizations can also provide current regional information on activities of would-be censors. An English department undergoing a censorship attack should maintain a thorough, written record of the incident to be shared with the broader professional community (see chapter 18 on professional support).

Does the department participate actively in textbook adoption and curricular development committees? The opportunity to adopt new texts or to revise curriculum always allows for a refreshing professional rejuvenation; but it also must be a time when departments are sensitive to, but not overly fearful of, innovations/revisions that may trigger new censorship attacks. Local teachers are in a prime position to recognize potentially volatile themes, topics, or language in new materials or curricular matters. They should use this expertise to make knowledgeable decisions arrived at departmentally, not individually. The community should be informed about new adoptions and the reasons specific materials were chosen.

Has the department done everything possible to familiarize the community with its program and to elicit community support? Perhaps the key to a strong defense during a censor's attack is the general support previously established between the school and the parents and community at large. Parents should certainly be invited to participate in the ongoing education of their children. Through regularly scheduled PTA/PTO meetings as well as additional school-sponsored events, such as back-to-school nights, student-author nights, and dramatic productions, the English department should create a constant, positive bond with the parents. Furthermore, through the local school meetings and the local media, parents should be kept thoroughly informed of the curricular process—new textbook adoptions, curricular revisions, etc. A parent or community member who feels she or he *knows* what is occurring at his/her school is less likely to take an adversarial stance out of ignorance or misconception and more likely to consider local educators as allies, not potential enemies.

Practices during Ongoing Censorship Attempts

The English department that can answer each of the following questions authoritatively has little to fear from attempts at censorship. Already armed with written policies outlining both their own curricular choices and their procedures for handling would-be censors, much of the anxiety such a frontal attack might create should be alleviated. The questions that the department must ask itself, at this point, are still not simple ones, but at least they are manageable.

How can the department react professionally and logically and not just emotionally? If the previous policies and procedures have been enacted, then the individual teacher or the department should be in a strong position of defense against would-be censors. The first thing to remember is to remain calm and dispassionate and to let the policies and procedures take their preplanned course. No teacher should find herself unsupported so long as she has followed the departmental policies and procedures. The battle becomes, by definition, a collective one—one in which all department members, as well the administration, have a vested interest. No decision should be made by an individual teacher in these instances; the full force of the professional community should be involved.

Has the material in question been endorsed by departmental policy? In the event of a censorship attack, a quick review should be made to ensure that the material in question has been properly endorsed by the department. Did the teacher complete the supplemental text rationale, and when was it endorsed by the department and administration? Perhaps at this point, the department, in conjunction with the administrator, might wish to communicate with the would-be censor, confirming the school's support for and previous experiences using the questioned material.

Has the would-be censor completed the "request for reconsideration" form? The would-be censor should be accountable for the same responsible actions that the department has already undertaken. That is, she or he should be encouraged to think logically about his/her concern and be willing to articulate that concern in writing, not just through oral communications. Let the would-be censor know that the department is concerned about the issue but needs to deliberate thoughtfully as it reconsiders the use the materials in question. The would-be censor's completion of the "request for reconsideration" form is a crucial step. Recollections of hotly contested, oral conversations rarely serve as accurate records. Adversarial diatribes never lead to amicable resolutions. The English department must begin its communication with would-be censors by *listening.* Any departmental response should only be offered *after* written documentation of the complainant's concern to the school's reconsideration committee.

Since the anti-censorship strategy should already be a part of departmental policy, all the department must do is comply with its own stated process. Administrators should certainly be part of this reconsideration process, as should librarians, parents, and, in the case of senior high schools, students themselves.

Has the department wisely used all of its allies to combat the censorship attempt? Having properly prepared itself for a censorship attack, the department should take the offensive in publicizing any attempt to censor the school's curricular choices. Rather than shunning publicity, which will almost certainly be sought by the would-be censor, the department should vigorously defend its curriculum and its curricular materials. Local, state, and national anti-censorship groups should be contacted to enlist their support, their aide, and their expertise (see chapter 15 on professional support). It would be a rare material, indeed, which has not previously come under the guns of censorship. The experience of others can only be a positive force in executing the department's defense.

The public, too, needs to be informed of the censorship attempt. The local curriculum belongs to the community. A vociferous minority must not be allowed to dictate curricular change. The best means of informing the community is through local media—newspapers, radio, and television/cable stations. Thriving as they do themselves on the First Amendment, the media are the natural allies of the "right to know." Share with media representatives information about the department's curriculum and the curricular materials under attack. The would-be censor will seek to introduce prejudicial information; this must be combated with the positive rationale for the questioned material's use in the school. Critical reviews of the questioned material and information about its educational value should be shared with media representatives. When the press is informed in this positive manner, they will promulgate the full and accurate story, not just the negative opinions of the would-be censors.

Practices Which Strengthen the Profession and Discourage Future Attempts at Censorship

A single, protracted incident of proposed censorship can dishearten even the most enthusiastic department, so it is vitally important that the department turn a potentially negative experience into a positive one. This can be accomplished by putting the documentation associated with the censorship attempt to good use in several different ways. First, the documentation should be used intradepartmentally. The department should review the entire censorship incident in light of any other previous attempt at censoring the school curricula or curricular materials. How is this incident like others in the past? Are there recurring themes/ issues the department needs either to reexamine its position on or to develop a more explicit policy statement about? Does this incident indicate any particular precautions in future practices; however, it must be quickly noted that departments should *not* allow such introspection to lead to oppressive self-censorship. The issue here is not what to avoid in the future but rather how to select and use materials that best serve the learning needs of the students in the school.

Second, the documentation from this particular incident can be used interdepartmentally: both to notify and to share experiences and outcomes with other English departments within and beyond the school district's boundaries, and further, to examine the possibility of similar concerns surfacing in other local academic departments. Finally, as part of all teachers ongoing concern for the profession in general, the incident should be reported to the appropriate state and local professional organizations (NCTE, ALAN, ALA, among others; see chapter 15) and submitted for publication in professional journals.

Expect no truce in the censorship war. As schools seek to individualize programs and to build flexible curricula to meet the needs of "all the children of all the people," more varied materials will be required.

Teachers will be called upon more and more to make individual material selections from a wider and wider variety of sources. As curricula shed the constraints of traditional molds and materials, more questions are bound to be asked by the community. Consequently, it is imperative that each teacher in each school become a better communicator, capable of developing rationales for curriculum and defending those choices. One must also be aware that reactions to curricular materials may come from any point on the political, social, religious, and economic spectrum.

Every school must have in place the machinery to provide for the reconsideration of challenged materials. Well-considered, locally conceived, professionally made curricular decisions are the first line of defense against censorship attacks (see chapters 12, 13, and 14). Censorship "basic" training for preservice teachers must provide beginning teachers with an understanding of the problems of censorship. Continuing in-service education is essential to keep teachers aware of the changing fronts, tactics, and objectives of those who would restrict the right of students to learn and to know.

15 What Do I Do Now? Where to Turn When You Face a Censor

Robert C. Small, Jr.
Radford University

M. Jerry Weiss
Jersey City State College

Censorship: An Everyday Problem

As the many cases cited in the preceding chapters indicate, teachers, librarians, authors, publishers, booksellers, and others who make books available to students face a regular barrage of censorious comments and criticisms. In some cases, the censors have merely felt a need to express a complaint and, having done so, are satisfied. In many cases, however, would-be censors make concrete and continuing efforts to remove books and magazines from school and public libraries, from classroom libraries and materials collections, from school curricula, and from required and suggested reading lists. And all too often those efforts are successful.

These would-be censors have many places they can turn for assistance. Phyllis Schlafley, the Gablers, and Beverly LeHaye represent only three of the better known of these promoters of censorship. Censors know where to turn for help, but where can a teacher, librarian, school board member, or school administrator turn when he or she is trapped in the midst of a censorship attack?

The purpose of this article is to describe some of the resources available to us when we are on the defensive. What follows is information about national organizations that you can turn to for help. We've matched each one with a letter shared with us by friends who have been on the receiving end of censorship. We thought you'd be interested in them.

A Letter to a Teacher

Dear English Teachers:

I have noticed a disturbing trend in the assignments that you give to my child and others in your school. These recently published books seem to have teenagers as their target, and they show children and adults in conflict, usually with most of the blame for everything that goes wrong falling on the adults. They also show teenagers drinking, using drugs, and having sex. Others show teenagers dying of AIDS and other diseases or committing suicide. These books promote wicked behavior and are depressing.

Now, I know that many of these books have received awards, but I also know that those awards have been given by people like you, not concerned parents like me. So, I don't think those awards justify the books in the school. I wouldn't let my child read them, and I certainly don't want them assigned to him.

Therefore, please remove these novels from your reading lists and from the school library and go back to studying the tried and true classics, books like those I studied when I was in high school.

Although I don't want to threaten you, I plan to contact the members of the School Board to alert them to what is being read in school and to call on them to help me rid the school of these novels.

Sincerely yours,

A Concerned Parent

Where You Might Turn:
The National Council of Teachers of English
1111 W. Kenyon Road
Urbana, Illinois 61801-1096
800-369-6283

NCTE works through its staff, a standing committee, at least two of its constituent groups, and a publications program to combat censorship and to help its members resist censorship efforts. At its headquarters in Urbana, the Director of Affiliate and Membership Services is assigned the task of coordinating requests for information and for assistance from affiliates and individual members. Currently, that director is Millie Davis. Through publications such as *Dealing with Censorship, The Students' Right To Know, The Students' Right To Read,* and *Celebrating Censored Books,* NCTE also provides information about and assistance to those of us who find ourselves fighting a battle against censorship. NCTE has taken several official positions on different aspects of censorship, including a "Statement on Censorship and Professional Guidelines."

Recently NCTE and IRA (see below) formed a Joint Task Force on Intellectual Freedom. Under then-chair James E. Davis, the task force prepared a statement on intellectual freedom principles that was approved by the executive committees of both groups. The task force then prepared a brochure containing that statement plus helpful information for combating censorship efforts. That brochure, *Common Ground*, is available at no charge from NCTE or IRA.

In addition to publications and staff support for the anti-censorship effort, NCTE has a committee, the Standing Committee Against Censorship, devoted to work in this area. Its charge is

> To solicit and receive reports of censorship incidents from NCTE members, constituent groups, and sources outside the Council; to maintain an annotated list of agencies and organizations concerned with censorship and to maintain informal liaisons with groups that are opposed to censorship; to coordinate its activities with other Council groups that deal with censorship; to serve as a resource on current patterns of censorship; to advise the Executive Committee, affiliate leaders, and others on strategies for dealing with censorship; to propose convention sessions and publications on the subject of censorship.

At this writing, its chairs are Geneva Van Horne of the University of Montana and Joyce Armstrong Carroll from Abilene, Texas.

The Conference on English Education of NCTE has established an ongoing Commission on Intellectual Freedom, designed to sponsor publications and programs and to recommend to the CEE Executive Committee actions that it should take to protect the integrity of the English language arts curriculum, instruction, and teacher education. At this writing, the chair of this commission is Jean Brown of the Saginaw Valley State University.

Also, the Assembly on Literature for Adolescents of NCTE (ALAN) has appointed an Intellectual Freedom Officer who serves as the liaison between the ALAN Board of Directors and the NCTE Standing Committee Against Censorship. The Intellectual Freedom Officer advises the ALAN Board about the state of censorship efforts in this and other countries related to the availability of literature to teenage readers and recommends actions that ALAN should take or support to defend the First Amendment rights of teachers and students. The current Intellectual Freedom Officer is Margaret Sacco of Miami University, Oxford, Ohio.

ALAN has also established a policy that, at its annual workshop in November, at least one session should deal with intellectual freedom issues, and that its journal, *The ALAN Review*, should regularly publish articles dealing with censorship. The co-editors of the journal are Patricia Kelly of Virginia Tech and Robert Small of Radford University.

NCTE is a member of the National Coalition Against Censorship.

For Local Support: Many NCTE affiliates have intellectual freedom committees or officers. Faced by a censorship challenge, we'd suggest that you contact, first, your affiliate president in order to see what help the affiliate can offer. If you can't contact your affiliate president, call NCTE.

A Letter to an Author

Dear Author:

We are pleased to inform you that we would like to include an excerpt from your novel in our new basal reading series. The chapters that we would like to include are those that deal with Washington crossing the Delaware. We feel that it is an excellently written depiction of an important event in our nation's proud history.

In order to make the excerpt suitable for our textbook series, it will be necessary to request that you agree to a few changes in the chapters. Specifically, it will be necessary to eliminate all references to Christmas Eve because of the religious nature of that date. Also, there are several references to the British soldiers drinking and smoking and celebrating Christmas Eve. Those references will have to be eliminated because of their negative moral implications.

We look forward to including your work in our text, which we are confident will place your fine writing in the hands of an even larger circle of readers than did the original publication.

Sincerely yours,

A Publisher

Where You Might Turn:
The International Reading Association
800 Barksdale Road
P.O. Box 8139
Newark, Delaware 19714-8139
302-731-1600

IRA has established the President's Advisory Committee on Intellectual Freedom. As its title suggests, it reports directly to the IRA president. Its charges are to

1. Monitor attacks on intellectual freedom and incidents of school or community censorship . . . and

2. Prepare position statements for Board action . . . and resolution(s) for the Delegates Assembly . . . for review by the Resolutions Committee on issues involving intellectual freedom.

In addition, each IRA affiliate is expected to appoint an intellectual freedom officer. The IRA IFC is in regular contact with these individuals, and at the annual conference of IRA in May, the IRA IFC sponsors a breakfast meeting for the members of the committee and these affiliate officers. At this meeting, an author, a scholar, or a teacher who has been involved in a censorship controversy discusses intellectual freedom issues. Following the breakfast meeting, the IRA IFC sponsors an open session dealing with censorship problems.

As a part of its charge, this committee advises the president of IRA on actions that the organization should take in defense of intellectual freedom. The current chair of the committee is John Ridley of Houghton-Mifflin.

IRA has a number of statements on different aspects of censorship, including "On Textbook and Reading Program Censorship," "On Opposing Abridgment or Adaptation as a Form of Censorship," and "Selection of Instructional Materials." The organization also has an official statement of censorship in general and guidelines for individuals face with censorship efforts.

IRA is a member of the National Coalition Against Censorship.

For Local Support: Most IRA affiliates have intellectual freedom committees or officers. Faced by a censorship challenge, we'd suggest that you contact, first, your affiliate president in order to see what help the affiliate can offer. If you can't contact your affiliate president, then call IRA headquarters or the chair of the IRA IFC.

A Letter to a School Librarian

Dear Librarian:

It has come to my attention that school system funds have been used to purchase contemporary books written for adolescents for the school library. In these times of restricted budgets for education, we cannot afford to spend school monies on such ephemeral works. All available funds must be spent to purchase the best of our literary heritage in order to reverse the cultural literacy crisis in this country.

Therefore, please let me instruct you (a) to purchase no more of these titles and (b) weed those already purchased from your materials collections and the school library and plan a book sale to raise money to replace them with copies of the traditional classics.

Sincerely,

Chair, School Board

Where You Might Turn:
The American Library Association
50 East Huron Street
Chicago, Illinois 60611
800-545-2433

Perhaps the most active of the professional organizations in the United States in defense of intellectual freedom, ALA has established the Office for Intellectual Freedom (OIF) at its Chicago Headquarters. The director of this office is Judith Krug. The ALA OIF gathers information concerning censorship attacks on libraries, including school libraries; defends librarians who are under attack; and is responsible for a number of publications, including the *Intellectual Freedom Newsletter*. The OIF also provides support for much of ALA's other work in combating censorship.

The principal focus of ALA's member activities in support of intellectual freedom is the ALA Intellectual Freedom Committee. The committee reviews individual cases and decides what actions ALA should take, regularly proposes updates of the ALA Library Bill of Rights, considers publications, and generally acts as ALA's watchdog on these issues. The current chair of the ALA IFC is Arthur Curley of the Boston Public Library.

ALA is divided into eleven divisions, most of which have their own intellectual freedom committees. The divisions most closely related to the work of English language arts teachers are the American Association of School Librarians, the Association for Library Service to Children, the Young Adult Library Service Association, and the Public Library Association. The intellectual freedom committees of these divisions advise the boards of directors of their divisions on censorship issues, prepare support materials for division members, and sponsor programs at the annual ALA conference in late June. The charge to the YALSA IFC, for example, reads as follows:

> To serve as a liaison between the division and the ALA Intellectual Freedom Committee and all other groups within the Association concerned with intellectual freedom; to advise the division on matters pertaining to the First Amendment of the U. S. Constitution and the ALA Library Bill of Rights and their implication to library service to young adults and to make recommendations to the ALA Intellectual Freedom Committee for changes in policy on issues involving library service to young adults; to prepare and gather materials which will advise the young adult librarian of available services and support for resisting local pressure and community action designed to impair the rights of the young adult user.

The current chair of the YALSA IFC is Patricia Mueller of the Arlington, Virginia, Central Library. This IFC has published a packet of materials to help librarians faced with censorship efforts, *You Are Not Alone*, and a collection of rationales entitled *Hit List*, and has sponsored programs at most recent ALA conferences.

In addition, ALA sponsors the Intellectual Freedom Roundtable. Its charge is

> To provide a forum for the discussion of activities, programs and problems in intellectual freedom of libraries and librarians; to serve as a channel of communications on intellectual freedom matters; to promote a greater opportunity for involvement among the members of the ALA in defense of intellectual freedom; to promote a greater freedom of responsibility in the implementation of ALA policies on intellectual freedom.

ALA also works closely with the Freedom To Read Foundation, which provides funds to resist censorship, especially in court cases, and sponsors several awards for service to intellectual freedom, most notably the Immroth Award.

ALA is a member of the National Coalition Against Censorship.

For Local Support: Many ALA affiliates have Intellectual Freedom Committees or Officers. Faced by a censorship challenge, we'd suggest that you contact, first, your ALA affiliate president in order to see what help the affiliate can offer. If you can't contact your affiliate president, then call the ALA OIF.

A Letter to a Teacher

Dear English Teacher:

It has been brought to our attention that you have been spending a great deal of time teaching literary works by writers whose personal lives are, at best, questionable. I am referring to such writers as Oscar Wilde, Walt Whitman, Edgar Allan Poe, O. Henry, Ernest Hemingway, William Faulkner, and Lillian Hellman, to mention only a few. Do you really believe that the values as represented by the lifestyles of these individuals should be presented to our students? They are drunkards, homosexuals, and communists. The best literature is surely that which has been created by moral individuals, not people like these.

Perhaps there is a place for the study of such authors in college English courses like those you took, but our children already are confronted daily with television programs and newspaper and magazine articles that reflect a rapid decline in American values and culture. We feel that we should not praise those whose personal lives are a disgrace. We call upon you, therefore, to eliminate works by the authors listed above and in the enclosed publication.

Sincerely,

A Minister

Where You Might Turn:
National Coalition Against Censorship
2 West 64 Street
New York, New York 10023
212-724-1500

NCTE, IRA, ALA, and many other national organizations are members of the National Coalition Against Censorship (NCAC), both an organization of organizations and one that individuals can join. This organization advises and gives direct assistance to schools and citizens in local communities when censorship controversies erupt. It also works through the network of participating organizations to stimulate and assist them in anti-censorship activities and informs and educates the wider public about censorship activities and how to oppose them. In addition, it publishes *Books on Trial*, a report on school book-banning court cases, through its National Clearinghouse on Book-Banning Litigation. The executive director of NCAC is Leanne Katz.

To support the work of NCAC, an individual can become a "friend" by sending a tax-deductible contribution of $25.00 or more to its headquarters. Friends receive NCAC's quarterly newsletter, *Censorship News,* and special reports. They are also invited to attend special seminars and luncheons on topics related to censorship.

———

A Letter to an Author

Dear Author:

I thought that you ought to know that we have used many of your books in our academic program. However, we have noticed that your publisher's address includes the number 666. These are Satanic numerals. After discussing this problem with a number of people in my community, I have been asked to suggest that you find another publisher or risk losing our patronage. We can't afford to support evil in our reading program.

We are praying for you.

Sincerely yours,

A Parent

Where You Might Turn:
PEN
PEN American Center
568 Broadway
New York, New York 10012
212-334-1660

The Freedom-to-Write Committee of PEN American Center works on behalf of writers caught in censorship cases and deals with issues of censorship in about thirty countries each year. Since 1980, the committee has become increasingly concerned with violations of the First Amendment and other forms of censorship in the United States: book bannings in school libraries, restrictions imposed on foreign travelers under the ideological provisions of the 1952 Immigration Act, misuse of libel laws, and government jamming of the Freedom of Information Act. The following statement appears in the Charter of International PEN:

> The PEN stands for the principle of unhampered transmission of thought within each nation and between all nations, and members pledge themselves to oppose any form of suppression of freedom of expression in the country or community to which they belong.

Liberty Denied: The Current Rise of Censorship in America, written by Donna A. Demac and published by PEN, is a valuable resource. It is available from PEN American Center at the address listed above at a cost of $6.95. PEN is a member of the National Coalition Against Censorship.

A Letter to an Author

Dear Author:

Although we previously signed a contract with you for you to speak to our students three weeks from now, we have, since signing that contract, read several of your books. Unfortunately, because we discovered that you use such words as "ass" in those novels, we are forced reluctantly to cancel our agreement. We do not feel that such language is appropriate for our students, and we are confident that the appearance that we are promoting such language through your appearance in our school would cause a commotion in our community.

Given your popularity, we feel confident that you will be able to make arrangements for another appearance, despite this short notice.

Sincerely yours,

A Superintendent of Schools

Where You Might Turn:
National School Boards Association
1680 Duke Street
Alexandria, VA 22314-3493
703-838-6722

A Letter to a School Superintendent

Dear Superintendent of Schools:

We are parents of students in our local high school. It has come to our attention that the English teachers there are asking our children to give their opinions about characters and incidents in the books they study and to relate those books to their own personal lives. Doing so is a violation of the rights of our children as well as an intrusion into the moral education of those students, which belongs in the home.

We feel that the teachers should use more objective tests to deal with the facts presented in the literature studied. Open-ended questions such as the ones being used promote situation ethics as well as holding up to ridicule the beliefs we have taught our children.

We look forward to hearing from you that the testing program has been corrected so that it evaluates the facts of literature, not the opinions of immature students.

Sincerely yours,

Citizens for Moral Evaluation

Where You Might Turn:
People for the American Way
2000 M Street, NW
Suite 400
Washington, D.C. 20036
202-467-2381

In a statement of its purposes, People for the American Way has stated that it "is the leading national organization in the fight against censorship in our children's schools. . . ." In that same statement, the organization concludes: "In our battles against the forces of intolerance, no contest is more important than our efforts to protect the freedom to learn."

People for the American Way publishes several important monographs on censorship, including *Attacks on the Freedom to Learn: People for the American Way 1989–1990 Report* ($7.95 for members; $8.95 for nonmembers), and *Protecting the Freedom to Learn: A Citizen's Guide* (member $4.95; nonmember $5.95). Membership in People for the American Way is twenty dollars.

In recent years, a number of books, pamphlets, and newsletters have been published that are useful to teachers, librarians, schools, and school systems caught in censorship controversies. We have included, toward the end of this essay, a short list of materials that have proven helpful in such situations.

People for the American Way is a member of the National Coalition Against Censorship.

———

Other Organizations That Will Help

American Association of School
    Administrators
1901 North Moore Street
Arlington, VA 22209
703-528-0700

American Association of
    University Professors
1012 Fourteenth Street, NW
Suite 500
Washington, D.C. 20005
202-737-5900

American Civil Liberties Union
    ACLU Washington Office
122 Maryland Avenue, NE
Washington, D.C. 20002
202-737-5900

Association for Supervision and
    Curriculum Development
1250 North Pitt Street
Alexandria, VA 22314-1403
703-549-9110

Association of American
    Publishers, Inc.
2005 Massachusetts Avenue, NW
Washington, D.C. 20036
202-232-3335

National Association of
    Elementary School Principals
1615 Duke Street
Alexandria, VA 22091
703-684-3345

National Association of
    Secondary School Principals
1904 Association Drive
Reston, VA 22091
703-860-0200

National Education Association
1201 16th Street
Washington, D.C. 20036
202-833-4000

Some Publications That Might Help

American Library Association. 1989. *Intellectual Freedom Manual.* 3rd ed. Chicago: American Library Association.

American Library Association Young Adult Services Division. 1989. *Hit List.* Chicago: American Library Association.

Children's Legal Foundation, Inc. 1990. *Victory Agenda: A Battle Plan for America.* Phoenix, AZ: Children's Legal Foundation, Inc.

Delfattore, Joan. 1992. *What Johnny Shouldn't Read*. New Haven: Yale University Press.

Demac, Donna A. 1988. *Liberty Denied: The Current Rise of Censorship in America*. New York: PEN American Center.

Hoffman, Frank. 1989. *Intellectual Freedom and Censorship: An Annotated Bibliography*. Metuchen, NJ: Scarecrow Press.

Karolides, Nicholas J., Lee Burress, and John M. Kean, eds. 1993. *Censored Books: Critical Viewpoints*. Metuchen, NJ: Scarecrow Press.

Kelly, Patricia P., and Robert C. Small, Jr., eds. 1986. "Censorship or Selection?" *Virginia English Bulletin* 36.1 (Spring).

Krug, Judith F., ed. *Newsletter on Intellectual Freedom*. Los Angeles: Intellectual Freedom Committee.

Marsh, David. 1991. *50 Ways to Fight Censorship and Important Facts to Know about the Censors*. New York: Thunder Mouth Press.

Moffett, James. 1988. *Storm in the Mountains: A Case of Censorship, Conflict, and Consciousness*. Carbondale: Southern Illinois University Press.

National Coalition Against Censorship. 1985. *Books on Trial: A Survey of Recent Cases*. New York: National Coalition Against Censorship.

———. *Censorship News*.

National School Boards Association. 1989. *Censorship: Managing the Controversy*. Alexandria, VA: National School Boards Association.

Reichman, Henry F. 1988. *Censorship and Selection: Issues and Answers for Schools*. Chicago: American Library Association; Alexandria, VA: American Association of School Administrators.

Underwood, Murray. 1989. *Censorship: Challenging Your Freedom*. St. Louis: Missouri Coalition Against Censorship.

So Where Can You Turn?

As you can see, when a case does hit you, you do have many places to turn. After the initial terror has subsided, pick up the telephone and call—first, your NCTE affiliate president. Nothing more may be necessary. If your affiliate is prepared as it should be, the network will kick into action.

If not, well, call NCTE headquarters. Then, call your ALA affiliate, or, if you aren't a member of ALA—as you should be—call your school librarian and get him or her on the case, calling the ALA affiliate censorship chair.

Next, try the IRA affiliate chair. Are you a member of IRA? Why not? But if not, call an elementary teacher friend and get a telephone number for the IRA affiliate president.

Although national organizations can and will help, they can be accused of being "outsiders." Consequently, we'd suggest that you start with your local and state affiliates of NCTE, ALA, IRA, and the other groups reviewed in this chapter. But if you feel you're not getting anywhere, call the national organizations—their numbers are listed above. Tell whomever answers about the problem you're having, what you've already done, and then ask for help.

IV Taking Action for Intellectual Freedom

In the first chapter of this section, Dee Storey presents a series of scenarios of potential censorship problems that novice teachers and even experienced ones may encounter. She makes a case for including preparation in coursework to prepare teachers. The next chapter of the section is by two high school teachers who share their censorship experiences. Linda Kapron and Rita Paye relate their experience with administrative censoring of the high school literary magazine that they directed. Their detailed account covers the experience from the grant they received to initiate the magazine to the lawsuit they filed. The third chapter is by Margaret T. Sacco, who advocates effective communications through the use of the media to address censorship issues. She also reaffirms the need for a positive collegial relationship between teachers and librarians/media specialists. In the final chapter of the section, C. Jane Hydrick recounts "a teachable moment" in her classroom. She involved her students in a simulation after reading about local residents calling for the banning of the book *Slugs*. She then involved her students in a spirited examination about banning books.

16 Caution, Novice Teachers: The Promotion of Reading, Writing, and Thinking Could Be Grounds for Censorship

Dee Storey
Saginaw Valley State University

Novice teachers have a tendency to enter their first teaching assignment using skills, insights, and talents they developed during professional methodology courses, field/practicum classes, and especially student teaching. Their attitudes and beliefs have been influenced by a number of instructors and experiences in hopes that they will be able to create educational episodes that will be thought provoking and meaningful for their own students. Frequently, novice teachers begin teaching by using activities and/or practices that were role played in their methodology classes. Because they were taught such practices by revered college professors, they believe that they can also be employed in the average public school.

With unexpected disappointment, novice teachers found that sometimes success was not to be had. In a number of instances, the novices had properly connected theory into practice, but in doing so had stumbled, quite innocently/naïvely into censorship: "You should have considered the wants and needs of our community. Ignorance of community concerns is no excuse if you are going to teach in this town."

> *Censor:* originally a Roman magistrate whose duty it was to take the census of all segments of the population: senators, knights, commoners, and slaves. Since Roman law required that many civil and religious offices be held by a senator or knight, part of the censor's job was to determine who met the qualifications for membership in those groups. Most qualifications were financial, but since religious offices were involved, a knight or senator also had to be of good moral character. (Hole 1984, 147)

It is the everyday dealing with the concerns of the curriculum, the needs of the students, and the makeup of the community that could "set up" the novice teacher to fall prey to the censor's ire. The following situations are real scenarios that happen all over the country much too frequently.

Scenario #1: Expurgation

> The dirtiest book of all is the expurgated book.
>   —Walt Whitman

In the past few years publishers of basal readers have included stories that originated in trade book/library editions. Editors and teachers knew that children would read a favored story over and over. Such redundancy in reading is one way to build comprehension. With that in mind, many "modern" stories from trade/library books are included in a reading series in an effort to interest children and because the stories are accessible in their school library.

Knowing that the redundancy factor was important, Teacher #1 made sure that multiple copies of *Molly's Pilgrim* (Cohen 1983) were available in the classroom after the children read the story in their basal. However, before the day was out, the children indicated that the story in the basal did not read the same as the one in the library book.

How will Teacher #1 explain to eight year olds that the differences in texts have to do with "expurgation: any excision of words, lines, or sections of a work deemed politically or morally unsuitable for some audiences" (Bradford 1986, 53). How will Teacher #1 clarify why the library edition contains information about how the Pilgrims learned about the concept of Thanksgiving from the Jews and that the basal reader doesn't contain religious ideas having to do with the worship of God?

Was it an oversight that the basal reader story and the trade/library book story were really not the same book after all? Was it planned to leave the teacher and the students ignorant that author Barbara Cohen knowingly allowed the "changes" to be made in order to have the story made "suitable" for a wider range of readers than a religious story? Would Teacher #1 be able to quote Cohen when she said, "I found out something. Censorship in this country is widespread, subtle, and surprising. It is not inflicted on us by the government. It doesn't need to be. We inflict it on ourselves" (Cohen 1983, 99).

While some may argue the pros and cons regarding the practice of expurgation, it could be noted that a "single library book is much less likely than a single textbook to violate the First Amendment. A text is required reading and is a student's main introduction to the area of study. A library book, on the other hand, is simply one of many books available; its biases may be balanced by other available books" (Moshman 1989, 126).

Thus, it may be considered that Thanksgiving, whether it is Sukkot celebrated as a religious holiday by Jews, or a more "American" one celebrated by the people in the United States, should not be intended to "force" religious belief on children who are the audience of a basal. The main purpose of the basal is to teach youngsters how to read, not to develop a religious bias.

Expurgation practices are also promoted in some paperback book club titles that are aimed at children and adolescents. Again, it is not *prominently* noted that the paperback book does not contain the same information, terms, or events that were presented in the hardcover edition. Thus, the teacher is left hanging, once again, having to defend two versions of one story. This practice continues "because it appears obvious that parents and parents alone are why book clubs are unlikely soon to discontinue expurgating . . . the books they sell to children" (Hartzell 1985, 44).

Scenario #2: Omission

> It is impossible for ideas to compete in the marketplace if no forum for their presentation is provided or available.
>
> —Thomas Mann

Teacher #2 knew that February was National Black History Month. Rather than only study the contributions of African Americans for one month, Teacher #2 planned on having the fourth graders read about such individuals throughout the school year. However, after consulting the school and public libraries, Teacher #2 noticed that such a plan was not feasible because there weren't enough books on the subject and the titles that were available were very dated and stereotypical.

How prepared will Teacher #2 be to explain to students that in one study of all children's books published in the United States between 1973–1975, only 14.4 percent had at least one black character (Sims 1983). Such a finding caused Rudine Sims to surmise that "the Supreme Court outlawed segregated schools in 1954, but a decade later the world of children's books had not even arrived at separate but equal" (150).

Does Teacher #2 know that such a shortage of books about African Americans is a controversial issue? Does Teacher #2 know how the late author John Steptoe, winner of the Caldecott Honor Medal for excellence in illustrations in children's books and winner of the Coretta Scott King Award for excellence in illustrations for books that convey the spirit of African Americans, believed an ulterior motive was being practiced because there was such a shortage of books about African American characters?

In an interview Steptoe was asked: "Do you see any relationship between censorship and racism?" He responded:

I'm afraid so. After doing this type of work for nearly twenty years, I've concluded that the industry is inherently hostile toward blacks ... when you realize how few blacks are in the picture book field, it's hard not to conclude that it isn't an accident. As I see it, this is a form of censorship. It might be indirect censorship, but it's just as effective as book banning. (West 1988, 94)

Scenario #3: Sexist/Nonsexist

20 ... but for Adam there was not found a helper like himself. 21 Then the Lord God cast a deep sleep upon Adam? and when he was fast asleep, he took one of his ribs, and filled up flesh for it. 22 And the Lord God built the rib which he took from Adam into a woman: and brought her to Adam. (Genesis 2: 20–22)

Teacher #3 believed that first graders should be aware of nontraditional roles for people in the work force. Teacher #3 also wanted the children to learn the nonsexist labels for different occupations. Teacher #3 held that *both* women and men in the 1990s quite commonly share professions; thus, children should learn why sexist/nonsexist language and terminology regarding traditional/nontraditional roles were very important issues.

While Teacher #3 felt a lot of positive feelings were being discussed in class, some parents objected to what was being taught. Some parents complained that their children did not have to be a captive audience to materials that went against their religious upbringing. The parents who protested noted that according to their religious beliefs, God indicated that women were to be helpmates to men and that women should be at home raising children. The parents objected to having their youngsters attend a school where secular humanism was a primary basis for the curriculum (Murray and Woods 1982).

The parents wanted to remove their children from the classroom during the time the unit was taught and to instruct their children about workers in the community in home-based lessons. Given the community feelings, did Teacher #3 know that the parents may have based their objections in accordance with the case of *Mozert v. Hawkins County Public Schools*, heard in Tennessee in 1986 (Hulsizer 1987)?

Although the original ruling was eventually overturned, Federal Judge Thomas B. Hull stated that parents had a right to remove their children from reading classes and teach them reading at home because stories in the basals went against certain religious beliefs of the parents, particularly by having stories taught from a Christian perspective. In reaction to the case, Rowell noted "how unfortunate if schools must attempt to teach only that which offends no one. Parental intervention cannot be allowed to destroy the school's function as a place where children learn how to handle conflicting options" (Rowell 1987, 14).

Scenario #4: Freedom of the Press

> To limit the press is to insult a nation; to prohibit reading of certain books is to declare the inhabitants to be either fools or slaves.
>
> —Claude Adrien Helvetius

Teacher #4 decided that a literary newspaper would be an excellent forum for seventh graders to study literary genres, propaganda techniques, and journalistic writing. Teacher #4 decided that "problem novels would be a good choice of reading material because they would provide the students with material that could be viewed from more than one point." Teacher #4 was operating from the premise that "we owe our students powerful reading experiences which include them in a total way. Great thinking emerges from great questions, and nothing is as memorable in a classroom as book-inspired discussion. . . . A book with a moral choice that has no clear-cut solution will keep a classroom alive for a long time" (Lepman-Logan 1989, 111).

As a group the students critically discussed the use of fact and opinion in the news. They weighed the pros and cons of sensationalistic journalism versus objective reporting. Many students read the same books so that the content could be covered a number of ways in the paper. They worked in pairs, going through the writing process from rough drafts to finished copy. After a lot of soul-searching and productive writing-process sessions, their work was done; the hard copy of the classroom paper was sent to the office to be duplicated.

When the classroom newspaper was printed, to their astonishment, the students found that any articles related to Marion Dane Bauer had been omitted. Bauer wrote in *Rain of Fire* about a fictional soldier's belief that the United States should not have dropped the atomic bomb on Japan. Gone from their classroom paper were also letters to the editor discussing the young soldier's critical evaluation of his own government's amoral decision.

Their thoughtful articles were replaced by recent school sports scores and the lunch menu for the upcoming month. The students felt that the principal had violated their First Amendment rights because the administrator had not discussed the removal of the articles before the final edition of the paper was "sent to press." Ultimately, the principal surmised that the articles based on *Rain of Fire* were not a "fair and balanced" portrayal of the American image.

Seemingly in keeping with *Hazelwood School District v. Kuhlmeier* in 1988, the principal declared that the paper was not an official paper of the school. It was a class assignment that was under administrative control because it was part of the language arts curriculum, and the duplication of said paper was paid for by the school. Unfortunately for Teacher #4 and the students, *Hazelwood* breaks dangerous new ground, however, in suggesting that public schools are constitutionally permitted to provide this important educational opportunity to students who hold and wish to express ideas the school agrees with and to withhold it from students who wish to express alternative views or to address controversial topics (Moshman 1989, 108).

Scenario #5: Content/Intent of Spelling Lists

What's in a word?

Teacher #5 knew that youngsters frequently became more involved in the correct spelling of words when they used these same words actively in their writing. Teacher #5 was aware that youngsters had to "bond" to the words in terms of communication, appropriate context, and the need for consistent spelling: all issues a writer is concerned with when addressing an audience (Stoodt 1988).

Keeping in mind that children had a tendency to learn to spell words that they had an individual interest in, Teacher #5 allowed children to develop individualized spelling lists that incorporated words of their choosing and words determined to be important by the selected curriculum. The pupils found this to be a workable give and take in the educational process.

However successful the program was with the students and the teacher, parents and pressure groups were dismayed with many words selected by the youngsters and approved by Teacher #5. Consider the following lists:

List 1	*List 2*	*List 3*
archangel	demon	peace-keeping force
Christianity	cadaver	armed conflict
créche	graveyard	oxymoron
nativity	hobgoblin	Patriot Missile
Saint Nicholas	Halloween	military advisors

List 1 was criticized because it promoted Christian ideals which did not comply with the spirit of separation of church and state. List 2 was found to be the opposite of the spirit of life celebrated by a Christian philosophy. List 3 proved to be too much for critics who were sure that youngsters would believe the words to be anti-American. Objectors were concerned that students would find that list 3 would promote the questioning of American values, which, in itself, was humanistic and unfit for the American schools (Gabler and Gabler 1987).

Scenario #6: The Selection of Library Books

Appropriate is in the eye of the beholder.

Teacher #6 attended graduate courses in order to maintain certification. One of the courses taken was children's literature. The teacher was pleased to have opted for this course when the building principal had announced at a faculty meeting that their library had the most books in the system and that a large proportion of the books were recent.

Teacher #6 had difficulty using the building library in order to meet the requirements of the course. Yes, the books were recent, but they did not pertain to most subjects covered in a graduate-level children's literature course. While the library had recent books on how to raise cranberries, on how icebergs develop, and atlases that had kept up with the different and new countries in the world, the library was woefully short on books that could be used in problem solving and bibliotherapy.

When Teacher #6 asked the school librarian about the collection, the librarian noted that the library had undergone a number of changes, given the new administration and current public opinion regarding what elementary school children should be reading. As it turned out, two forces had been in operation in the state of the collection: book selection and purging.

The librarian, cautious about the political atmosphere, began to only use three book selection journals from which to purchase books. In doing so, the librarian was practicing self-imposed precensorship by selecting "safe titles." Watson found that "book selectors avoid selecting children's books containing objectionable content as identified by someone else" (Watson 1981). Watson warned that a novice educator would place the collection standards in the hands of someone who might not be in favor of titles that require problem solving or critical thinking. Watson noted that review journals, in themselves, could also be seen as censorship aids if the book buyers only select from conservative journals.

The librarian said that about five years ago, a community committee decided which books should or should not be in the library. After they had deselected the books, they then made funds available for purchase of "appropriate" books, considering public opinion. The librarian, given a few guidelines by the community committee, then began to search the conservative book review journals for books that would not irritate, cause readers to question, or provide information that was too mature for elementary-age readers.

Thus, one action lead to another. Unfortunately, a large number of recent books does not necessarily make a useful library. Olson termed this type of book selection and purging as having adults who are blind in one eye: thus the blind spots in collection development are bound to happen when concern for the public overrides concern for a library that promotes literary quality and an atmosphere for intellectual development (Olson 1985).

Scenario #7: Critical Thinking

> Critical thinking and reading is crucial to both lifetime learning and participatory democracy.
>   —Dennis Adams (1986)

Teacher #7 was excited about having sixth, seventh, and eighth graders participate in panel discussions. Teacher #7 knew that such a format required a more formal presentation and that the information had to be delivered by experts. Teacher #7 decided to also increase the development of critical-thinking, reading, and listening skills in order to integrate the language arts skills into the social studies curriculum (Bromley 1992).

The students finally decided to make their presentations about the American involvement in Operation Desert Storm. In their "expert" presentations they were to also include:

1. information relating to themselves on the topic;
2. look for assumptions;
3. interpret the data (facts and opinions);
4. find analogies, metaphors, and similes used to describe the involvement in Operation Desert Storm; and
5. criticize and analyze the information. (Hyde and Bizar 1989, 20–21)

Some of the information the "audience" for the panel discussion had decided to listen for included:

1. Should Americans have become involved in Operation Desert Storm?
2. Did the Americans leave the Middle East too soon?
3. Should the Americans go back and help the refugees?

4. Why should soldiers receive such a hearty welcome when American Vietnam veterans were treated so poorly upon their return?

The teacher knew that it would be impossible to find library books related to the topics, so the students also used interviews. Although newspaper and magazine coverage of the war was extensive, the teacher found that print material was not always the best source. One researcher found that when pupils studied a war "for the most part, the subject entered our students' consciousness not through literature or the curriculum but through television" (Adams 1986, 304). Teacher #7 also decided to allow students to use interviews as a primary source of material.

Adams stated that censorship was definitely in action because the current textbooks did not cover the recent wars or armed conflicts, thus limiting American students from any understanding as to *why* the fighting began or *why* the politics were such that fighting was the ultimate alternative. He commented that "no one wants to assume the risks of knowing. We are in the second decade of 'dumbing down' literature—making sure that as few people as possible object to a story line. The war in Vietnam and nuclear weapons are just the most obvious examples. The various educational-reform movements of today are finding prior censorship on subjects from evolution to armed conflict. By keeping these issues out of schoolbooks we help make television the universal curriculum" (Adams 1986, 304).

Editor-in-chief of a publishing firm, Briley (1982) stated that she took into account the suggestions made from concerned groups in America before something was added or omitted from a book her company published. She noted that trends in public leadership had created the impetus for change—*not* precensorship. However, "there are times when it is perfectly reasonable to object to the use of certain words and references, and there are other times when the same words and references are so germane to what is being said that it would be objectionable not to include them" (Briley 1982, 115).

Teacher #7 was impressed with all the work that the students were doing; however, their panel discussions were never delivered. A group representing teachers, parents, and concerned citizens deplored the action of the critical nature of the information that was to be presented. Some criticized that the material was secular humanism in nature and that children had no right to question the adult authority (Gabler and Gabler 1987). Unfortunately, while the students had learned a lot, they were never given the opportunity to meet with or present to their audience.

What Happened?

> The censor is right: reading is a risky activity.
>
> —Hamida Bosmajian (1987)

In the scenarios discussed above, the novice teachers made a conscious decision to include a variety of skills throughout their teaching. Their intent was to show language as it is used today. They set about to create atmospheres where learning was quite naturally combined with creative and critical thinking. The novice teachers were using ideas that were common activities explained and acted upon in undergraduate K–8 professional methodology courses. Where had these novice teachers gone wrong?

Should they each have cleared their teaching strategies with their building principals? (Then they would be perceived as not able to make decisions.) Should they have not strayed from the stated curriculum and specified textbooks that were selected and approved by the administration? (Then they would be perceived as not being flexible and creative.) Should they have opted to select another occupation instead of more teaching? (Then they would be perceived as being unresponsive to children and as having no commitment to their selected profession.)

It is naïve to say that all teachers, whether novice or master, should know about the issues surrounding censorship and how to deal with censorship. They should know, because ignorance on the topic is *no* excuse. However, one researcher found that "most surveys indicate that fewer than 50% of public schools have policies for selecting materials or dealing with citizens complaints about learning materials" (Burress 1985, 22).

Perhaps the novice teachers should return to the place of their education and question why issues surrounding censorship weren't discussed in professional methodology classes. However, at some point in their education, continuing certification, and successive years of teaching, the novice teacher becomes one with expertise that could be shared with a student teacher. Such expertise could be subject matter in nature and, of course, framed within the basis of censorship.

Works Cited

Adams, Dennis M. 1986. "Literature for Children: Avoiding Controversy and Intellectual Challenge." *Top of the News* 42 (Spring): 304–8.

Bauer, Marion Dane. 1983. *Rain of Fire*. New York: Clarion/Houghton-Mifflin.

Bosmajian, Hamida. 1987. "Tricks of the Text and Acts of Reading by Censors and Adolescents." *Children's Literature in Education* 18 (Summer): 89–96.

Bradford, J. Kenneth. 1986. "To Be or Not to Be: Issues on Changes in Literature Anthologies." *English Journal* 75.2 (October): 52–56.

Briley, Dorothy. 1982. "Are Editors Guilty of Precensorship?" *School Library Journal* 29 (October): 114–15.

Bromley, Karen D'Angelo. 1992. *Language Arts: Exploring Connections.* Boston: Allyn & Bacon.

Burress, Lee. 1985. "Facets: My Biggest Worry about Censorship." *English Journal* 74 (January): 22.

"Censorship in the Eighties." 1982. *Drexel Library Quarterly* 18 (Winter): 1–103.

Cohen, Barbara. 1983. *Molly's Pilgrim.* New York: Morrow.

———. 1986. "Censoring the Sources." *School Library Journal* 32 (March): 97–99.

Gabler Mel, and Norma Gabler. 1987. "Humanism in Textbooks (Secular Religion in the Classroom)." *Communication Education* 36 (October): 362–66.

Hartzell, Richard. 1985. "Eye on Publishing." *Wilson Library Bulletin* 58 (September): 44–45.

Hole, Carol. 1984. "Who Me, Censor?" *Top of the News* 40 (Winter): 147–53.

———. 1985. "Yeah, Me Censor: A Response to Various Critics." *Top of the News* 41 (Spring): 236–43.

The Holy Bible. 1950. Chicago: The Catholic Press.

Hulsizer, Donna. 1987. "Religion in the Public Schools." *Educational Leadership* 44 (May): 13–16.

Hyde, Arthur A., and Marilyn Bizar. 1989. *Thinking in Context.* New York: Longman.

Lepman-Logan, Claudia. 1989. "Books in the Classroom: Moral Choices In Literature." *The Horn Book Magazine* 65 (February): 108–11.

Moshman, David. 1989. *Children, Education, and the First Amendment: A Psycholegal Analysis.* Lincoln: University of Nebraska Press.

Murray, Charles W., Jr., and L. B. Woods. 1982. "'You Shall Know the Truth': The New Christian Right and Censorship." *Drexel Library Quarterly* 18 (Winter): 4–25.

Olson, Lowell E. 1985. "Blind Spots in Collection Development." *Top of the News* 41 (Summer): 371–76.

Peter, Laurence J. 1977. *Peter's Quotations: Ideas for Our Time.* New York: Bantam.

Rowell, C. Glennon. 1987. "Implications of the Tennessee Textbook Controversy for Public Education." *Educational Leadership* 44 (May): 14–15.

Sims, Rudine. 1983. "What Has Happened to the All-White World of Children's Books?" *Phi Delta Kappan* 65 (May): 650–53.

Stoodt, Barbara D. 1988. *Teaching Language Arts.* New York: Harper and Row.

Watson, Jerry. 1981. "Self-Censorship: The Proof Is in the Selection." *Newsletter on Intellectual Freedom* 30 (March): 35, 53–54.

West, Mark, ed. 1988. *Trust Your Children: Voices against Censorship in Children's Literature.* New York: Neal-Schuman.

17 Who's Protecting Whom and From What?

Lynda K. Kapron
Carlson High School
Gibraltar, Michigan

Rita E. Paye
Carlson High School
Gibraltar, Michigan

Censorship is the language arts teacher's nightmare. Fear of public criticism prevents some teachers from acting on their dreams. Censorship can happen when the unwary fulfill student dreams of getting published.

In the spring of 1988 we dreamed ourselves into a whirlwind which stirred our atmosphere every day for the months of May and June. In the fall of 1987 we had applied for and received a Wayne County Intermediate School District (WCISD) mini-grant to produce a high school literary magazine. The booklet would furnish a needed forum for literary and artistic expression at our Michigan high school of over 1,300 students, where comprehensive year-long English classes cover literature, grammar, and writing. The only English electives are yearbook and speech and drama. The booklet would encourage independent literary expression and afford a "reward" for creativity. It would showcase student talent in short story, poetry, essay, and art. Copies would cost a minimal two dollars after free ones went to contributors.

In December a cover contest billed our project, based on the results of a telephone survey to all of the nearby public schools, "the Downriver area's only student literary magazine." Later, other magazines floated into our hands, magazines with no official school logo, of which secretaries and English language arts teachers seemed totally unaware when contacted to determine whether their district published a literary magazine. We did not then know that area sponsors chose to remain low-profile due to censorship problems they had encountered. One sponsor who contacted me after our censorship experience had spent a night in jail because of his. Censorship is emotional and overblown. Sample magazines eventually solicited from Detroit-area public and parochial schools provided models and a source of inspiration, particularly in layout and design.

We knew from the dream stage that some of the cost of publication would be out-of-pocket since our appropriately named mini-grant of $254.06 was not enough even for Speedy Printers, who quoted the best price in a competitive photocopy market. A back-page ad for the teachers' local, the Gibraltar Education Association (GEA), paid another $70, similar in price to the ad the GEA buys in the yearbook. Both the administrators' union and the school board declined without comment Kapron's offer to purchase ads, although both regularly buy ads in the yearbook.

A pun on jib sail and Gib, short for Gibraltar, became the name of the magazine. Growing up in a community with acres of dockage on the confluence of Lake Erie and the Detroit River, most of our students have boating experience. *The Jib's* first cover and frontispiece featured sailboats.

We did not yet have student editors, so the two of us undertook the entire project except the typing. As students dropped off contributions, student volunteers typed them, using whatever typewriters and computers they had available. Over the spring holidays, we met at my home to make final selections, finish typing, and organize selections. Artistic pupils submitted work to visually express various themes. We chose what we found to be the most creative, clearly phrased writing and the most interesting, most reproducible art. At the same time, we attempted to represent a variety of topics of interest to our high school students, and to publish a wide cross-section of students, from learning disabled to advanced. We wanted their dreams to come true.

Early in April of 1988, Carlson's principal of seven years, James Vollmar, furnished a shared substitute so that we could finalize the magazine for printing. The mock-up of final selections expanded from the planned 32-page booklet to 58 pages to accommodate the gratifying number and quality of submissions. The book retired to print in mid-April.

Printed copies arrived May 1. We distributed free copies to contributors as planned, and began selling books to contributors, parents, and teachers. We proudly handed a complimentary copy to the principal, and delivered one to the central office to be displayed with elementary accomplishments. We even mailed a copy to each school board member, hoping that they would spread the word about student achievement. We made plans to sell copies at the awards banquet that week and began organizing an author/artist reception for June.

The morning of the awards banquet, however, Vollmar called us into his office. He thought it not a good idea to sell *The Jib* at the banquet; school board members had received two anonymous notes and were very upset about the magazine's contents. One note, he said, alleged Satanism in a picture of a dragon. The other referred to language use. Since Superintendent Pavlov was investigating the charges of impropriety, Vollmar thought it would be better to wait until things cooled down before continuing sales. Although stunned and disappointed, we complied.

The next day, students tumbled into class distressed about comments allegedly made by a board member at the awards banquet. One girl, who had sat with the board member at dinner, said that she had found herself unexpectedly defending *The Jib*'s contents, even though she was not a contributor. She said she had questioned the board member's apparent acceptance of anonymous complaints as valid. The irony in one poem— about putting cats to sleep, and why not fathers?—she had explained eloquently. She was well prepared to take on such issues after a recent unit on censored books in her English class. She explained the irony of American attitudes toward euthanasia and defended student freedom of expression.

Another student offered to help the magazine's sponsors in any way possible. Others asked questions: "What's wrong with the language? It's used in quotation." "What will happen next?" "Don't these people understand irony?"

These were tough questions because no one but our principal expressed anything to us but approval of *The Jib*, and his negative statements seemed to represent less his own views than those of the school board and the superintendent—who had not yet spoken to us. Vollmar said he appreciated the achievement represented by the magazine, which he read in its completed form for the first time only after its publication. He had not previewed it prior to publication, deeming that to be the responsibility of the mini-grant coordinator, or of the ISD. He may have cautioned against the language use in one piece had he read it prior to publication, he said, simply because he knew it "would raise eyebrows" in our conservative district. On the other hand, the ISD's annual contest often honored pieces with such language, so he did not see it as a concern, having read and shared with us the contest publications in years past. One week after publication of *The Jib*, our principal formally responded to Pavlov's request for information regarding our funding, our requests for submission of student writing, and our publication procedures. In his letter, Vollmar protested having "to respond to inquiries that are not substantiated by signatures," adding that he had "not received one negative phone call." He documented distribution and sales. Of 200 copies printed, 139 had been distributed. All of the grant dollars were accounted for: a check from the district for $254.06 had gone directly to the printer. The remaining printing costs of $113.09 had been paid by Kapron's personal check, which was partially reimbursed by the GEA's back-page ad payment of $70. Sales were accurately documented. In his opinion, the teachers had followed prescribed grant procedures and logical, professional publication procedures for literary magazines.

Despite this report, *The Jib* continued to cause waves the following evening at the regular monthly school board meeting, when a board member hoisted it in the air, asking what would be done about "this literature." The board president recommended that the matter be discussed behind closed doors, at the advice of the board's attorney. Another board member said he'd read and appreciated *The Jib*. He later told me that the board had scarcely discussed the magazine in its private session that night. Five board members remained publicly silent on the issue.

Board members gave the situation to the superintendent to deal with as he saw fit. Pavlov was not slow in acting on this authority. The next morning, Wednesday, May 11, 1988, he took the alarming step of ordering confiscation of all remaining, unsold copies of *The Jib*. Kapron delivered 61 copies of the 200 published to the central office after school with a letter protesting the confiscation and requesting that the books be returned "in same condition" at the close of the superintendent's investigation.

We filed grievances that same day, alleging "unsubstantiated censorship and seizure of product produced by county grant monies." It was an infringement, we argued, of our academic freedom. *The Jib* was not journalism; it was not even produced in class. It was a product of after-school activities, not to be controlled by in-class directives or rulings. The situation was, we thought, covered under the academic freedom clause of our contract. As local union negotiators who had, in the fall of 1987, helped bring in our then-current contract, we first turned, naturally, to the most familiar avenue for redress; only after all local options were exhausted would we go "outside." At the direction of Pavlov, Vollmar denied our grievance.

On Monday, student contributors reported that their parents had received letters asking if their writing was done "during class time" or "outside of class." How should they answer this unprecedented student survey? We recommended: "Honestly." The students were personally alarmed. Was she in trouble, one girl asked tearfully. She had thought it OK to submit poetry to the magazine. Now she wondered. We told students that the superintendent was investigating our actions, not the students', *per se*.

The English department chair, we soon learned, had been called to the central office with the yearbook sponsor to answer questions: Was *The Jib* in the curriculum? Was it done on school time? Did the English department discuss it at meetings? The answers given, our colleagues told us, were all "no." English staff were, of course, aware of *The Jib;* posters hung in their classrooms. Though it may have been informally discussed at lunch or in the hallway, and though other members of the department had encouraged student submissions, *The Jib* was an individual grant project, not part of department curriculum.

At last we had, we thought, opportunity to face our accusers. Late that Monday afternoon, two weeks after *The Jib* first came out, seated around a large conference table, we faced Pavlov and two other central office administrators, one of whom, Stanley Kochanski, later became our principal.

Instead of discussing the contents of *The Jib* as we'd hoped, however, we were asked a bewildering barrage of questions about procedure. Although censorship seemed to us to be the crux of the issue, we were asked: Was it done in class? Was it done on school time? *In* school? Did we consult with the principal? What about the GEA ad on the back page? What about *the money?* Not until much later did we realize that these seemingly irrelevant questions arose from the recent U.S. Supreme Court *Hazelwood* decision. As we later learned, this decision in January of 1988 allowed censorship of two class-produced school newspaper articles, a case we had dismissed as irrelevant to ours.

While answering, we fired back questions of our own: Why was *The Jib* confiscated? When and under what conditions would it be returned? Why weren't we, the teacher-editors, contacted first, before the principal, the students, their parents, the department chair, the yearbook sponsor, and the local newspaper? What did this student survey mean? Acrimonious and accusatory on both sides, the meeting ended without resolution. We were convinced that the real issue was our role in the 1987 teachers' strike, though that has never been confirmed.

Over the following week, the storm continued. Students wrote lengthy explanations of their time spent working on contributions. Parents tried to obtain but were denied access to the magazine at the board office. Students signed a waiting list to purchase booklets when/if they became available. We took our grievance to the formal, written step, adding "subversive evaluation" to our list of grievances. We sent a letter to the central office in a futile attempt to obtain an explanation of the seizure, since none had been forthcoming at the meeting. All these written and personal communications failed to calm the storm.

Further muddying the waters, a local newspaper quoted Pavlov's justification for the seizure, "alleging misuse of federal money, publishing of a magazine without proper authority and questionable material in the booklet itself"; the board president: "I don't care for some of the contents"; and the board member who waved it in the air at the May school board meeting: "the booklet contained some of the sickest, meanest things to come out of the high school . . . If they want this trash, they should buy it from the newsstand." In the same article, Paye is quoted in defense of her students' writing and artwork: "It was 'just a slice of life in the '80s.'"

The newspaper article became the focus of the next meeting between us and central office administrators, on June 2. This time we had union representation. The news story had articulated the superintendent's objections, our MEA Uniserv representative said. Was the story accurate? Pavlov called the news reporter in our presence and denied that he was accusing us of misuse of federal funds, though he still had "questions about money in the expenditure of a federal grant," despite the principal's letter spelling out exactly where each dollar went.

As the superintendent well knew, we could account for the money, so what was the real problem? Pavlov finally cited four pieces in the booklet, not mentioning the dragon drawing referenced in the one anonymous note, and adding two previously unmentioned pieces and a computer graphic. He demanded that these four be deleted:

Dream

I had a dream last night. A small boy stepped
into his first hour
Algebra class, walked to his desk and sat down
    without saying
a word.
Back straight.
Feet flat on the floor.
Hands crossed in front of him on the desk.
Halfway through class William's teacher became
    puzzled with his
queerness and asked him to answer the problem
    on the board. William
promptly stood, reached into his bright yellow
    duffel bag and produced
a small pistol. He aimed it at the teacher,
    answered the question, and
pulled the trigger three times. He stood rigid,
    poised straight as an
arrow and placed the end of it into his mouth.
The trigger was squeezed once more.
    You know, children shouldn't eat
    gunpowder for breakfast.

        —M. D. P.

The allegation was that, to a suggestible reader, "Dream" promotes shooting teachers and committing suicide. We argued that the last two lines express the opposite.

Convenience

I don't like my cat. She urinates on the floor.
She coughs up hairballs and scratches the furniture. I think I'll
have her put to sleep.
I have the power to do that. If I don't like something I can just
get rid of it—kill it at my convenience.
Pay the man my precious bill of rights to inject the eternal venom
and destroy a Life—at my convenience.

I don't like my Dad, he makes me mad. I think I'll have him put to
sleep. I have the power to do that.

—M. D. P.

"Convenience" was said to be objectionable in that it promotes violence prohibited in the Carlson High School Student Code of Conduct, ironically using language developed by the ACLU in the late 1960s to protect freedom of expression. Administrators asked if we'd referred the writer to his counselor. (The poem was later reproduced in the local newspaper in an article about the court case that eventually resulted from censorship of *The Jib.*)

Overheard

Madonna was on stage in
Toronto. She was singing
"Crazy for You." This guy was
yelling, "I want you. You are
so sexy." Madonna just ignored him.
A few moments later he grabbed her
boob. She just ignored it. Then
he did it again.
        "You asshole. Who in the hell
do you think you are?" She
slapped his face. "You are
disgusting!"

—K. G.

"Overheard" was described as "too graphic," "sexual" in the use of the word "boob," and inappropriate for younger readers who might pick up the magazine at home and read it. Probably fiction, "Overheard" succinctly expresses conflict and plot while using character-revealing conversation correctly, a difficult task for many student writers.

Superintendent Pavlov said the computer graphic in figure 1 "encourages drinking." Questioned, he admitted that he had not read the essay

—M. T.

Fig. 1. Illustration slated for censorship from *The Jib*.

opposed to out-of-control drinking bouts which accompanied the drawing of champagne glasses, but formed his opinions on first impression
and partial understanding of the literature. Carlson High School's sports
calendar in 1988, which all teachers were asked to post, advertised
alcohol at a party store, a local saloon, and a board member's "Champagne Limousine Service."

These four pieces, we were told, violated the student code of conduct
and board policy, which requires all official communications to be
approved by the principal. We would have to censor the four pieces in
some unspecified way and include a waiver in the 61 unsold copies,
stating that the opinions expressed did not represent the school or the
school board. We agreed to the waiver, but not to the censorship.

One month after the magazine was first published, both of us received
written reprimands. We responded with a second grievance that the
reprimands were "without just cause." Grievance denied. On Wednesday, we received a letter from the superintendent, refusing all possible
settlements except censorship and the waiver. In the same mail, ironically, we received a Certificate of Special Recognition from the ISD for
our work on *The Jib*. At the June school board meeting, Pavlov said he had
sent a full communication to the principal: "It's in his hands now." It was
up to Vollmar, who personally disagreed, to enforce the superintendent's
censorship orders. We had been reprimanded, and the superintendent
apparently felt he had successfully resolved the problem.

A student and a parent also spoke at the June school board meeting, both protesting censorship and insisting that the teacher-editors should be commended rather than reprimanded. The parent protested her lack of choice. She was not being allowed to decide whether or not to buy the booklet, and thus whether or not to read it.

The school year ended minus the author/artist reception. Submitting *The Jib* to the NCTE contest, we hoped, would help us more objectively judge our students' achievement, and plan for the 1989 *Jib*. The student with the best résumé (yes, it was typed, on bond paper) became editor. Then we put together a pile of documentation and mailed it with a cover letter to the American Civil Liberties Union in Detroit.

The ACLU was immediately interested, but waited for the resolution of the labor grievance before filing a lawsuit against the school district for unconstitutional censorship. In February 1989, a state arbitrator ruled that the reprimands must be removed from our files; we had followed every known procedure. But, since the magazine was indeed a voluntary, outside-of-school activity, the arbitrator could not find that its seizure had violated our contractual right to academic freedom.

Superintendent Pavlov interpreted this as a total win. He declared the arbitration decision upheld administrators' absolute right to censor any student's writing on school premises.

In the meantime, we studied censorship, especially the U.S. Supreme Court's *Tinker* and *Hazelwood* cases. The *Tinker* case, involving the wearing of black arm bands to protest the Vietnam War, held that students do not shed their rights at the schoolhouse gate, a standard maintained until just before we were censored in 1988. That spring's *Hazelwood* decision, which allowed censorship in a class-produced, teacher-edited school newspaper, a decision we'd assumed had little impact on us—classroom English teachers putting together a publication after hours—was causing a stir in the lower federal courts.

Belatedly, we educated ourselves on the history of censorship. Like many Americans, we had naïvely ignored the gradual restriction of speech and publication rights in this country during the 1980s. When they went after traitors, communists, and devil worshippers, we weren't harmed, were we? Like many English teachers, we were fairly knowledgeable about journalism cases and attacks on books by the far right. When they went after other English teachers, we were concerned, and we had read language arts publications to keep up on the trends over the years. But now "they" were after us and we read everything we found or someone dropped in our mailboxes concerning first amendment rights, from cartoons to law journals.

Also, in the interim, we applied for and received another WCISD mini-grant, though the grants are not usually repeated. Because of our situation, ISD forms were more clear, now explaining the "mini-grant coordinator" and the district's control of the grant payout. This time the grant was for only $100, but it was enough to go forward with a second publication in May of 1989. Our new principal, Stanley Kochanski, formerly a central office administrator involved in the censorship, was careful to insist from the outset that he wanted to read the mock-up. We allowed him the courtesy of reading student literary submissions. He censored one piece, a love poem which ended ". . . And the blood sets us free." Kochanski, when pressed for a reason to suppress the poem, told Paye it might be interpreted by someone somewhere as referring to Charlie Manson. Paye was at an unusual loss for words. When she asked the student author for an explanation of his poem, he explained it in Christian terms, but Kochanski refused to speak with the author.

Our objections to the censorship of this poem, and to the new principal's insistence upon conducting prepublication review of the booklet, became count two (prior restraint of the lawsuit which was filed in February of 1990 against the school district, the board, the superintendent, principal Kochanski, and two board members).

A number of students joined the suit. They were *all* contributors to either the 1988 or the 1989 publication, or to both. All felt strongly that their rights had been denied, whether in lack of access to extra copies of the first *Jib*, or in fear of censorship in the second *Jib*. The pieces objectionable to the superintendent and school board were not objectionable to our students. One piece satirizing student groups had cheerleaders hot, but not board members. Adults objected to the language, not students, who admitted "cleaning up" their language when around adults. Who was protecting whom and from what? What was objectionable to our students was their lack of choice in whether to purchase or to read the confiscated magazines. They were insulted that adults seemed to think that teenagers are too stupid to resist stimuli and to make their own decisions of right and wrong. The suit asked for an order that all 61 confiscated copies of *The Jib* be returned, and that the censorship be declared unconstitutional.

The second *Jib* was generally found to be inferior in quality to the first. Even Kochanski, in his deposition, noted that he had a hard time finding pieces to like in the second publication. The writing was good but bland. As one student told Paye, "I ain't gettin' in trouble" for submitting a thoughtful piece. Censorship had chilled student enthusiasm for the dream of publication.

After the ACLU took the case in the winter of 1990, though, submissions poured in for the third issue of *The Jib*. Apparently, students' enthusiasm had warmed at news of the lawsuit. Despite the usual funding problems, the 1990 issue swelled to 78 pages. While assembling this booklet, we met several times with Kochanski to try to formulate a procedure should a problem occur with this and subsequent issues. Kochanski was unable to come to agreement though he said that he, too, wanted a policy. We proposed that a committee decide, as already occurs in case of a challenge to a library or textbook. Kochanski would not, or was not allowed to, agree. He questioned one piece in the 1990 *Jib* and deleted another, though this time, perhaps because of the lawsuit and the procedural discussions, he agreed to sit down with the censored student authors individually and discuss his reasons for censorship. One poet withdrew his "too graphic" piece from consideration and another questioned poet agreed to delete one anti-abortionist line so her poem could be published. This particular deletion seems directly related to *Hazelwood*.

Though unable to come to a procedural agreement, we were aware of costs; rather than go through an expensive and time-consuming jury trial, therefore, the attorneys for both sides agreed to submit the case to a judge for a decision based on stipulated facts. The attorneys submitted briefs to Federal Judge Robert DeMascio in December of 1990. Many of the board's arguments were focused not on whether the board had the right to censor, but whether the students and teachers had the right to sue. The board's attorney first argued that the plaintiffs lacked standing: all of the students had graduated by the time the case was filed, and we, the editors, were not contributors of written work. If that were true, cooperating ACLU attorney Lee W. Brooks countered, then no decision on the issues raised in our suit could ever be obtained from the courts, because the affected students will almost always graduate before the case can be resolved. As for us, the teacher-editors, he argued, we had continued, under a system of prior restraint, to publish subsequent booklets, and 61 copies of the first issue were still gathering dust in a box in the superintendent's office.

Brooks's brief focused not on these technicalities, but on an explanation of how the actions of the defendants had violated our well-established constitutional rights. The Supreme Court wrote in *Tinker*, in 1969, that independent student expression which does not disrupt class, create disorder, or invade the rights of others is protected by the First Amendment and cannot be punished or silenced by public school officials. Because *The Jib* contained independent student expression, and because the only disruption connected to its publication was created by the defendants' acts of censorship and confiscation, that censorship and confiscation, we believed, infringed upon the student-authors' rights, and on our rights under the First Amendment.

The brief further argued that the 1988 *Hazelwood* decision did not change the law applicable to our facts. In *Hazelwood*, the censorship involved the removal of two pages containing articles the Hazelwood principal found objectionable from a six-page newspaper. Our case, on the contrary, involved a literary magazine produced by teachers and students at a particular school, but which was not produced in a class or as part of the regular high school curriculum. Though we received a small grant to aid in publication, the magazine was produced also with our own funds and was primarily created off-campus and outside school hours. And the censorship in our case was more extreme than in *Hazelwood*. Copies of the first issue of *The Jib* were confiscated in their entirety, so that they could not be distributed. The administration intended to continue its censorship, based on no standards whatsoever, for as long as we kept producing the magazine. Under these circumstances, the Supreme Court's allowance of censorship in *Hazelwood* would not, we argued, be taken to mean that the censorship of *The Jib* was constitutional. In fact, there appears to be no case other than ours which has sought a decision from the federal courts on the First Amendment rights of those who produce *high school* literary magazines. Much litigation swirls around university student concerns. High school students are not citizens able to sue, though they are not children without the ability to care for themselves in every way, either.

Hazelwood had established precedent of which we were unaware but which impacted on our situation. Thus, the case we had dismissed as irrelevant in 1988 and therefore did not understand contained this new test: "open forum." Even when we did read the language of the Supreme Court decision, we thought that, of course, our school was an "open forum" based on our layperson's understanding of the term. Wrong. A school is not an "open forum" unless the administration so designates. According to the courts, a school which is *not* an open forum *can censor* not only in print but in play production and speeches. The more restrictive the administration, the less open the forum and the stronger the right to censor. The court ruling does not suggest that schools *should* censor, but that was our superintendent's written recommendation to his administrators.

It took over three years for our case to be resolved. Judge DeMascio ruled in August of 1991 that the (by then former) students involved in the suit had no standing in court, a position taken by the school board attorney. We would have had no standing in court either, except that one had invested money, and the other had published a drawing of hers in the disputed booklet. The day we worked in school, with subs in our rooms, made the project curricular, according to the ruling. The school was not an open forum. The superintendent's objections were "reasonably related to pedagogical concerns," though the actual pieces, or their merits (or demerits) were not mentioned in the summary disposition. Therefore, we infer, if an administrator's objection is reasonably related to pedagogical concerns, it matters not what the piece actually says or even implies. It matters not that objections were grounded on anonymous notes, nor that the superintendent had not read the booklet. It matters not that the students were *not* advocating illegal acts; to the court it matters that our superintendent had concerns reasonably related to the student code of conduct, no matter how ludicrous we might think that relationship.

In their depositions, school board members said they thought that publication of *The Jib* had been stopped. It had not. We continued to publish yearly throughout the three-year suit, we continued to be censored, and we began publishing yearly disclaimers. We simply did not send copies to board members, inferring at this point that such optimistic showcasing of student accomplishment would not be well received in our district. We continued submitting *The Jib* to the NCTE contest, winning fourths, and a third the year we sued.

Today, we continue to use the partial policy drawn up in hopes of amicable settlement, though we always hit the wall of "Because I said so," even with a new superintendent. The objections have remained consistent over the years, so that we can now tell students what will not pass, such as the word "sex," or any reference to the devil. Board members had attended a workshop on the prevalence of area Satanism in early 1988, part of the national Satanism hysteria of the time. Although Satanism was dropped in the suit, it is apparently still on our Christian administrators' minds. Knowing we can expect this makes it easier to counteract the natural student inclination to self-censor material which would *pass* the censor. Our yearly inclusions of well-written pieces (we refuse to self-censor) and our yearly objections to the inevitable one exclusion, an administrative insistence on what is perhaps token censorship, make it easier for students to get published in our district.

This process also ensures careful reading on the part of both the principal and the assistant principal, who was not involved in the lawsuit but now gets called in to help in the decision-making process, and on the part of the new superintendent. All are more aware now of student achievement in writing than they would otherwise have been, and they are becoming more aware of how their own interpretations sometimes paint violence and sex into innocent student expression, and how they "get" allusions much more quickly than most high school readers, let alone younger, less-sophisticated readers. When facing the individual student writer, they find it much harder to ignore feelings, harder to say "Because I said so." In order to make a decision, administrators must review the criteria they established to win the suit.

It is our hope that our story will help others to successfully prevent censorship, or, if censorship occurs, to successfully assert their and their students' rights to freedom of creative expression. Would we do it all over again? Yes, more calmly. Ours are lessons worth learning. Dealing with it effectively takes away the nightmare quality of censorship.

English language arts teachers need not avoid it. Instead, they can accept censorship attempts as inevitable political actions which they can counter. They can aggressively educate themselves about the law before an emotional storm gathers, stay attuned to variances and nuances in student expression, forge clear inclusive policies in their districts, and network with other language arts professionals and local journalists to defend students' rights to read and publish without fear. If censorship occurs, they need to be able to act quickly, effectively, and calmly.

Students involved in our suit went on to obtain a dorm grant to publish a literary magazine in a college dorm, to write college papers and speeches on censorship, to create alternative basement play productions, to write and produce rock songs and to d.j. a radio show. Their firsthand experience of unwarranted but legal censorship informs their writing, speaking, and publishing decisions. The censored students got especial pleasure from seeing their pieces published in the local paper in an article asking readers to judge for themselves if they were bad enough to cause such a storm.

Students need not be voiceless and ignored by the courts. They can be educated to advocate for themselves. Teachers must work within the system and against the system to make dreams come true. Freedom can be protected by knowledgeable teachers, students, parents, administrators, and board of education members.

Works Cited

Hazelwood School District v. Kuhlmeier. 1988. 484 U.S. 260.
Paye v. Gibraltar School District. 1991. 90CV70444DT.
Tinker v. Des Moines Independent Community School District. 1969. 393 U.S. 503.

18 Using Media
to Combat Censorship

Margaret T. Sacco
Miami University

Since many censorship problems arise from poor communication, the effective use of media can be used to combat censorship. Parents, students, teachers, administrators, and the general public need to be instructed about the evils of censorship and how censorship jeopardizes the school curriculum as well as a democratic society. Additionally, parents and community members need to know how instructional materials are selected and used in the classrooms, particularly books that are required reading. One of the best ways to educate the community about the dangers of censorship and what educational materials are used and how they are used is to effectively utilize mass media, school-produced media, and/or commercially prepared media to educate administrators, parents, and the community.

Teachers and library media specialists can work together and formulate goals and objectives for combating censorship, then select or produce the best media for conveying the information. English teachers can use their writing skills to write scripts, and library media specialists can produce media for conveying their messages.

Once a censorship problem occurs it may be too late to get effective information to the community. So do it now! Some teachers and librarians do not want to publicly discuss censorship because they are afraid that talking and writing about censorship will cause censorship problems. However, if teachers and librarians do their homework and work to combat censorship, they will be a lot better off when a problem does occur. Ignoring the problems of censorship will not make them go away. Futhermore, when the censors win, censorship activity does not stop with just one book. The censors' victory builds momentum, and other books and teaching materials are banned too.

Effective audiovisual media or mass media can be used as a powerful weapon to combat censorship for the following reasons:

192

1. visual aids make a presentation more persuasive;
2. with the use of visual aids people can grasp more information;
3. visual aids add variety and emphasis to presentations;
4. a message is presented both visually and orally so that a presenter can communicate with an audience whose members may process information aurally or visually;
5. visuals help presenters organize a presentation;
6. visuals help presenters be concise so the audience will not be bored with too much detail;
7. visuals can facilitate meetings or discussions by capturing and keeping audience attention; and
8. audiences today are used to being exposed to mass media and information technology. (Raines 1989, 4; Heinich et al. 1986, 4)

In the following paragraphs, suggestions will be given on how audiovisual media and mass media can be produced and/or be used effectively to combat censorship.

Research on the results of media production techniques suggests that inexpensive, locally produced visuals can be just as effective as polished, professional materials (Simonson and Volker 1984, 47). However, in order to produce an effective audiovisual presentation, it is necessary to establish goals and objectives. Clear, well-written objectives will give focus to a media production and make the effectiveness of audiovisual media easier to evaluate. Once a group or groups are targeted, the next step involves audience research. One needs to know the educational level, demographic information, and socioeconomic facts about the targeted population. Different strategies can be employed with different groups. For example, visual portrayal of how censorship could result in an economic loss to a community could be effective in gaining support from a business group.

On the other hand, visuals of burning books or empty library or classroom bookshelves would have little impact on a group of nonreaders. However, visuals of Nazis or Communists burning books, or celebrities at a public forum with tape on their mouths, could be more effective.

The next step involves the composition of a storyboard which contains the narration or script and a description of the visuals that will be produced. Storyboards assure that the presentation is in an appropriate sequence to convey the message and help teachers communciate to library media specialists. Slides are a good medium because they can be used with both a large group and small group; they can be easily produced; their order can be rearranged; slides can be easily transfered to a videocassette using a rear projection unit; some of the same slides can be used with different groups; and the equipment is portable. Also, if you have two screens, you can use transparencies with slides or two slide projectors with a dissolve unit. A good cassette tape to accompany a slide show only requires a well-written script, careful production, and a warm, friendly, audible voice.

Tips for a Successful Audiovisual Presentation

The following hints may help teachers and library media specialists have a successful media campaign:

1. Do not preach, talk down to the audience, or be afraid to stop the presentation for audience questions. These questions can be a learning experience and give one ideas for improving the production.
2. Use humor frequently in your visuals and/or narration. People remember funny moments longer. Well-selected cartoons that convey one's message can be very helpful in achieving goals and objectives.
3. Field test your presentation before it is used with any group. A class that has been trained in visual literacy and/or a teachers' group may be a good preview audience.
4. Do not use other controversial topics, language, and/or visuals to convey your message. The Legion of Decency, a former censorship organization, produced a film to educate the public on what is pornography, and it was lurid. The Supreme Court cannot define pornography, so leave that topic alone. Additionally, the American Library Association laid an egg when it produced and distributed an anti-censorship film called *The Speaker: A Film about Freedom* (1977). This film, which *does* effectively show how censorship works and effects the community, divided the membership by offending its African American members and created a censorship battle that embarrassed this reputable professional organization which has a long history of combating censorship.
5. Use emotionally laden visuals to sell the idea that the only censorship that works is self-censorship and/or that books should be judged in their entirety. Visuals of gory war scenes of young men and women dying carrying an American flag, and enumeration of the values of a democratic society that they died for, and how the

school's literature program teaches these values could be effective. A study of World War II propaganda films can be quite useful to learn how media can be used to change attitudes.

6. Slides made using the collage technique appear two dimensional and may be attention grabbers. Pictures from newspapers and magazines with 3/8" press-on letters can be used to make slides with a 35mm camera on a tripod with a close-up attachment to photograph pictures at a close range and photoflood lights. For example, if the presenter wants to depict burning books, pictures of books could be pasted on construction paper with flames made with red acetate sheets pasted on the books, and then be photographed.

7. Since library media specialists are knowledgeable about the research on effective media presentations, it is best to let these professionals do the production work. For example, since audiences have seen so many quality video productions, they are usually very critical, so a poorly produced video could turn your audience off.

Mass Media Opportunities for Combating Censorship

The mass media offer many opportunities for educators to voice their opinions about censorship and to influence public attitudes. Earlier, Charles Suhor (1979, 176–77) advocated some of the following suggestions on how to use the various communciation channels:

Community Cable Television Programs. Each community has a television channel for community affairs. This provides schools with an opportunity to educate the public about censorship, the English curriculum, and how and why certain instructional methods are used. People outside the field of education have a right to know how their tax dollars are being spent by educators.

Television Editorials. A message about the importance of intellectual freedom can be presented on television channels. English teachers should have enough clout to have their messages endorsed by local teacher organizations and community groups and delivered by a spokesperson on television. Television station managers welcome informed public opinion and give airtime for rebuttals, too.

Newspapers. Some local newspapers and magazines need fillers. Get to know the editors and feature writers. Usually newspapers support school efforts for combating censorship because the press is threatened by the censors, too. A series of articles about censorship, the importance of intellectual freedom, and/or the value of literature can be written.

Community Groups. Many influential people belong to local organizations and clubs. These clubs are always looking for interesting speakers. So get a spokesperson's name in a library's community-speaker resource file. A well-produced slide/tape that conveys an anti-censorship position can be used to inform the public and recruit possible important allies. Additionally, one may want to ask members of the audience what book or books have influenced them the most. Then pass around a paper for them to sign if they are willing be interviewed on tape by a student about their favorite books for a class project. Subsequently, the tapes can be used to motivate student reading as well as an article for the school newspaper.

Call-In Talk Shows. An opportunity exists to express an educated opinion against censorship. So many of these shows often feature wacky opinions of uninformed and oftentimes ridiculous people.

Public Forums. School newsletters and PTA meetings offer many opportunities to sell your literature and library programs to the parents and community members. Frequently, teachers lament that parents do not attent high school PTA meetings. Perhaps one can get a well-known local celebrity and local merchants to donate door prizes to increase attendance when the literature program is being discussed. Newsletters and school meetings are ideal to educate the public on teaching methods and which research studies support these methods. Many people outside the field of English education are not aware of the research support for response-based literature programs and journal writing. Additionally, an enthusiastic presentation of Rosenblatt's (1983) theories of the transaction between the book and reader and a demonstration of the response-based literature method soliciting audience participation may be effective. A teacher can read a literature passage, and the audience can be given paper and pencils to write a response. Then members of the audience can be asked to share their responses because adults bring a lot of experience to literature. A lecture at a public meeting will probably turn off your public, but a short effective videotape or sound/slide tape may motivate interest.

Community Adult Education Programs. One of the best ideas for educating parents about books is discussed by June Berkley in

Dealing with Censorship (1979, 180–86). A demonstration and discussion of this article is available on film and videotape as *Books Our Children Read* (1984). Berkley describes how she successfully utilized an adult education class to combat censorship of the school's literature program.

In conclusion, English departments and library media specialists should not wait for censorship to occur before they educate parents, school administrators, and the community about their literature and library programs and the dangers of censorship. They can work together and develop effective strategies and media campaigns to ensure that their students have the right to read and know.

Works Cited

Berkley, June. 1979. "Teach the Parents Well: An Anti-Censorship Experiment in Adult Education." In *Dealing with Censorship,* edited by James E. Davis, 180–86. Urbana: National Council of Teachers of English.

Books Our Children Read. 1984. [Film]. Chicago: Films Incorporated.

Heinich, Robert, Michael Molenda, and James Russell. 1986. *Instructional Media and the New Technologies of Instruction.* 2nd ed. New York: Macmillan.

Raines, Claire. 1989. *Visual Aids in Business: A Guide to Effective Presentations.* Los Altos, CA: Crisp Publications.

Rosenblatt, Louise M. 1983. *Literature as Exploration.* 4th ed. New York: Modern Language Association of America.

Simonson, Michael R., and Roger P. Volker. 1984. *Media Planning and Production.* Columbus, OH: Charles E. Merrill.

The Speaker: A Film about Freedom. 1977. [Film]. Chicago: Vision Associates/ American Library Association.

Suhor, Charles. 1979. "Basic Training and Combat Duty—Preventive and Reactive Action." In *Dealing with Censorship,* edited by James E. Davis, 168–79. Urbana: National Council of Teachers of English.

19 *Slugging* It Out: Censorship Issues in the Third Grade

C. Jane Hydrick
Entz Elementary School
Mesa, Arizona

Wednesday morning. Next to Sunday's paper, Wednesday's newspaper is my favorite. Barefooted, I darted outside on a still-warm September morning to grab the local daily that burgeoned with coupons and the coming week's grocery specials.

I scanned the front page quickly, eager to get to the inserts. My eyes caught on the words, "library ban" and I stopped. "Bugged by slugs. Mom seeks library ban on book about critters." This latest target for censorship was David Greenberg's book *Slugs* (Trumpet Club, 1983). I didn't care for the book, but my six-year old daughter, Libby, and my twelve-year-old son, Kip, both loved it. The article continued, ". . . it contained disgusting rhymes and grotesque pictures." I had to agree, but it was those same disgusting rhymes and grotesque pictures which had delighted my two children. The following statement was my call to arms: "The library's book complaint review committee meets at 6:30 p.m. today to decide whether to take *Slugs* off the children's bookshelves."

By coincidence, David Greenberg, author of *Slugs,* had visited my daughter's school the day before to autograph books, to share his experiences as an author and to compare notes with fellow writers in Libby's first grade, so I had a handy, freshly autographed copy of *Slugs.* I arrived at my own elementary school an hour later with *Slugs* and the front page of the *Mesa Tribune,* eager to share with my third-grade team an idea I had for using *Slugs.* My colleagues were almost as eager as I—until I shared the newspaper article. They readily admitted that they were too reluctant to slug it out with what was now a publicly controversial book.

I remembered then that one of these colleagues had not completed reading Roald Dahl's *Witches* as a read-aloud rather than agonize over how to avoid the references to dog droppings. This same colleague had altered an entire class set of books for a literature study group by drawing a bathing suit over the barely showing buttocks of a swimming boy in one of the book's illustrations. She had anticipated the children's reaction to the picture and didn't want the unpleasantness of dealing with parents who might object. In these colleagues' classrooms, there are no *National Geographic* magazines because of the sometimes-controversial subject matter and more-than-occasional nudity of members of indigenous tribes.

Despite the refusal of my teammates to share *Slugs* with their classes, I introduced the book to my third graders that morning. I began by telling them simply that the author, David Greenberg, had been at my daughter's school the day before and had signed the book for her. After reading each page, I held up the book for all the children to see pictures by illustrator Victoria Chess: brightly colored depictions of huge, brown slugs being nibbled and devoured alive, served up on pans, stomped, and slurped as juice.

> Nibble on its feetsies
> Nibble on its giblets
> Nibble on its bellybutton
> Nibble on its riblets

When I reached page eight, the children's reactions to both text and illustrations ranged from delighted "Yea! Rad! Neat!" to disgusted "Yuck! Sick! Gross!" Some children's faces had lit up with glee, others exhibited curled lips or frowns.

> Perch one on a doorknob
> Or on a toilet seat
> Sizzle them on light bulbs
> Squash them with your feet

By the time I read page fourteen, the children were watching each other's reactions as closely as they were looking at the illustrations. Christy stuck her tongue out and rolled her eyes ceiling-ward.

> Slugs are small and portable
> Just stuff 'em up your nose
> They'll fit beneath your armpits
> Or right between your toes

Suddenly on page twenty-seven, the tables turned in favor of the slugs. Some children reacted with disbelief. "What?" "Wait a minute!" "They can't do that!" Others lent their loud and enthusiastic support. "All right, slugs!"

> They'll chop you into pancakes
> And turn you inside out
> So your liver's on the outside
> And your brain is sauerkraut

Poetic justice was served on page thirty-one as three adult-person-size slugs crammed a hapless human victim into a garbage can.

> And after how *you've* treated Slugs
> It surely serves you right!

I closed the book, put it on the table and said, "Well, what did you think?"

Alison was the first one to react. "It was awful. I hated it. It was terrible."

"I can understand why you feel that way," I said. "And do you know what? There's a group of moms who agree with you, Alison." I picked up the morning paper, showed the class the article, and read the headlines. "Bugged by slugs. Mom seeks library ban on book about critters." "See? These moms were so disgusted with this book that they are going to meet at the library to have *Slugs* taken off the shelves."

Alison looked rather pleased with herself. Some of the children sat, just listening, while others began to squirm uncomfortably, to look at each other, to shrug, to widen their eyes, or to raise eyebrows.

Tyson spoke up hesitantly. "But I liked it. I thought it was funny."

Ryan agreed, slowly. "Yeah, so did I. I think."

I promptly set them straight. "Sorry, guys, you're out of luck on this one. Alison doesn't like *Slugs* and neither do these moms. In fact, Alison, it seems that your opinion is pretty good because these moms agree with you and they're willing to go to the library over it. Are there any other books that you feel strongly about? There wouldn't be any problem removing them from our class library. And we could probably get Mrs. Edgell to remove them from our school library. And—if enough kids and moms agree, we could probably have them removed from the city library."

The room was buzzing and the children were giving each other questioning looks, affirming, disagreeing. Traditional boy-girl polarization and friends' support that had surfaced before on many other issues didn't seem to be holding true on this issue. Alison's voice came over the confusion: "Well, I don't really like the Hardy Boys."

I interrupted her. "Alison, wait a minute. You're getting hot here. Let me go to the board and write these down." I began writing "Alison's Books to Go."

"Go ahead, Alison."

"Well, *Slugs* and Hardy Boys and Alvin Schwartz's books are gross."

Laura broke in. "Hey! *Scary Stories* are neat!"

Laura's speaking up gave Tyson the support he needed to regain his voice: "Yeah. I like *Scary Stories*, too."

More rumblings seemed to support Tyson than Alison, so I said, "Okay, maybe I was wrong. Maybe it's Tyson's list we should go by and not Alison's." I erased Alison's list and wrote "Tyson's Books to Go."

"Okay, Tyson," I said. "You decide which books should go and which books should stay. What do you like?"

Cassie had a puzzled look. "Ms. Hydrick," she asked, "Why should we go with Tyson's list?"

"Look, Cassie," I said. "You obviously don't understand. If a book bothers someone, we need to see that the book is removed from the library so that it won't bother anyone else. We just need to come up with a list and then we can start removing books. Do you agree with Alison's list or Tyson's list?"

Cassie was thoughtful and hesitated long enough for Mike to pop in, "Why do we have to take Alison's or Tyler's list?"

I turned to Mike. "We don't have to. We can take your list, Mike. I don't care whose list we take."

"Well," began Mike, "I really like *Sideways Stories from Wayside School.*" The whole class rallied behind this favorite of ours.

"I don't know," I said thoughtfully. "As long as we're talking about books bothering people, I'm afraid we're going to have to pull this one off the shelves. I've heard several teachers and parents complain about how silly it is. And Mrs. Gorf is definitely a witchy-type person. Yes, we should probably have it pulled."

"No!" said Stevie, very emphatically. "That's a great book."

"That's just your opinion, Stevie," I said. "I'm not sure we ought to have people bothered by books even though you like them."

"Well, they don't have to read it," said Mike. "Let 'em get something else to read."

"But if a book is going to bother someone, shouldn't we make sure that the book isn't there on the shelves?" I asked.

Holly, usually quiet during group discussions, spoke up. "No. Like Mike says, let 'em get something else." Others agreed with nods and single-word assents.

At that point, I read the entire newspaper article to the class. Their discussion of the issue continued, but the focus was no longer on which books they liked or disliked. They had discarded the notion of lists, and both lovers and haters of *Slugs* were concerned now with whether the book would be pulled off the Mesa City Library shelves.

Later that day, two *Slugs* haters, Ryan and Rachel, asked to write a review of the book for our class newspaper. Their review ended with this: "Some of us liked it, some of us didn't. *Slugs* is on any library shelf. If you want to read it you can and then you can decide if you like it or not."

That morning, the third graders didn't use the term "censorship," but for the rest of that school year, when intolerance or dominant opinion reared their heads, the children would remind each other of the "*Slugs* talk," and that would be the cue for the children to remember a notion they evolved from their reactions to *Slugs:* that people have different likes and dislikes, that people have different reactions to things, and that it's okay because we don't want to be stuck forever with Alison's list or Tyson's list or even Mike's list.

The literature study book bathers still have bathing suits drawn on them, there are still not *National Geographic* magazines in those third-grade classrooms, and *Witches* is no longer used as a read-aloud. Every year, across the grade levels, other books will not be shared or encouraged because of language or subject matter. Unpleasant or "sticky" current events will not be discussed. In time, when the potency of the "*Slugs* talk" fades from my third graders' memory, will Alison's passion to protect a book she dislikes give way to her zeal to assert Alison's list?

Obviously, there's no way of knowing whether the "*Slugs* talk" will follow these children throughout their lives. I'd like to believe, though, that in the future, when they're faced with an issue of censorship or intolerance, they'll remember Rachel and Ryan's words—"some of us liked it, some of us didn't"—and make a judgment based on intellectual inquiry, not thoughtless bias.

V Legal Implications of Limiting Intellectual Freedom

This volume concludes with three chapters that explore the legal implications of decisions that deal with issues of intellectual freedom. Lief Carter and Daniel Carroll present an insightful look at the application of constitutional law to issues in the schools. Their historical review of court cases provides a framework for understanding the legal implications for education. Mel Krutz, in the next chapter, examines, in depth, the implications of the *Hazelwood* decision. She examines other court decisions that have cited *Hazelwood* as they have established a separate definition of freedom for students and the schools. In the final chapter, Ken Holmes looks specifically at the provisions of the *Hazelwood* decision. He then offers helpful suggestions for teachers and advisors of student publications.

20 Mind-Control Applications of the Constitutional Law of Censorship in the Educational Environment

Lief H. Carter
University of Georgia

assisted by
Daniel Carroll

Introduction

It is simplest to define the Constitution of the United States as the law that governs the government. The First Amendment's prohibition on enforcing laws that abridge freedom of speech and press prohibits the federal government from punishing spoken and written communication. The due process clause of the Constitution's Fourteenth Amendment also prohibits state and local governments, including the public schools, from limiting expression. The government may punish speaking or publishing obscenities, on the theory that obscenity by definition has no communicative value. And government may restrict speaking and publishing non-obscene messages where speaking and writing raise a clear and present danger of an immediate disturbance. The government may arrest a person for disturbing the peace who insists on reading loudly from Shakespeare throughout a church service, and it may arrest someone who publishes secret plans for troop movements in time of war. Beyond that, it would seem that the Constitution protects our freedom to say and write what we wish.

Since the Constitution governs public school officials who supervise teachers and students, these officials and their policies, in turn, must obey the Constitution. Teachers and students would thus seem free to teach and learn what they wish as they wish, provided only that they obey the bureaucratic routines necessary for schools to function at all.

But schools are different. Limits on speaking and writing that courts would instantly strike down in the adult world survive in schools. Education promotes social cohesion and stability by transmitting the society's basic beliefs and values to its children. Not just any beliefs and values will do. Furthermore, the law puts children and their needs in a special category. These differences inevitably make public schools an arena in which rights and interests clash.

Rights clash in schools on several dimensions. First, teachers cannot possibly teach all the available material published in any one particular field. Choices must be made. The problem arises from the competition between the teachers' academic freedom and the students' right to learn, on one hand, and the choices that limited time and resources force us to make when devising any curriculum, on the other. Second, process values collide. We believe in popular democratic control of public education, but what if popular control violates the Constitution? Curricular choices should not erect a barrier against the infusion of new ideas, for education seeks to produce individuals who confidently think for themselves. As Amy Guttmann has stated:

> Even if the school board's intention is to lay the foundation of human decency and patriotism by banning books, it should not attempt to achieve this end by shielding students from understanding why some people use indecent language, hold radical political views, and break laws. Such understanding constitutes an important part of what it means to be an informed citizen.[1]

But must the courts, the least democratic and responsive of our political institutions, define what democracy requires?

The Supreme Court, through its involvement in academic freedom and censorship issues, has tried to define who makes curricular choices and how. Unfortunately, vague Supreme Court decisions regarding education have failed to resolve these problems. This essay surveys the significant court decisions from this century. Recent decisions, that is, decisions since the election of Ronald Reagan in 1980, have substantially eroded constitutional rights with regard to student and teacher freedom of expression, academic freedom generally, and textbook and library content. This essay concludes by suggesting a philosophical basis for resolving the clash of rights in a democracy more effectively.

Case Law on Free Expression in Education

In 1952 Justice William O. Douglas, dissenting in *Adler v. Board of Education*'s challenge to the Feinberg Law,[2] first introduced the concept of academic freedom in modern First Amendment law. Condemning this statute's "black list" encroachment on teachers's freedom of expression, Douglas stated that a "system of spying and surveillance . . . cannot go hand in hand with academic freedom."[3] Justice Frankfurter reiterated Douglas's thoughts later that year in a majority opinion in *Wieman v.*

Updegraff[4] overturning an Oklahoma law that barred employment to teachers who would not submit to a loyalty oath. In 1967, in *Keyishian v. Board of Regents*,[5] the Court declared the Feinberg Law unconstitutional. A bare majority spoke against imperiling academic freedom. Justice Brennan wrote, "Our Nation is deeply committed to safeguarding academic freedom, which is of transcendent value to all of us and not merely to the teachers concerned."[6]

This initial period in which the Court enhanced the academic freedom of teachers through the First Amendment has given way to a jurisprudence that balances First Amendment rights against other nonconstitutional values and interests. In recent years, the constitutional definition of academic freedom has shifted its emphasis from institutional neutrality to what is in practice nearly its opposite, institutional autonomy.[7]

The erosion of a teacher's freedom of speech came only a year and a half after *Keyishian*. In *Pickering v. Board of Education*[8] the board of education had dismissed a teacher for publishing a newspaper article criticizing the board's allocation of school funds between educational and athletic programs. The Court, rejecting Pickering's claims of protection by the First Amendment, based its decision on a balancing between "the interest of the teacher, as a citizen, in commenting upon matters of public concern and the interest of the state, as an employer, in promoting the efficiency of the public services it performs through its employees."[9]

The Court narrowed academic freedom of expression further when it applied the *Pickering* balance test[10] in *Connick v. Myers*.[11] This case, though it dealt with the dismissal of a female assistant district attorney in New Orleans, implicitly accepts as constitutional a highly restrictive atmosphere both inside and outside the classroom. Myers, after objecting to a job transfer, and after a colleague told her that others in the office did not share her objections to office policy, solicited the general views of her co-workers through a questionnaire. She was summarily dismissed after her superiors learned of her actions. The Supreme Court upheld this dismissal. It disregarded the reasoning of *Keyishian*, which stated that "when one must guess what conduct or utterances may lose him his position, one necessarily will steer far wider of the unlawful zone."[12] The impact of Myers and its progeny on academic freedom is a far cry from those sentiments expressed by Douglas and Frankfurter.

The case law surrounding the content of textbooks and the selection of books in school library holdings is similarly vague, and recent decisional trends are equally troubling. *Presidents Council, District 25 v. Community School Board No. 25 (New York City)*[13] first considered whether a school board had the authority to remove books from the shelves of a public school library in 1972. Citizens had requested removing from the school library a book containing allegedly offensive language and sexual depictions. The U.S. Court of Appeals for the Second Circuit upheld the school board's decision to revoke access to the books based on the declared responsibility of school boards to select books and prescribe the curriculum.

In contrast, *Minarcinni v. Strongville (Ohio) City School District*[14] ruled against a school board and upheld both the librarians' right to disseminate information and the students' right to receive it. The U.S. Court of Appeals for the Sixth Circuit rejected the absolute right of the school board from removing books based on any particular disfavor. The court also held that outside access to sources did not minimize the responsibility of the school board to provide access. In 1978 a trial court relied on this precedent in *Right to Read Defense Committee v. School Committee of the City of Chelsea*,[15] where it struck down the Chelsea (Massachusetts) School Committee's banning of a poetry anthology. The federal district court found that the committee's authority did not extend to banning works simply on the allegation that they were vulgar.

In 1980, in *Zykan v. Warsaw (Indiana) Community School Corporation and Warsaw School Board of Trustees*,[16] however, the focus of federal courts again began to shift from institutional neutrality to institutional autonomy. The issue was a school board curriculum review in which the board discontinued certain courses, removed some books from the curriculum, dismissed some teachers, and terminated publication of the high school newspaper. A student brought suit seeking to reverse the decision of the school board limiting the use of certain textbooks and library books and deleting courses from the curriculum. The U.S. Court of Appeals for the Seventh Circuit ruled that a school board has the right to establish a curriculum at its own discretion without imposing "orthodoxy" on the classroom. Further, the decision, although recognizing the right of students to file legal complaints regarding curriculum, held that claims must meet a relatively high threshold before being suitable for federal consideration.

The issues raised in *Mozert v. Hawkins County (Tennessee) Public School*[17] further confused educators. Here the school board had refused to remove three books in a junior high school reading series at some parents' request. The parents charged that the books taught beliefs that fell under the heading of secular humanism (although this was not the entire focus of the case). The U.S. Sixth Circuit of Appeals ruled against the parents, and thereby overturned the lower court ruling. While *Mozert* was progressing through the courts, a more egregious assault on textbooks occurred in *Smith v. School Commissioners of Mobile County, Alabama*.[18] Judge Brevard W. Hand had lobbied for and then adjudicated a suit to permit a moment of silence for prayer in Alabama public schools. The Supreme Court overturned Judge Hand's decision, so he devised another suit which alleged that forty-four textbooks promoted a religious belief in secular humanism, and therefore violated the religious liberties of children and their parents. The Eleventh U.S. Circuit Court of Appeals reversed Judge Hand's decision, but did not answer the question of whether secular humanism was a religion. Instead, it ruled more narrowly that the forty-four texts did not promote secular humanism.

Looking to broader Supreme Court rulings for a philosophy that would clarify the murky waters of censorship law has proved futile. The history of the constitutional rights of students within public schools actually began in the 1920s with *Meyer v. Nebraska*[19] and *Pierce v. Society of Sisters.*[20] These decisions upheld the liberty to engage in private education freely, but they did not develop a theory about public school student rights. Indeed, these cases approve strong parental control of student life. The Supreme Court has stated and endorsed the parental power of the state over minors most clearly in its obscenity rulings. In *Ginsberg v. New York,*[21] the Court recognized a compelling interest to safeguard children from obscenity "even where there is an invasion of protected freedoms," because "the power of the state to control the conduct of children reaches beyond the scope of its authority over adults." [22]

The Court has not, however, followed this standard consistently either. In 1969, in *Tinker v. Des Moines Independent Community School District,*[23] the Court nullified the suspension of high school students who mounted an anti-war protest by wearing black armbands to school. The Court stated that students "do not shed their constitutional rights to freedom of speech or expression at the schoolhouse gate."[24] The Court did allow discretion by the school administration to limit student speech, but only if officials could "show that its actions were caused by something more than a mere desire to avoid the discomfort and unpleasantness that always accompany an unpopular viewpoint."[25] Consistent with First Amendment cases generally, the Court placed the burden of proof on schools to show the necessity of limiting freedom.

The decision reached in *Pico v. Board of Education*[26] held that removing nine books from the library shelves by the school board violated the First Amendment rights of students. Yet the decision is not clear cut. The bare majority makes a broad distinction between the function of a curriculum in the classroom and books in the school library. The court focused on the motivation of school authorities for suppressing ideas and condemned this motivation. The protection afforded school libraries did not extend to curricular choices only indirectly affecting the academic freedom of teachers.

The Supreme Court further protected the autonomous discretion of school administrations in two recent cases. In *Bethel School District v. Fraser*,[27] the Court upheld a student's suspension for giving at an assembly a sexually suggestive speech questioning the potency of a candidate for school office. The Court ruled that the school board's discretion to select the student's manner of speech does not violate the First Amendment rights of students. The Court, by deeming the student's speech vulgar, also created a new standard for regulating student speech without subjecting the speech to the *Ginsberg* obscenity standard.

The Supreme Court held in *Hazelwood v. Kuhlmeier*[28] that a Missouri high school principal's action to censor a student newspaper did not abridge the First Amendment rights of students because the newspaper could not be characterized as a public forum.[29] The principal had deleted from the paper two full pages that analyzed the problems of teenage pregnancy and divorce because they were too mature for the audience and because readers might learn the identities of principles in the story, thereby invading their privacy improperly. The Court ruled that this form of censorship was acceptable because it was done in a reasonable manner. (Chapters 21 and 22 explore the *Hazelwood* decision and its implications.)

These decisions have left "the nation with an amorphous line of demarcation between free student speech and censorship."[30] The problem is highlighted when trying to utilize an operational definition of censorship based on Supreme Court decisions. *Tinker's* "substantial disruption" standard held that schools may not regulate student expression which neither disrupts classwork nor invades the rights of others.[31] Therefore, any more stringent censorship would violate the First Amendment. Yet, *Pico* shifted the burden of proof from the school, as set forth in *Tinker*, to the students to prove the unconstitutional motives of presumably professional and impartial school officials. *Pico* held that school administrators may regulate library content on any rational basis as long as their motives are without the intent of suppressing ideas or producing political orthodoxy.[32]

Despite its reliance on the *Tinker* precedent, the *Hazelwood* majority all but overturned the "substantial disruption" standard. The Supreme Court applied the constitutional rubber stamp known as the "rational basis" test.[33] This test hinges the concept of censorship on the fact that administrators' actions need only be "reasonably related to legitimate pedagogical concerns."[34] Given competition "between a liberal paradigm emphasizing the importance of student free speech and the need for judicial protection, and a communal paradigm stressing judicial deference to the community's concern for effective performance of the educational mission,"[35] it is easy to recognize that this latest decision squarely supports popular control of schools, not free expression.

Resolving the Clash of Rights

Thus far this essay has implied that a conservative Court has failed to read the Constitution properly. If so, it would follow that we could restore respect for constitutional values by aggressively educating voters and their leaders in the true civic value of liberty. Unfortunately, at least for libertarians, the Court has not gotten the Constitution wrong. The Constitution does little more than articulate the paradoxes of civic life. The democratic value of public control of government *is* just as much a part of the Constitution as the value of free expression. Both are good, and they can collide head on.

We conclude this essay by suggesting a way to resolve the clash of rights that gives us a real purchase on the censorship problem. We cannot, however, do so by demonstrating which right is "righter" in any legal way. Rather, we must recognize that rights are neither objective moral truths nor political absolutes. Rather, they are the rhetorical tools we use to debate who we are and why we claim to share a community, a common national life. Censorship is a practice that limits the access and exposure to ideas and concepts that help people describe themselves as democratic citizens. Censorship is not so much unconstitutional as it is incoherent. If public education is responsible for "inculcating fundamental values necessary to the maintenance of a democratic political system,"[36] those values must include a free dissemination of information that exposes individuals to various ideas.

A democracy that opposes the free flow of ideas is incoherent for the same reason anything is incoherent. Its parts don't fit together. It is untrue to itself, and it becomes untrustworthy. This claim does not depend on any proof that democracy is the correct form of government. The same coherence standard applies in reverse to the early Bolshevik state. In 1920 Lenin, in a speech in Moscow, attacked the free flow of ideas:

> Why should freedom of speech and freedom of press be allowed? Why should a government which is doing what it believes to be right allow opposition by lethal weapon? Ideas are more fatal than guns. Why should a man be allowed to buy a printing press and disseminate pernicious opinions calculated to embarrass the government?[37]

Lenin's ideas were just as coherent for his system as our notion of free expression is to ours. Hence we do not so much argue for the objective correctness of free information as we do for the ethical principle that we be true to ourselves.

Traditionally, censorship has been viewed as the activities of fundamental and conservative groups spouting Christian dogma for its justification. Recently though, an upsurge in the advocacy by feminist groups and minority groups for censorship calls for a reevaluation of this stereotype. In fact, it has been argued that feminist groups are among the most successful in altering textbook and library content.[38] But, regardless of the nobility of a particular purpose, limiting communicative freedom is counterproductive to the ideals of a democratic education.

It is quite acceptable to censure—to express moral outrage—at a particular aspect of a certain curriculum. But when censure is allowed to move freely into the realm of censorship in which the outrage succeeds in banning a book from library shelves or removing a class from a curriculum, then the openness of education is inhibited precisely because the censorship prevents us from debating what outrages us in the first place. It is more central to our self-identity to preserve our capacity to talk about who we are than it is to preserve any one right, but at minimum this requires us to protect talk. L. H. LaRue makes a helpful distinction in this regard:

> [W]e ought to be clear about the difference between asking people to do something and telling them that they have to do it. We are being dishonest with ourselves, and others, if we don't specify which one of these two very different enterprises we are engaged in.[39]

Defining liberal society as "one whose ideals can be fulfilled by persuasion rather than force, by reform rather than revolution, by the free and open encounters of present linguistic and other practices with suggestions for new practices,"[40] exalts freedom as its goal. In this context, censorship ultimately limits language—language that could be used to further intelligent discourse. By narrowing the scope of language, censorship inevitably deprives individuals of the opportunity to generate new visions and new ideas, instead slowing the tide of progress and resulting in a recurrence of tired debates. Discourse which relies on fear and coercion to prevent a free dissemination of information in any intellectual pursuit can only debilitate the transfer of ideas from one generation to the next. Limiting the freedom of expression and creativity of future generations leaves society to quibble over words, instead of describing new conceptions with a fresh language.

These new languages are learned in the classroom where:

> . . . the sparks that leap back and forth between teacher and student, connecting them in a relationship that has little to do with socialization but much to do with self creation, are the principle means by which

the institutions of a liberal society get changed. Unless some such relationships are formed, the students will never realize what democratic institutions are good for: namely, making possible the invention of new forms of human freedom, taking liberties never taken before.[41]

Applying this theory of learning in accordance with an educational mission that strives to inculcate fundamental values establishes teachers as role models of good democratic skills. Students are consequently encouraged to become proficient communicators by internalizing role models. Contrasting theories promote information acquisition and storage based on value neutral ideas or those values that have survived the censors ever watchful eyes. If "students [are] regarded as closed-circuit recipients of only that which the state chooses to communicate,"[42] inculcation crosses over into the area of indoctrination.

The current of thought mentioned in Lenin's speech runs contrary to the First Amendment values under which a student's freedom of expression, textbook content and library choices, and academic freedom are all protected. As Ronald Dworkin (1978) says:

> [T]hose constitutional rights that we call fundamental like the right of free speech, are supposed to represent rights against the Government in the strong sense; that is the point of the boast that our legal system respects the fundamental rights of the Citizen.[43]

It is the clash of rights that presents us with the censorship problem. Once it is realized that the "Enlightenment merely transferred the office of Censor from a civic to a private trust,"[44] the competition between openness and participation is more easily understood. But, it must be further understood that openness "trumps" participation when these two rights compete in the realm of censorship.[45] Openness, through which diverse ideas can be expressed both within the classroom and on the shelves of school libraries, creates unfettered discourse without which participation would only reflect those ideas that were deemed acceptable by the censorial vanguards. Openness ultimately reinforces the diversity and plurality on which we model our perhaps peculiar civic life.

Notes

1. Amy Guttmann. 1987. *Democratic Education*. Princeton, N.J.: Princeton University Press, 97–98.

2. N.Y. EDUC. LAW 3022 (McKinney 1981), a New York state statute that made ineligible for employment in the public schools any member of any organization declared by the board of regents to advocate the overthrow of the government by illegal means.

3. 342 U.S. 485, 510-11 (1952).

4. 344 U.S. 183 (1952).

5. 385 U.S. 589 (1967).

6. Id. at 603.

7. Walter P. Metzger. 1988. "Profession and Constitution: Two Definitions of Academic Freedom in America." *Texas Law Review* 66 (June): 1265–322. 8. 391 U.S. 563 (1968).

8. 391 U.S. 563 (1968).

9. Id. at 568.

10. The Pickering balance test. Six factors: (1) the necessity of harmony in the workplace; (2) whether the government's responsibilities require a close working relationship to exist between the plaintiff and co-worker when the speech in question has caused or could cause the relationship to deteriorate; (3) the time, manner, and content of the speech; (4) the context in which the dispute arose; (5) the degree of public interest in the speech; and (6) whether the speech impeded the employee's ability to perform his or her duties. 461 U.S. 138, 151,2 (1983).

11. 461 U. S. 138 (1983).

12. 385 U.S. 589, 604 (1967).

13. 457 F.2d 289, (2d. Cir. 1972), 409 U.S. 988 (1972).

14. 541 F.2d 577 (6th. Cir. 1976)

15. 454 F.Supp. 703 (D. Mass. 1978).

16. 631 F.2d 1300 (7th Cir. 1980).

17. F.2d (6th Cir. 1986).

18. 655 F. Supp. 939 (S.D. Ala. 1987), 827 F. 2d 684 (11th Cir. 1987).

19. 262 U.S. 390 (1923). The Court invalidated a Nebraska statute prohibiting the teaching of German to students below the eighth grade because the law did not promote the production of civic-minded children.

20. 286 U.S. 510 (1925). An Oregon law requiring children to attend public school between the ages of eight and sixteen was held unconstitutional because the government's interest in child development was not served by an abolition of private schools.

21. 390 U.S. 629 (1968).

22. Id. at 638. See also *Miller v. California* 413 U.S. 15 (1973). A three-part test for identifying obscene material based on an expanded definition contained in *Roth v. U.S.* 354 476 (1957). *FCC v. Pacifier* 438 U.S. 726 (1978). A two-tiered strict scrutiny test established for state legislation.

23. *Tinker v. Des Moines Independent Community School District.* 393 U.S. 503 (1969).

24. Ibid.

25. Id. at 513–14.

26. 457 U.S. 853 (1982).

27. 478 U.S. 675 (1986).

28. 108 S. Ct. 562 (1988).

29. The public forum doctrine is used to determine when the government's interests in restricting its property to its intended purpose is greater than the

interest of the speaker seeking to exercise her right to freedom of speech. See e.g., *Cornelius v. NAACP Legal Defense & Education Fund* 473 U.S. 788 (1985), *Perry Education Association v. Perry Local Educators' Association* 460 U.S. 37 (1983).

30. Deborah Jane Clarke. 1989. "Constitutional Law: First Amendment Rights: Good-bye to Free Student Press?" *Oklahoma Law Review* 42 (Spring): 101.

31. 393 U.S. 503, 513–14 (1969).

32. 457 U.S. 853, 871 (1982).

33. See e.g., *McCulloch v. Maryland* 17 U.S. 316 (1819) in which Chief Justice Marshall wrote: "Let the end be legitimate, let it be within the scope of the Constitution, and all means which are appropriate, which are plainly adapted to that end, which are not prohibited, but consist with the letter and spirit of the Constitution, are constitutional." Id. at 421.

34. 108 S. Ct. 562, 571 (1988).

35. C. Thomas Dienes and Annemagaret Connolly. 1989. "When Students Speak: Judicial Review in the Academic Marketplace," *Yale Law & Policy Review* 7: 356.

36. *Ambach v. Norwick* 441 U.S. 68, 77 (1979).

37. Quoted from Sue Curry Jansen. 1988. *Censorship: The Knot That Binds Power and Knowledge.* Oxford, UK: Oxford University Press, 189.

38. See e.g., Robert Lerner and Stanley Rothman. 1990. "Newspeak, Feminist-Style," *Commentary* 89 (April): 54–56.

39. L. H. LaRue. 1988. *Political Discourse: A Case Study of the Watergate Affair.* Athens, GA: University of Georgia Press, 70.

40. Richard Rorty. 1989. *Contingency, Irony and Solidarity.* Cambridge, MA: Cambridge University Press, 60.

41. Richard Rorty. 1989. "Education without Dogma: Truth, Freedom and Our Universities," *Dissent* (Spring): 204.

42. *Keyishian v. Board of Regents* 385 U.S. 589, 603 (1967).

43. Ronald Dworkin. 1978. *Taking Rights Seriously.* Cambridge, MA: Harvard University Press.

44. Sue Curry Jansen. 1988. *Censorship: The Knot That Binds Power and Knowledge.* Oxford, UK: Oxford University Press.

45. Dworkin defines individual rights as "political trumps," xi.

21 *Hazelwood:* Results and Realities

Mel Krutz
Central Community College
Columbus, Nebraska

In 1677 William Berkeley, the Colonial Governor of Virginia, expressed an attitude which underlies a basic issue inherent in the *Hazelwood* decision. He said, "Thank God that there are no freeschools nor printing in this land, for learning has brought disobedience and heresy into this world, and printing hath divulged them" (Mitchell 1988, 12).

The Supreme Court has struggled to maintain a balance between First Amendment rights and indoctrination, a tipping of which could make the difference between students who search or who are manipulated. Theodore R. Mitchell, of Dartmouth, states:

> Intolerance of student expression is at odds with one of the central missions of every school: to teach democratic values, principles and actions. Ideals and practice cannot be divorced. A school preaching democracy while practicing tyranny is one in which hypocrisy and duplicity become de facto parts of the curriculum. Schools which fail to protect the constitutional rights of individuals (according to John Dewey) "strangle the free mind at its source and teach, youth to discount important principles of our government as mere platitudes." (Mitchell 1988, 12)

Mitchell's attitude was also the clear attitude under educational practice and the courts through the *Tinker* decision of 1969 until January 18, 1988—until *Hazelwood,* which "rests more on fear of disobedience and disorder than on . . . hope for liberty and democracy . . . to our peril as a republic" (Mitchell 1988, 12).

Educational psychologist David Moshman (see chapter 3, this volume), author of *Children, Education, and the First Amendment* (1989), says, "The *Hazelwood* decision seriously tips the delicate balance between liberty and learning in the public schools" (Moshman 1988, 3).

Before *Hazelwood* the sequence of cases determining students' rights leaned toward the support of the First Amendment to assure those rights, but *Hazelwood* made other distinctions. The following prior cases illustrate the difference.

Meyer v. Nebraska 262 U.S. 390, 43 S Ct. 625, 67 L. Ed. 2d 1042 (1923) clearly held that students, teachers, and parents have constitutional liberties that cannot be interfered with.

West Virginia State Board of Education v. Barnette 319 U.S. 624, 63 S. Ct. 1178, 87 L.Ed. 1828 (1943) struck down a West Virginia law requiring public school students to salute the flag and pledge allegiance, stating that the government may "present ideas to convince by persuasion and example, but it may not require belief" (1189).

Burnside v. Byers 363 F. 2d 744 (5th Cir.) (1966) stated that objection to the wearing of symbols such as armbands cannot be sustained unless it materially and substantially interferes with the requirements of appropriate discipline in the operation of the school.

The landmark decision of a 1965 event, *Tinker v. Des Moines Independent Community School District* 393. U.S. 503, 89 S. Ct. 733, 21 L.Ed. 731 (1969), established that children are legally persons with constitutional First Amendment rights which hold in public schools as well as anywhere, establishing that "school officials do not possess absolute authority over their students (739). . . . Students in and out of school are 'persons' under the constitution . . . [with] fundamental rights which the state must respect (734) . . . and may not be confined to the expression of those sentiments that are officially approved" (739). School officials could limit free expression only if it would cause "material and substantial" (740) disruption of school activities or an invasion of the rights of others. Simply disagreeing with the views of the school does not constitute disruption of other students or of education. Thus *Tinker* recognized that a student's right under the First Amendment does not stop at the school door. This acknowledgment of students as complete citizens under the First Amendment, unfortunately, was undermined by the *Fraser* decision of l966.

Bethel School District v. Fraser 478 U.S. 675, 106 S. Ct. 3159, 92 L.Ed. 2d 549 (1986), the Supreme Court ruling on a 1983 event, decided seven to two in favor of the school, citing "obscene, vulgar, lewd, and offensively lewd remarks" (3166) and "exceeding permissible limits" (3167) as rationale, allowing administrators broad discretion. Thus the scope of *Tinker* was limited by the *Fraser* decision. An impact was felt. Although *Tinker* was not overturned, the extent of that limitation would soon be tested in the courts.

Hazelwood School District v. Kuhlmeier 484 U.S. 260, 108 S. Ct. 562, 98 L.Ed. 2d 592 (1988), also a ruling on a 1983 event, was that test case. This January 13, 1988, decision entrenched the attitude presented by *Fraser*. The Supreme Court ruled for the administration, presenting, in effect, major variations from past decisions (562).

The following four aspects of *Hazelwood* have been selected for focus because of their frequency of use as precedent in decisions of subsequent cases from January 1988 to November 1990. Examples of their impact indicate the reach and power shift that *Hazelwood* has brought about. These four aspects are

1. That the rights of high school students in school settings can differ from those of adults in other settings (*"Hazelwood* Guide," 1988, 563, 564).
2. Determination of when a school event is or is not a public forum (562, 564, 567, 568, 569).
3. That schools can censor if that censoring relates to "legitimate pedagogical concerns" (563, 565).
4. That "the education of the nation's youth is primarily the responsibility of parents, teachers, and state and local officials and not of federal judges" (571).

The first of these—that the rights of high school students in school settings can differ from those of adults in other settings—was used to establish precedent in at least three later cases.

City of Milwaukee v. K. F. 145, Wis. 2d 24, 426 N. W. 2d 329 (1988), in which "youths were found guilty of violating a curfew ordinance" (329). The Supreme Court held in favor of the administration, citing *Hazelwood* to affirm that "while juveniles possess fundamental rights, they are not automatically coexistent with the rights of adults" (338).

Poling v. Murphy 872 F.2d 757 (6th Cir.) (1989), in which a student was disqualified as a candidate for student council president for making "discourteous and rude remarks" about the assistant principal during a speech at a school-sponsored assembly (757). The circuit court cited *Hazelwood,* saying that "educators do not offend the First Amendment by exercising editorial control over the style and content of student speech in school-sponsored expressive activities that are reasonably related to legitimate pedagogical concerns" (758). "Limitations on speech that would be unconstitutional outside the schoolhouse are not necessarily unconstitutional within it" (762).

Alabama Student Party v. Student Government Association 867 F.2d 1344 (11th Cir.) (1989). The Student Party of the University of Alabama objected to "restriction of distribution of campus literature three days prior to election day and on election day and limitation of open forums and debates" (1344). *Hazelwood* was cited as a rationale for recognizing that "the First Amendment rights of students in the public school are not automatically coextensive with the rights of adults in other settings" (1346). The students lost.

Because of each of these citations from *Hazelwood*, student rights were negated. This was clearly not the attitude under *Tinker*.

A second aspect of the *Hazelwood* decision concerned determination of when a school event is or is not a public forum. School facilities may be deemed to be public forums, *Hazelwood* said, only if school authorities have by policy or by practice opened the facilities for indiscriminate use by the general public, or by some segment of the public, such as student organizations. As long as they are not public forums, the administration has the possibility of complete control. This determination was applied to the following cases.

Burch v. Barker 651 F. Supp. 1149 (W.D. Wash. 1987), Rev'd., 861 F.2d 1149 (9th cir.) (1988). A suit challenged the Renton, Washington, School District policy which required submission and approval of any material to be distributed at the high school, including that which was non-official, and therefore in the public forum. The Ninth Circuit Court of Appeals reversed a district court decision. The appeals court found the school policy "overly broad" (1149). *Hazelwood* was cited to affirm that the case involved material over which the school held no sponsorship and therefore regulation of it violated the First Amendment (1159). The students were supported.

Stewart v. District of Columbia Armory Board 863 F.2d 1013 (D.C. Cir.) (1988). There were objections to religious banners being removed from a football stadium display. The stadium, owned by the District of Columbia Armory Board, was ruled to be a public forum by the circuit court, as opposed to *Hazelwood*'s newspaper being a nonpublic forum. The case was sent back to district court to be reconsidered. The students were supported (1013, 1017, 1021).

Garnett v. Renton School District No. 403, 865 F.2d 1121 (9th Cir. 1989). Renton, Washington, school students brought action when the public school refused to permit their religious meeting on school property. The court held that refusal to allow a student religious group to meet did not violate the First Amendment and that "the public school did not have 'limited open forum'" (1126), and therefore was not required to allow student religious groups to hold meetings. Citing *Hazelwood* to define schools as nonpublic forums, the court held in favor of the authorities of the school, stating that First Amendment rights were not violated (1126).

Chicago Tribune Company v. City of Chicago 705 F. Supp. 1345 (N. D. ill.) (1989). The Tribune sought "to prevent the city airline from relocating newsboxes in the passenger concourse area at the airport" (1345).

Hazelwood was cited to establish whether 'the airline concourses are public or non-public forums." If non-public, the City of Chicago's view could be upheld, since *Hazelwood* gives authority to administrations unless a forum is public. The concourse was recognized as public. The newspaper publishers were supported.

Student Government Association v. Board of Trustees of the University of Massachusetts 676 F.Supp. 384 (D.Mass. 1987), aff'd. 868 F. 2d 473 (1st Cir.) (1988). Students challenged the "termination of legal services" (473) by the university, citing *Hazelwood* to point out that the contrast between the two cases related to the existence of public forum, stating that analysis of public forum was inapplicable to this issue. The court supported the university (473, 480).

Searcey v. Crim 681 F. Supp. 821 (N.D. Ga.) (1988). "Peace Activists" were denied the opportunity to participate in career day at a Georgia public high school, when they wanted to hand out material and discuss the "merits of military service" (821). Although their participation was upheld, *Hazelwood* was cited as legal precedent that the school facility became public forum when deemed so by policy or practice, and "that educators are entitled to exercise greater control over 'curricular' programs to assure (that) . . . listeners are not exposed to material inappropriate for their level of maturity" (827, 828). Other arguments gave the plaintiffs access to the career event, but administrative authority was noted in spite of the outcome (830).

Planned Parenthood of Southern Nevada, Inc. v. Clark County School District 887 F.2d 935 (9th Cir.) (1989). The school district rejected Planned Parenthood's advertisements in school student publications (the high school newspapers, yearbooks, and athletic event programs). The court upheld this rejection, identifying the publications as "non-public fora" (939).

Kirkland v. Northside Independent School 890 F.2d 794 (5th Cir.) (1989). The Fifth Circuit Court of Appeals, reversing a district court opinion, held in favor of the school when a teacher claimed that his contract was not renewed as "an attempt to censor the contents of [his] supplemental reading list for the world history class" (794). *Hazelwood* was cited both to define the school setting as a nonpublic forum, and therefore under the jurisdiction of the administration, and to affirm that "school officials may impose reasonable restrictions on the speech of teachers and other members of the school community" (801).

Board of Education of the Westside Community School v. Bridget C. Mergens 110 S.Ct 2356 (1990). The Supreme Court, in a reverse decision from that of the Washington Circuit Court in the case of *Garnett v. Renton School District*, No. 403 above, upheld students' right to equal access to school "premises during non-instructional times" (2356). In this case the Court focused its argument primarily on the Equal Access Act and on questions of school curriculum inclusion. When it referenced *Hazelwood*, it did so to seek its definition of noncurriculum (2365, 2379) and to support school authority (2365). The questions of curriculum border the question of determination of public forum. Curriculum-included activities are designated by *Hazelwood* to be under administrative determination, and not in the public forum.

Gregoire v. Centennial School District 907 F.2d 1366 (3rd Cir.) (1990). Campus Crusade for Christ "brought action seeking access" (1366) to use of the school auditorium. The court allowed access, but denied "religious worship or distribution of literature. Both parties appealed" (1367). The court of appeals found in favor of the religious organization, using *Hazelwood* as used in the *Mergens* case above (1374, 1375, 1380). However, the dissenting opinion cited *Hazelwood* directly, as precedent that "the decisions of school administrators in these matters must be accorded deference" (1939).

United States v. Kokinda 110 S. Ct. 3115 (1990). A "political advocacy group" solicited contributions and sold materials "on a sidewalk near the entrance to a U.S. Post Office" (3116). The Fourth Circuit Court of Appeals reversed the Maryland district court and held in favor of the group, citing *Hazelwood* among its list of cases which define public forum (3127).

In this section concerning the citing of schools as nonpublic forums, referencing *Hazelwood*, four cases held in favor of the administration, seven held in favor of students' or others' rights, but of these, three also made noted reference to cognizance of administrative authority.

A third application of the *Hazelwood* decision as precedent was to allow schools to censor, if that censoring related to "legitimate pedagogical concerns," i.e., if the school presented educational justification "or if the material or action [could] be perceived to bear the imprimatur [i.e., sanction] of the school" (563, 565). A question that needs to be asked is, who decides what constitutes "educational justification"?

Citing this standard, in the following cases, the courts consistently favored the administration, even in the last, where, though it ruled in favor of the plaintiff, it reaffirmed its supportive position.

Virgil v. School Board of Columbia County, Florida 677 F. Supp. 1547 (1988); aff'd 862 F.2d 1517 (11th Cir.) (1989). Parents of a student objected to a text anthology, *The Humanities: Cultural Roots and Continuities, Vol. 1*, because it included adaptations of Aristophanes's "Lysistrata," and Chaucer's "The Miller's Tale," which these parents found to contain "explicit sexuality and excessively vulgar language" (1518). The text had been approved by the Florida Department of Education. The superintendent recommended that the text be discontinued. The district court upheld his decision, as did the circuit court, which cited *Hazelwood* saying that "the decision was reasonably related to legitimate pedagogical concerns" (1520).

Crosby by Crosby v. Holsinger 852 F.2d 801 (1988). Students objected to the Fairfax, Virginia, High School "principal banning the school's 'Johnnie Reb' symbol," which the principal felt justified in doing after reviewing complaints from some students and parents (801). *Hazelwood* was cited to support that "school officials need not sponsor or promote all student speech, (particularly) anything the public might perceive to bear the imprimatur of the school," and further that "there is a difference between tolerating student speech and affirmatively promoting it" (802). The district court found in favor of the principal. The court of appeals affirmed this finding (801, 803).

Wise v. Pea Ridge School District 855 F.2d 560. 566 (8th Cir.) (1988). Students brought action against the school district alleging that disciplinary actions denied them due process rights. "The court held their rights were not violated (by 'two licks on the buttocks with wooden paddle')" (561). *Hazelwood* was cited in support of "maintaining order in the schools" (586) and therefore in support of administrative authority.

Torres v. Wisconsin Department of Health and Social Services 859 F.2d 1523 (7th Cir.) (1988). In a sex discrimination suit, male correctional officers protested the hiring of only female guards at a women's maximum security prison. The dissenting opinion cited *Hazelwood* to support that "special demands placed on public school administrators, like the demands placed on prison administrators, necessitate special leeway" (1534), and "that prison officials were asked to meet an unrealistic and unfair burden when required to produce evidence (to support) only female correctional officers" (1523). Administrative considerations were again primary.

Searcey v. Harris 888 F.2d 1314 (11th Cir.) (1989), a successive suit to *Searcey v. Crim*, of 1988, cited in the previous section. Searcey (the Atlanta Peace Alliance) in further pursuit of access to participation in the public schools' "Career Days," sought freedom to present information on the disadvantages of careers (namely military), without restrictions by the board of education. *Hazelwood* was cited to reaffirm the power of "school officials to regulate speech . . . where such regulation would not be upheld in a nonschool setting" (1319), and to reassert that "the education of the nation's youth is primarily the responsibility of parents, teachers, and state and local school officials, and not of federal judges," who "must defer to reasonable educational decisions made by educators" (1319).

Thus emphasis was again placed on the authority of the school, but the case was decided in favor of the plaintiffs' freedom of speech. The court found "no valid educational purpose as to require judicial intervention" (1319–20).

And finally, *Hazelwood* established that "the education of the nation's youth is primarily the responsibility of parents, teachers, and state and local officials and not of federal judges" (571). In most of the cases citing this facet of *Hazelwood*, the court held in favor of the administration, using that exact quote.

Schaill by Kross v. Tippecanoe County School Corporation 679 F. Supp. 833 (N.D. Ind. 1988). Student athletes in the Tippecanoe, Indiana, school objected to having to submit to random urinalysis for drug testing for eligibility for sports. Their motion was denied. *Hazelwood* was cited to support the authority of school administrators. The court stated the law was "clear [that] the court's role is not to set aside decisions of school administrations *even where the school's position might be viewed as lacking in wisdom or compassion*" (855; emphasis added).

Palmer v. Merluzzi 689 F. Supp. 400 (D.N.J. 1988), aff'd 868 F.2d 90 (3rd Cir.) (1988). A "high school student brought action against school officials after being suspended for smoking marijuana and drinking beer on school property" (400). The student lost. *Hazelwood* was cited to affirm that "the education of the nation's youth is primarily the responsibility of parents, teachers, and state and local school officials and not of federal judges" (414).

Lewis v. Sobol 710 F. Supp. 506 (S. D. N. Y. 1988). Parents withheld immunization from their daughter on religious grounds. The Yonkers School District Commissioner of Education held that the parents' religious beliefs were not sincere. The court held that the beliefs were sincere (506). The parents' stand was upheld citing *Hazelwood*, which stated that the "education of the nation's youth is . . . [etc., as above]" (512).

Thus between January 1988 and November 1990, when citing *Hazelwood* as precedent, the courts obviously favored school authority in the vast majority of cases. The effect is a potentially devastating blow for scholastic journalism and all school programs, for *Hazelwood* exerts comprehensive and unlimited reach to all "school-sponsored non-forum student activity that involves student expression" ("*Hazelwood* Guide," 1988, 38). Are there any areas where student response, communication, or expression does not or should not exist in education?

Already in 1974, administrative control was found to be the "fundamental cause for triviality, innocuousness and uniformity that characterizes the high school press" (Nelson 1974, 48), according to *Captive Voices*, the report of high school journalism, which cites "a free vigorous student press" as necessary to "a healthy ferment of ideas and opinions, with no indication of disruption or negative side effects on the educational experience of the school" (49).

The unfortunate effects of *Hazelwood* include the limitation of topics, even making some taboo—a limiting of comprehensiveness; a cause for content to become abstract and less meaningful to students' reality— "bland" (111) safe exercises in the routine (i.e., unrealistic journalistic situations; "not encouraging free expression, independent inquiry, or investigation of important ideas") (111); not proposing to completely teach, therefore influencing failure to achieve the ultimate purpose of a good curriculum to provide a professional learning experience. Fortunately, the scope of *Hazelwood* is not unlimited and can be challenged ("*Hazelwood* Guide," 1988). For example:

1. It does not deny the possibility for other protection, such as under state constitutions, statutory laws, individual school board or other regulations which might deny censorship to school officials (38).

2. *Hazelwood* does not strip high school students of all First Amendment rights. It does not apply to student publications that are considered public forums, i.e., alternate, unofficial or underground student publications, even when these are school-sponsored. The Hazelwood school did not recognize its publication so much a forum as it did a class. It was the *first* student paper found "*not* to be a forum for student expression" [36; emphasis added]. When publications are designated as a forum, *Tinker* standards apply, and when censorship is found to "serve no educational purpose," the court hopefully will protect student rights (37).

3. *Hazelwood* does not mandate that school administrations and school boards must assume broader power. Levelheaded administrators have done nothing differently because of *Hazelwood*. They have elected to continue to operate their schools as forums for exploring all facets of ideas, consciously choosing to keep them as places to test and try, experience and live democracy.

Though the power of the *Hazelwood* decision will continue to be tested in the courts, the evidence is clear that the attitude of the present court is to favor administrative control. In spite of this, there are things that teachers need do and need not do:

1. Not be self-censoring, pulling topics felt to be controversial. If others want to censor, let that be their decision, not that of a teacher or a journalism sponsor.

2. Not try to guess what might be offensive to someone. Anything can be offensive to someone. This leads to watered-down *journalism*.

3. Do urge schools to adopt a protection policy for school publications.

4. If censored, appeal. Ask for specific objections in writing. If the problem is a mechanical, syntactical, or factual inadequacy, improve these. If it concerns choice of topic, professionally and calmly discuss the journalistic rationale with the objector. An administrator can only censor if the school board permits. Appeal to the board, or the superintendent, but don't give up too soon.

5. Use public pressure to your advantage. Get parents, community, librarians, the press, other media, fellow faculty, and students to petition or take other public action, including debate. Probably no school wants to be labeled as censoring.

6. Support and reward administrators and others who are committed to upholding and defending freedom of speech in the schools. Establish an award to honor them.

7. Seek assistance from organized groups such as the State and National Councils of Teachers of English, the Student Law Center, the State and National High School Press Associations, the State and National Library Association, the State and National Coalitions Against Censorship, etc.

8. Use alternative publications not affected by *Hazelwood*, public forums that are open whether school-sponsored or underground.

9. Push for state legislation to protect student First Amendment rights, as Iowa, Massachusetts, Colorado, California, and other states have already done (Items 1, 4, 5, 7, 8, 9, "What to Do," 1988, 39–40).

The tension is real between order and control in education and students' open and free expression in the schools. It is a tension a democratic society accepts. It is a tension recognized as necessary prior to the *Hazelwood* decision of January 13, 1988, which has changed the climate since the *Tinker* decision of 1969. *Hazelwood*'s results have been visible and strong, leaning toward broad and unrestrained administrative power. The extent of the power of the *Hazelwood* decision can lead America back to the prerevolutionary attitudes of William Berkeley's autocratic society. Students, parents, teachers, administrators, local and state governments can and must counteract its potential indiscretion, for ironically but realistically, the restriction of democracy for any affects us all.

Works Cited

Alabama Student Party v. Student Government Association. 1989. 867 F.2d 1344 (11th Cir.).

Bethel School District v. Fraser. 1986. 478 U.S. 675, 106 S. Ct. 3159, 92 L.Ed.2d 549.

Board of Education of the Westside Community School v. Bridget C. Mergens. 1990. 110 S.Ct 2356.

Burch v. Barker. 1987. 651 F. Supp. 1149 (W.D. Wash. 1987). Rev'd. 1988. 861 F2d 1149 (9th Cir.).

Burnside v. Byers. 1966. 363 F. 2d 744 (5th Cir.).

Chicago Tribune Company v. City of Chicago. 1989. 705 F. Supp. 1345 (N. D., ILL.).

City of Milwaukee v. K. F. 1988. 145, Wis. 2d 24, 426 N. W. 2d 329.

Crosby by Crosby v. Holsinger. 1988. 852 F. 2d 801.

Garnett v. Renton School District. 1989. No. 403, 865 F.2d 1121 (9th Cir.).

Gregoire v. Centennial School District. 1990. 907 F. 2d 1366 (3rd Cir.).

"*Hazelwood:* A Complete Guide to the Supreme Court Decision." 1988. *Student Press Law Center Report.* Washington, D.C.: Student Press Law Center. Spring.

Hazelwood School District v. Kuhlmeier. 1988. 484 U.S. 260, 108 S. Ct. 562, 98 L.Ed.2d 592.

Kirkland v. Northside Independent School. 1989. 890 F.2d 794 (5th Cir.).

Lewis v. Sobol. 1988. 710 F. Supp. 506 (S. D. N. Y.).

Meyer v. Nebraska. 1923. 262 U.S. 390, 43 S Ct. 625, 67 L. Ed. 2d 1042.

Mitchell, Theodore R. 1988. "The High Court and *Hazelwood:* Chipping Away at Rights." *Christian Science Monitor* (25 January): 12.

Moshman, David. 1988. "Liberty and Learning in the Public Schools." *About "Hazelwood": Documents for Further Information,* 1–3. Academic Freedom Coalition of Nebraska. 17 September.

———. 1989. *Children, Education, and the First Amendment.* Lincoln: University of Nebraska Press.

Nelson, J. ed. 1974. *Captive Voices: The Report of the Committee Inquiring into High School Journalism.* New York: Schocken.

Palmer v. Merluzzi. 1988. 689 F. Supp. 400 (D.N.J.). Aff'd. 1988. 868 F.2d 90 (3rd Cir.).

Planned Parenthood of Southern Nevada, Inc. v. Clark County School District. 1989. 887 F.2d 935 (9th Cir.).

Poling v. Murphy. 1989. 872 F.2d 757 (6th Cir.).

Schaill by Kross v. Tippecanoe County School Corporation. 1988. 679 F. Supp. 833 (N.D. Ind.).

Searcey v. Crim. 1988. 681 F. Supp. 821 (N.D. Ga.).

Searcey v. Harris. 1989. 888 F.2d 1314 (11th Cir.).

Stewart v. District of Columbia Armory Board. 1988. 863 F2d 1013 (D.C. Cir.).

Student Government Association v. Board of Trustees of the University of Massachusetts. 1987. 676 F.Supp. 384 (D.Mass.). Aff'd. 1988. 868 F. 2d 473 (1st Cir.).

Tinker v. Des Moines Independent Community School District. 1969. 393. U.S. 503, 89

S. Ct. 733, 21 L.Ed. 731.

Torres v. Wisconsin Department of Health and Social Services. 1988. 859 F.2d 1523 (7th Cir.).

United States v. Kokinda. 1990. 110 S. Ct. 3115.

Virgil v. School Board of Columbia County, Florida. 1988. 677 F. Supp. 1547. Aff'd. 1989. 862 F.2d 1517 (11th Cir.).

West National Reporter System. St. Paul, MN: West Publishing Company. [All case information is taken from this source.]

West Virginia State Board of Education v. Barnette. 1943. 319 U. S. 624, 63 S. Ct. 1178, 87 L. Ed. 1828.

"What to Do if It Happens to You." 1988 (Spring). *Fighting Censorship after "Hazelwood."* Student Press Law Center Report. Washington, D. C.: Student Press Law Center.

Wise v. Pea Ridge School District. 1988. 855 F. 2d 560. 566 (8th Cir.).

22 The *Hazelwood* Decision: Thought Control in the High School? Or from *Tinker* to *Hazelwood*, to Chance?

Ken Holmes
Lincoln Senior High School
East St. Louis, Illinois

Prior to the *Hazelwood* decision, the U.S. Supreme Court had said that public school students didn't give up their constitutional rights upon entering the school building's doors. This landmark decision was handed down in the 1969 *Tinker v. Des Moines Independent School District* and, from the time of its writing until the *Hazelwood* decision, had been used as a guide for what was considered to be allowable speech on the part of high school students. The *Tinker* case was brought about by students who were forbidden to wear black armbands in peaceful protest of the war in Vietnam. The Supreme Court, in this case, decided that the First Amendment supports the rights of students to communicate with each other and that the school may intercede in that communication only in some narrowly defined instances.

In the intervening nineteen years between the *Tinker* and the *Hazelwood* decisions, some local circuit courts gave broad interpretation to the issue of school censorship, but there were still some wide variances. With the Hazelwood incident, the ACLU saw a chance to make a standardization for the whole country. Some states had a prior review stance wherein material could be censored before printing. Such was the case in Missouri, where the Hazelwood incident took place; hence the ACLU's belief that a case could be made for the whole country.

Justice Byron White (1988), speaking for the courts, ruled that "educators may exert editorial control in instances so long as their actions are reasonably related to legitimate pedagogical concerns. . . . A school need not tolerate student speech that is inconsistent with its 'basic educational mission.' . . . School officials may impose reasonable restrictions on the speech of students, teachers, and other members of the school community" (263).

Speaking as one of the dissenters, Justice William Brennan (1988) called the *Hazelwood* decision a "license for thought control in the high schools" (268). Glen Gray (1989), then president of the Colorado Language Arts Society, feared that "high schools will have even less to do with the real world, furthering themselves and their students into dominions governed by administrators" (6). Gray's prophesy is echoed in the concerns of Peggy Jackson (1989), a honors and journalism teacher at Morgan Park High School in Chicago. She decries that often students can't write about the world they live in. She fears that administrative censorship strikes out the very ideas that students should grapple with, especially in print (7). John Bowen (1988), an adviser to the suburban Cleveland *Times* and the chair of the Journalistic Education Association Scholastic Rights Commissions, wrote at the time of the decision that "[I]t was a terrible limiting, overreacting, outlandish decision. It was overkill. It opened the door to highly non-educational and non-realistic censorship" (n.p.).

There are those, however, who would agree with John Rignell, the past chair of the Media Instruction Department at Southern Illinois University. Professor Rignell (1990) believes that some of the response to the *Hazelwood* decision is overreaction ("Interview"). Richard Nugent (1989), a teacher at Niles North High School in Skokie, Illinois, thinks that the school's image is at stake. He takes the position that a paper is owned by the school and that the newspaper staff is in the position of speaking for the board. Nugent believes that the paper's purpose is to be a public relations tool for forming students attitudes toward the school and in building favorable opinion in the community. If the paper did not do that, Nugent believes the students would be using the board's own publication to their advantage (8). David A. Splitt, a lawyer from Washington, D.C., who specializes in school law, doesn't react as strongly as Nugent, but he does disagree with the decision. In the January 1989 issue of *The Executive Editor,* a magazine for school officials, lawyer Splitt wrote, "The name of the game here is reasonable limits. The Courts seem willing to back up those who enforce reasonable limits [to student expression]" (6).

Recap of What the *Hazelwood* Decision Does

1. It gives discretion to principals or other school officials to act as publishers. The court seems to equate a school official with an editor-in-chief, ignoring the implied fiscal and legal liability that

comes when one exercises such control. In some states the professional journalists are supportive of the principal being the censor. Their reasoning is that the editor-in-chief tells them what to pull. There are others, however, who see error in the analogy: the principal is a government official. In the analogy, the mayor of the city doesn't tell a reporter what to write.

2. It allows for censorship of material that is not pedagogically part of the school's educational program.

3. It gives broader powers to control expression through any school-sponsored activity.

4. It allows school officials advance review privileges, even in the absence of guidelines that define what will or won't be censored.

What Can a Teacher Do?

John Rignell, cited above, says that his advice to a new teacher would be to the effect that an instructor may interfere with material to the degree that the publication of the newspaper is tied into pedagogy. Unless there is a close connection with pedagogy, Rignell says, it's best not to get involved with the situation. If a teacher wants to be legal, the paper should be totally separated from pedagogical instruction and "let the chips fall where they may." The paper then would be judged by any other standards under the First Amendment. If that's not possible, Rignell says, then "grit your teeth, make the newspaper a class project and participate in the editorial decisions." Rignell would suggest becoming proactive rather than reactive. He fears many of the voices crying out today are reacting to the decision rather than acting within the scope of the ruling (1990, "Interview").

If a newspaper goes off campus, censorship of the publication violates First Amendment rights. Such is the interpretation of a decision given by the Ninth Circuit Court of Appeals in the case of *Burch v. Barker* No. 87-3612, November 18, 1988. (The Ninth Circuit is comprised of most of the states west of the Rockies.) The decision given in this case is of special importance since it was based specifically in *Hazelwood v. Kuhlmeier*. Judge Mary M. Schroeder (1988) wrote, "In *Kuhlmeier* the Supreme Court reaffirmed the principles laid down in *Tinker v. Des Moines*" (16). The judge drew a clear distinction between whether the First Amendment requires a school to tolerate particular student speech (the issue that was addressed in *Hazelwood*) or whether the First Amendment requires a school affirmatively to promote particular student speech (the issue that was addressed in *Kuhlmeier*).

In a letter dated February 3, 1988, to state directors of the Journalism Education Association, that organization's Press Rights chairman, John Bowen, outlined some actions that might be taken in light of the *Hazelwood* decision. In a recent telephone conversation with this writer, Mr. Bowen reiterated those suggestions. Some of his outline of action follows:

1. Within your state, move on making contacts with legislators to propose a change in your state's constitution or educational codes to guarantee students the rights provided for them in the U.S. Constitution. You could use the California law or a model bill available from the Student Press Law Center, 800 18th St., NW, Suite 300, Washington, D.C. 20002, 202-466-5293.

2. Write, and urge other journalism students and educators to write, letters to the editor or other op-ed pieces for local publications. Bring the educators' side to the local media through suggesting stories, being interviewed, going on talk shows. It is important to continue to bring the ramifications of the *Hazelwood* case before the public, stressing the impact on academic freedom, student learning, and guaranteed freedoms.

3. Work, or continue working, to educate influential groups within your communities about the advantages of having a sound and educationally valid journalism program. Groups to approach might be Rotary, PTA, city council, and others. Remember, the court did not say that schools had to censor and that recognized forums could still not be censored.

4. Don't give up hope. Work to educate your own board and administrators. Strive to develop an editorial policy establishing your paper/course as a forum. Point out that a policy protects the board as well and that liability only comes with reviewing. Stress the professional goals you and the students have set (Bowen 1990, "Letter").

Works Cited

Bowen, John. 1988. Letter to Journalism Educators Association. 3 February.
———. 1990. Telephone interview. 20 June.
Brennan, William. 1988. U.S. Supreme Court Report 484 US 268.
Burch v. Barker. 1988. Ninth Circuit Court Report. Case No. 87-3612.
Gray, Glen. 1989. *Newsline: Newsletter for Colorado High School Publications* (November/December): 6.
Hazelwood School District v. Kuhlmeier, et al. 1988. U.S. Supreme Court Report 484 US 260.

Jackson, Peggy. 1989. *Newsline: Newsletter for Colorado High School Publications* (November/December): 7.

Nugent, Richard. 1989. *The Executive Editor* (January): 8.

Rignell, John. 1990. Personal interview. 28 June.

Schroeder, Mary M. 1988. In *Burch v. Barker*. Ninth Circuit Court Report. No. 87-3612: 6.

Splitt, David. 1989. *The Executive Editor* (January): 6.

Tinker v. Des Moines Independent School District. 1969. U.S. Supreme Court Report 339 US 503.

White, Byron. 1988. U.S. Supreme Court Report 484 US 263.

Afterword

James E. Davis
Ohio University
Past President, NCTE

Banning books is not done to improve education but to placate those among us who have a closed-minded certitude, those who demand absolute conformity to their own particular brand of "truth." Censorship in schools is actually a process by which agreed-upon procedures are subverted. While these procedures will vary from state to state, they all follow a similar model. Some office, such as a superintendent of education at the state level, hired professionals, administrators, and teachers establish guidelines for the curriculum and the curriculum itself. The general public has its involvement at the ballot box. Censors use various tactics to subvert legal procedures. The integrity of schools is threatened by this subversion.

Every region of the country experienced challenges in the 1980s, and in the 1990s acceleration of those challenges has been the pattern. Organized censors target school board positions, legislative seats, and judgeships. And they are continuing to influence local testing and book-adoption policies. Objectors are increasingly unwilling to settle for their own children's exemption from whatever they object to; they want it banned for everyone. They believe that education should be a vehicle for ensuring conformity to a particular ideology. Those who believe otherwise must constantly act to preserve intellectual freedom.

How? Joining with professional groups at all levels can help to do such things as:

- create and/or disseminate self-help packets for dealing with censorship,
- develop intellectual freedom statements,
- prepare selection policies, and
- provide legal support.

Working with state legislators or departments of education is vital to accomplishing such things as right-to-read laws. NCTE has a suggested model for right-to-read legislation. It specifies such things as the need for written, well-understood, and publicized procedures for reviewing citizens' requests to have teaching materials withdrawn. Large numbers of school districts lack such written procedures; a recent survey of librarians showed that a fourth of secondary schools polled have no written policy. Absence of such policies may lead to costly and exhausting conflicts with those who seek to ban books.

NCTE's model policy on book complaints appears in *The Students' Right to Read*. It calls for complainants to fill out a form detailing their objections and answering questions that assure they have actually read the objectionable work. The written complaint is then reviewed by a local committee, the majority of its members, according to NCTE recommendations, to be selected from teachers of the grades where the book in question is used. The committee would have twenty school days to file its recommendation about retaining the book with the local school board. The proposed model policy specifies that teachers decide whether a book should be listed as required or optional, and it provides for districts to file their review committee actions with state superintendents as a matter of public record. The important thing is to encourage people to discuss effective ways to combat attacks on books and teaching materials and eventually to get intellectual freedom written into school laws.

Learning and the right to it deserve the clamor that too often belongs, by default, only to those with closed-minded certitude. Those of us who believe the world can be improved by learners who have thoughts we have not had must join the fight more vigorously. The country's and the planet's dilemmas cannot be resolved merely by continuing to think and operate along the lines we have been and still do now. We must begin to think in bold, new, daring, and even dangerous ways. Preserving intellectual freedom is a high-stakes enterprise!

Index

Editor

Jean E. Brown, professor of teacher education at Saginaw Valley State University, chairs the Conference on English Education's Commission on Intellectual Freedom for NCTE. She is a former high school English teacher and department chair. She is a past president of the Michigan Council of Teachers of English and is former editor of the Council's newsletter, *The Michigan English Teacher.* As SLATE representative for Michigan, she serves on the Executive Committee of the Michigan Council of Teachers of English. She has served on the SLATE Steering Committee for NCTE. She and Elaine C. Stephens are the co-authors of *Literature for Young Adults: Sharing the Connections.* She is also the co-author of *Toward Literacy: Theory and Applications for Teaching Writing in the Content Areas,* with Elaine C. Stephens and Lela Phillips. She has written over sixty articles and book chapters and has co-edited two books, with Elaine Stephens and Barbara Quirk, *Two-Way Street: Integrating Reading and Writing in the Middle Schools* and *Two-Way Street: Integrating Reading and Writing in the Secondary Schools.* She is the 1990 recipient of both the C. C. Fries Award from MCTE for service to the profession and the Saginaw Valley State University Faculty Association Award for Scholarly Achievement. In 1992 she received the research award from the Saginaw Chapter of Phi Delta Kappa. She is the 1994 recipient of the Earl Warrick Excellence in Research Award from Saginaw Valley State University.

Contributors

Hugh Agee is professor of English education in the Language Education Department at the University of Georgia. As a literature teacher he has been a longstanding advocate of intellectual freedom, and he has given conference presentations and written articles on censorship issues. His special interest is young adult literature, which has been a frequent target of complaint in schools and libraries.

Philip M. Anderson is associate professor of secondary education and youth services at Queens College of the City University of New York. Formerly a public school English teacher, he earned a Ph.D. from the University of Wisconsin–Madison, and has since served on the faculty at Ohio University and Brown University. He is the author of numerous articles and chapters on the literature curriculum and censorship, the co-author of *Enhancing Aesthetic Reading and Response* and editor of *English Language Arts and the At-Risk Student*.

Ellen H. Brinkley is assistant professor of English at Western Michigan University. While president of the Michigan Council of Teachers of English, she served as primary author and project manager of the Michigan Proficiency Examination Framework for Writing, which was produced under contract between the Michigan Council of Teachers of English and the Michigan Department of Education. Among her publications are articles on writing assessment, writing centers, and attitudes about writing.

Daniel Carroll studied for his Master of Arts degree in political science at the University of Georgia from September 1989 to June 1991.

Lief H. Carter has taught at the University of Georgia since 1973. Before coming to Georgia, he received college and law degrees from Harvard, served in the Peace Corps in Bolivia, and earned his Ph.D. at the University of California, Berkeley. He has published major texts in constitutional law, legal reasoning, and administrative law. He was the first professor to twice win the University of Georgia's top award for teaching, and he has won national awards and recognition from the American Political Science Association. He has served as visiting professor at Brown University and the University of Washington. His book *Reason in Law* appeared in the fall of 1993 in its fourth edition. He is a member of St. Gregory the Great Episcopal Church in Athens and has an avid amateur interest in music.

Kathie Krieger Cerra's interest in the First Amendment and the freedom to read began in a high school-level United States history class in Parma, Ohio, and developed during graduate study at the University of Chicago, the University of Buffalo (SUNY), and the University of Minnesota, where she completed a Ph.D. Her research interests focus on elementary school teachers' attitudes and practices regarding book selection and intellectual freedom in the elementary school. She reviews children's books for *The Five Owls* and has contributed essays concerning censorship to that publication. She teaches language arts, children's literature, and reading in the teacher-education program at Macalester College in St. Paul, Minnesota.

James E. Davis, professor of English at Ohio University in Athens, is a past president of the National Council of Teachers of English (NCTE). He reviews regularly for the *ALAN Review* and is a frequent contributor to journals of NCTE and its affiliates. He has edited the *Ohio English Bulletin, FOCUS,* and the book *Dealing with Censorship.* He wrote, with Hazel Davis, *Presenting William Sleator* (1992) and co-edited with her the 1988 edition of *Your Reading,* the junior high/middle school booklist for NCTE. His *Teaching Shakespeare Today* (1993) is also an NCTE publication.

Ken Holmes is a twenty-seven-year tenured classroom teacher/department chair at Lincoln Senior High School, East St. Louis, Illinois. His undergraduate and master's degrees are from Southern Illinois University, and his earned doctorate in rhetoric and curriculum is from Illinois State University. He has long been active in the local and state affiliates of NCTE. He is past president of the Illinois Association of Teachers of English and has served on two NCTE nominating committees. His writings have appeared in the *Illinois English Bulletin, English in Texas, English Journal,* and the new *Encyclopedia of English Studies and Language Arts.* He has contributed to various publications and monographs published by the Illinois Department of Education, and he currently is serving as a writer for two commercial publishing houses as well as a consultant to and grant reviewer for the United States Department of Education.

C. Jane Hydrick is the current president (1993–94) of the National Council of Teachers of English and a fifth-grade teacher at Entz Elementary in Mesa, Arizona. The first elementary classroom teacher to preside over NCTE since its founding in 1911, she has served in many varied roles within the Council. A member of the Arizona English Teachers Association, she received its 1989 Excellence in Language Arts Teaching Award. She has also served on the Arizona State Technology in Education Task Force and was named Tempe Woman of the Year in 1985. Hydrick has written many journal articles and has been the editor of several publications, including *Whole Language: Empowerment at the Chalk Face, Ethics and Excellence in Computer Education: Choice or Mandate,* and *Tomorrow's Technology.*

Lynda K. Kapron, a graduate of Eastern Michigan University in social science, earned her M.S. in reading from Wayne State University in Detroit. For twenty years, she has taught English in Gibraltar, Michigan. Yearly, she organizes events such as the district awards banquet and has sponsored a student literary magazine since 1988. She serves in a variety of volunteer positions, including long-time Gibraltar Education Association secretary and current chief negotiator, and A.D.K. Beta Omicron treasurer.

John M. Kean is professor of curriculum and instruction at the University of Wisconsin–Madison. He is co-editor (with Nicholas Karolides and Lee Burress) of and contributor to *Censored Books: Critical Viewpoints;* the former chair of the NCTE Standing Committee Against Censorship; a member of the IRA Intellectual Freedom Advisory Committee; and a member of the CEE Commission on Intellectual Freedom.

Jim Knippling teaches American literature and composition at the University of Nebraska–Lincoln. He has written on the relations between literary forms and public culture in the U.S., and he is currently at work on a study of the Astor Place Riot of 1849.

Mel Krutz is a member of the National Council of Teachers of English's Standing Committee Against Censorship and its Task Force on Censorship and Nonprint Media. She is on the executive board, as SLATE chair, of the Nebraska English/Language Arts Council (NELAC), and is also past chair of NELAC's Advocates for Intellectual Freedom. She is founding chair of the Academic Freedom Coalition of Nebraska. She has published a number of articles and presented a number of papers on censorship. She teaches English at Central Community College in Columbus, Nebraska.

Adrienne C. May is assistant professor of education and director of student teaching at Mary Washington College, Fredericksburg, Virginia, where she has taught since 1984. An active member of the Virginia Association of Teachers of English, Phi Beta Kappa, Phi Delta Kappa, and the Association for Supervision and Curriculum Development, she works extensively with Virginia public school divisions in the areas of English curriculum development and interdisciplinary instruction. Her interest in censorship issues grew from her own thirteen years of experience as a public school English teacher.

David Moshman is professor and chair of educational psychology at the University of Nebraska–Lincoln, where he teaches adolescent psychology and a doctoral seminar in cognitive development. His research and publications focus on the development of reasoning and rationality and the role of intellectual freedom in fostering such development. He has also served as president of the UNL Chapter of the American Association of University Professors, the Academic Freedom Coalition of Nebraska, and the Nebraska Civil Liberties Union.

Roy C. O'Donnell, professor of language education at the University of Georgia, teaches graduate courses in English language, curriculum, and research. He has served as editor of *Research in the Teaching of English* and as president of the National Conference on Research in English. He is the author of numerous articles and monographs related to language and language learning.

Rita E. Paye has taught English in the southern Michigan Gibraltar School District for twenty-one years. She publishes a literary magazine and sponsors a writers club that pens scripts for a cable network teen show. She holds a master's degree in literature from Eastern Michigan University. She serves as a regional coordinator for the Michigan Council of Teachers of English and serves as a member of the NCTE Standing Committee Against Censorship. She has presented on the topic of censorship at MCTE and NCTE.

Margaret T. Sacco spent four years as a high school library media specialist, and for the past twenty-one years she has taught library media and young adult literature courses at Miami University of Ohio. She has contributed to *The ALAN Review, Emergency Librarian, The Ohio Media Spectrum,* and *ERIC Resources in Education.* She is the creator and editor of the National Database of Theoretical Rationales of Young Adult Literature, and she frequently presents at conferences. She is the Intellectual Freedom Chair of NCTE/ALAN and serves as a consultant to the Standing Committee Against Censorship.

Paul Slayton is Distinguished Professor of Education at Mary Washington College, Fredericksburg, Virginia. He was the founding chair of the Committee Against Censorship of the Virginia Association of Teachers of English and served the organization in that role for more than twenty years. He has fought many skirmishes against would-be censors and directed innumerable in-service workshops dealing with the censorship phenomenon.

Robert C. Small, Jr., is dean of the College of Education at Radford University in Virginia. He is a former chair of the Assembly on Literature for Adolescents (ALAN) and the Conference on English Education of NCTE. He is also former chair of the Intellectual Freedom Committee of the International Reading Association and a member of the Joint NCTE/IRA Task Force on Intellectual Freedom. He is currently the co-editor of *The ALAN Review* and chair of NCTE's Standing Committee on Teacher Preparation and Certification.

Elaine C. Stephens, professor of teacher education, Saginaw Valley State University, is a former classroom teacher, reading consultant, and professional development specialist. She and Jean Brown are the co-authors of *Literature for Young Adults: Sharing the Connections.* With Brown and Lela Phillips, she also co-authored *Toward Literacy: Theory and Applications for Teaching Writing in the Content Areas.* She is the 1992 recipient of the SVSU Landee Award for Excellence in Teaching and was recognized by the Michigan Association of Governing Boards of State Universities for distinguished teaching and extraordinary contributions to higher education in 1993.

Dee Storey was raised and educated in Michigan where she earned her doctorate in children's literature at Michigan State University. In 1981, she was a co-initiator of the Nebraska Golden Sower Children's Reading/Book Award Program. Her book *Twins in Children's and Adolescent Literature: An Annotated Bibliography* was published in 1993. Since 1987 she has taught children's literature and language arts at both the graduate and undergraduate levels at Saginaw Valley State University's College of Education.

Mary Ellen Van Camp is assistant professor of English education at Ball State University in Muncie, Indiana. She worked in elementary schools and taught high school English and speech for twenty years before becoming a university professor. Her teaching specialties include elementary language arts, children's literature, secondary English methods, and adolescent literature. She is a past president of the Michigan Council of Teacher of English and has been active in NCTE for many years, serving as an elected member of the SLATE Steering Committee, a member of the 1985 Resolutions Committee, and the CEE Commission on Intellectual Freedom.

M. Jerry Weiss is Distinguished Professor of Communications at Jersey City State College. Weiss is a former chair of ALAN and the Intellectual Freedom Committee of the Young Adult Services Division of the American Library Association and a member of the Joint NCTE/IRA Task Force on Intellectual Freedom. He is currently chair of the IRA Intellectual Freedom Committee.

Allison Wilson, currently a professor of English at Jackson State University, received her doctorate from Columbia University, where she specialized in college-level writing instruction. Her articles on the teaching of composition have appeared in such journals as *Journal of Basic Writing, English Journal, Freshman English News,* and *Teaching English in the Two-Year College* and in book-length collections published by Random House, NCTE, Modern Language Association, and the International Reading Association.